146-7

José B. Torres, PhD, MSW
Felix G. Rivera, PhD
Editors

Latino/Hispanic Liaisons and Visions for Human Behavior in the Social Environment

Latino/Hispanic Liaisons and Visions for Human Behavior in the Social Environment has been co-published as *Journal of Human Behavior in the Social Environment*, Volume 5, Numbers 3/4 2002.

Pre-publication REVIEWS, COMMENTARIES, EVALUATIONS . . .

"AN EXCELLENT EXAMPLE OF SCHOLARSHIP BY LATINOS, FOR LATINOS. . . . Quite useful for graduate social work courses in human behavior or social research. It would also make AN EXCELLENT TEXT for diversity courses. I will definitely use this book in my course and other training activities."

Carmen Ortiz Hendricks, DSW
Associate Professor
Hunter College
School of Social Work
New York City

"The chapters are WRITTEN BY EXPERTS who are keenly sensitive to the diversity that exists among Latino/Hispanic subgroups residing throughout the United States. This is a book that must be reflected upon in its entirety since EACH CHAPTER PRESENTS A MEANINGFUL CONTRIBUTION to the dialogue about the Latino/Hispanic experience."

Robert M. Ortega, PhD, MSW
Associate Professor
The University of Michigan
School of Social Work
Ann Arbor

"EXCELLENT AND USEFUL. . . . Stresses the interplay between social structural arrangements and human development. The authors cover a wide range of human behavior topics, including diversity among Latinos, adaptation to immigration, family stress, child development, and substance abuse."

Dr. John F. Longres
Professor
School of Social Work
University of Washington, Seattle

"There is no question that Torres and Rivera have provided the reader with studies that WILL IMPROVE THE VISIBILITY AND UNDERSTANDING OF LATINOS for human services professionals."

Alejandro Garcia, PhD
Professor
School of Social Work
Syracuse University
New York

"A compilation of well-selected readings by leading writers in social work. FILLS A MAJOR GAP IN THE SOCIAL WORK LITERATURE. Instructors will find this book insightful and SUITABLE FOR UNDERGRADUATE AND GRADUATE COURSES in social work, sociology, education, and related disciplines."

Steven R. Applewhite, PhD
Associate Professor
School of Social Work
University of Houston Texas

Latino/Hispanic Liaisons and Visions for Human Behavior in the Social Environment

Latino/Hispanic Liaisons and Visions for Human Behavior in the Social Environment has been co-published simultaneously as *Journal of Human Behavior in the Social Environment*, Volume 5, Numbers 3/4 2002.

The *Journal of Human Behavior in the Social Environment*™ Monographic "Separates"

Below is a list of "separates," which in serials librarianship means a special issue simultaneously published as a special journal issue or double-issue *and* as a "separate" hardbound monograph. (This is a format which we also call a "DocuSerial.")

"Separates" are published because specialized libraries or professionals may wish to purchase a specific thematic issue by itself in a format which can be separately cataloged and shelved, as opposed to purchasing the journal on an on-going basis. Faculty members may also more easily consider a "separate" for classroom adoption.

"Separates" are carefully classified separately with the major book jobbers so that the journal tie-in can be noted on new book order slips to avoid duplicate purchasing.

You may wish to visit Haworth's Website at . . .

http://www.HaworthPress.com

. . . to search our online catalog for complete tables of contents of these separates and related publications.

You may also call 1-800-HAWORTH (outside US/Canada: 607-722-5857), or Fax 1-800-895-0582 (outside US/Canada: 607-771-0012), or e-mail at:

getinfo@haworthpressinc.com

Latino/Hispanic Liaisons and Visions for Human Behavior in the Social Environment, edited by José B. Torres, PhD, MSW, Felix G. Rivera, PhD (Vol. 5, No. 3/4, 2002). *"AN EXCELLENT EXAMPLE OF SCHOLARSHIP BY LATINOS, FOR LATINOS . . . . Quite useful for graduate social work courses in human behavior or social research."* Carmen Ortiz Hendricks, DSW, Associate Professsor, Hunter College School of Social Work, New York City

Violence as Seen Through a Prism of Color, edited by Letha A. (Lee) See, PhD (Vol. 4, No. 2/3, 4, 2001). *"Incisive and important. . . . A comprehensive analysis of the way violence affects people of color. Offers important insights. . . . Should be consulted by academics, students, policymakers, and members of the public."* (Dr. James Midgley, Harry and Riva Specht Professor and Dean, School of Social Welfare, University of California at Berkeley)

Psychosocial Aspects of the Asian-American Experience: Diversity Within Diversity, edited by Namkee G. Choi, PhD (Vol. 3, No. 3/4, 2000). *Examines the childhood, adolescence, young adult, and aging stages of Asian Americans to help researchers and practitioners offer better services to this ethnic group. Representing Chinese, Japanese, Filipinos, Koreans, Asian Indians, Vietnamese, Hmong, Cambodians, and native-born Hawaiians, this helpful book will enable you to offer clients relevant services that are appropriate for your clients' ethnic backgrounds, beliefs, and experiences.*

Voices of First Nations People: Human Services Considerations, edited by Hilary N. Weaver, DSW (Vol. 2, No. 1/2, 1999). *"A must read for anyone interested in gaining an insight into the world of Native Americans. . . . I highly recommend it!"* (James Knapp, BS, Executive Director, Native American Community Services of Erie and Niagara Counties, Inc., Buffalo, New York)

Human Behavior in the Social Environment from an African American Perspective, edited by Letha A. (Lee) See, PhD (Vol. 1, No. 2/3, 1998). *"A book of scholarly, convincing, and relevant chapters that provide an African-American perspective on human behavior and the social environment . . . offer[s] new insights about the impact of race on psychosocial development in American society."* (Alphonso W. Haynes, EdD, Professor, School of Social Work, Grand Valley State University, Grand Rapids, Michigan)

Latino/Hispanic Liaisons and Visions for Human Behavior in the Social Environment

José B. Torres, PhD, MSW
Felix G. Rivera, PhD
Editors

Latino/Hispanic Liaisons and Visions for Human Behavior in the Social Environment has been co-published simultaneously as *Journal of Human Behavior in the Social Environment*, Volume 5, Numbers 3/4 2002.

The Haworth Social Work Practice Press
An Imprint of
The Haworth Press, Inc.
New York • London • Oxford

Published by

The Haworth Social Work Practice Press, 10 Alice Street, Binghamton, NY 13904-1580 USA

The Haworth Social Work Practice Press is an imprint of The Haworth Press, Inc., 10 Alice Street, Binghamton, NY 13904-1580 USA.

Latino/Hispanic Liaisons and Visions for Human Behavior in the Social Environment has been co-published simultaneously as *Journal of Human Behavior in the Social Environment*, Volume 5, Numbers 3/4 2002.

The development, preparation, and publication of this work has been undertaken with great care. However, the publisher, employees, editors, and agents of The Haworth Press and all imprints of The Haworth Press, Inc., including The Haworth Medical Press® and The Pharmaceutical Products Press®, are not responsible for any errors contained herein or for consequences that may ensue from use of materials or information contained in this work. Opinions expressed by the author(s) are not necessarily those of The Haworth Press, Inc.

Cover design by Thomas J. Mayshock Jr.

Library of Congress Cataloging-in-Publication Data

Latino/Hispanic liaisons and visions for human behavior in the social environment / José B. Torres, and Felix G. Rivera, editors.
    p. cm.
    " 'Latino/Hispanic liaisons and visions for human behavior in the social environment' has been co-published simultaneously as 'Journal of human behavior in the social environment,' vol. 5, nos. 3/4, 2002."
    Includes bibliographical references and index.
    ISBN 0-7890-1656-7 (alk. paper)–ISBN 0-7890-1657-5 (pbk: alk. paper)
    1. Hispanic Americans–Social conditions.   I. Torres, José B. II. Rivera, Felix G. III. Journal of human behavior in the social environment.
E184.S75 L3555 2002
305.868073–dc21
                                       2002017185

Indexing, Abstracting & Website/Internet Coverage

This section provides you with a list of major indexing & abstracting services. That is to say, each service began covering this periodical during the year noted in the right column. Most Websites which are listed below have indicated that they will either post, disseminate, compile, archive, cite or alert their own Website users with research-based content from this work. (This list is as current as the copyright date of this publication.)

Abstracting, Website/Indexing Coverage . . . . Year When Coverage Began

- *BUBL Information Service An Internet-based Information Service for the UK higher education community <URL:http://bubl.ac.uk/>* . . . **2000**

- *Cambridge Scientific Abstracts is a leading publisher of scientific information in print journals, online databases, CD-ROM and via the internet (HEALTH & SAFETY SCIENCE ABSTRACTS/ RISK ABSTRACTS) <www.csa.com>* . . . **1995**

- *caredata CD: the social & community care database <www.scie.org.uk>* **1995**

- *Child Development Abstracts & Bibliography (in print & online) <www.ukans.edu>* **1995**

- *CINAHL (Cumulative Index to Nursing & Allied Health Literature), in print, EBSCO, and SilverPlatter, Data-Star, and PaperChase. (Support materials include Subject Heading List, Database Search Guide, and instructional video) <www.cinahl.com>* **1995**

- *CNPIEC Reference Guide: Chinese National Directory of Foreign Periodicals* **1995**

- *Criminal Justice Abstracts* **1995**

- *Family & Society Studies Worldwide <www.nisc.com>* **1995**

- *FINDEX <www.publist.com>* **1995**

(continued)

Special Bibliographic Notes related to special journal issues (separates) and indexing/abstracting:

- indexing/abstracting services in this list will also cover material in any "separate" that is co-published simultaneously with Haworth's special thematic journal issue or DocuSerial. Indexing/abstracting usually covers material at the article/chapter level.
- monographic co-editions are intended for either non-subscribers or libraries which intend to purchase a second copy for their circulating collections.
- monographic co-editions are reported to all jobbers/wholesalers/approval plans. The source journal is listed as the "series" to assist the prevention of duplicate purchasing in the same manner utilized for books-in-series.
- to facilitate user/access services all indexing/abstracting services are encouraged to utilize the co-indexing entry note indicated at the bottom of the first page of each article/chapter/contribution.
- this is intended to assist a library user of any reference tool (whether print, electronic, online, or CD-ROM) to locate the monographic version if the library has purchased this version but not a subscription to the source journal.
- individual articles/chapters in any Haworth publication are also available through the Haworth Document Delivery Service (HDDS).

Latino/Hispanic Liaisons and Visions for Human Behavior in the Social Environment

CONTENTS

ABOUT THE EDITORS

José B. Torres, PhD, MSW, joined the faculty of the School of Social Welfare at the University of Wisconsin-Milwaukee in 1995. He is Associate Professor there, with primary teaching responsibilities in the areas of multicultural social work, direct practice, and clinical supervision. He is also Associate Scientist with the Center for Addiction and Behavioral Health Research at UWM. Dr. Torres has twenty-eight years of experience as a clinical social worker, providing individual, marital, and family therapy to diverse populations. He is a certified marriage and family therapist with an approved supervisor status in the American Association for Marriage and Family Therapy. He also maintains a limited private practice and provides training on cultural diversity in mental health, educational, and work settings. He has researched and published on multicultural mental health education and training, supervision of clinical training and practice, cultural aspects of gender roles, and domestic abuse.

Felix G. Rivera, PhD, is Professor in the School of Social Work, San Francisco State University, where he has taught community organization and social and evaluative research since 1973. Dr. Rivera has forty years experience as a grassroots organizer and has worked with community, state, local, and Federal government organizations as an evaluator, planner, and program developer. His research and publications have emphasized the dynamics and implications for practice of emerging communities of color and the implications of community power and leadership for social justice and social change. His co-edited book, *Community Organizing in a Diverse Society,* is in its third edition. Dr. Rivera has written about the ethical and moral issues associated with research, emphasizing the importance of action, participatory, and emancipatory research. He sits on the editorial boards of the *Journal of Community Practice,* the *Journal of Health & Social Policy,* the *Journal of Progressive Human Services,* and the *Journal of Ethnic & Cultural Diversity in Social Work.*

Introduction

Among the challenges faced by the social work profession has been the enhancement of educational programs and professional literature targeted to accelerate ethnic and cultural sensitivity in multicultural social work practice with diverse ethnic minority groups including Latinos/Hispanics. This special volume is devoted to further consideration of social work practice implications relevant to the rapidly increasing Latino/Hispanic population in the United States.

In the context of changing demographics and political realities in the U.S., debates over the impact Latinos/Hispanics will have on political issues and other socioeconomic elements of the nation are vague and inconclusive. Despite the projection that Latinos/Hispanics will become the nation's majority minority population by the year 2020, the debates, in fact, have failed to adequately describe the complex ethnic tapestry of this population. This failure has been limited, in part, by minimal in-depth knowledge of Latino/Hispanic diversity, attitudes, behaviors, and experiences (de la Garza, 1993).

Literature on Latinos/Hispanics reflects a dysfunctional and myopic cultural view in which Latinos/Hispanics are often depicted in stereotypic characteristics and as a homogeneous population. Their ethnic and cultural identity is not a monolithic phenomenon: rather, there is a hybrid cultural potpourri, composed of distinct nationalities that identify with a specific language, culture, or place. The literature available however, frequently presents misguided generalizations about Latinos/Hispanics when a significant portion of the discourse designated as "Hispanic" or "Latino," is in fact, about a single origin group, such as

[Haworth co-indexing entry note]: "Introduction." Torres, José B., and Felix G. Rivera. Co-published simultaneously in *Journal of Human Behavior in the Social Environment* (The Haworth Social Work Practice Press, an imprint of The Haworth Press, Inc.) Vol. 5, No. 3/4, 2002, pp. 1-7; and: *Latino/Hispanic Liaisons and Visions for Human Behavior in the Social Environment* (ed: José B. Torres, and Felix G. Rivera) The Haworth Social Work Practice Press, an imprint of The Haworth Press, Inc., 2002, pp. 1-7. Single or multiple copies of this article are available for a fee from The Haworth Document Delivery Service [1-800-HAWORTH, 9:00 a.m. - 5:00 p.m. (EST). E-mail address: getinfo@haworthpressinc.com].

1

Mexican Americans (Baca Zinn & Wells, 2000; Mazzey, Zambrana, & Bell, 1995). This pattern of generalization often results in minimizing and further masking the extraordinary significant inter and intra group differences that exist among Latinos/Hispanics (i.e., Mexican Americans, Puerto Ricans, Cubans, and Central and South Americans). Grouping together Latinos/Hispanics into an undifferentiated single collective, subsequently leads to cultural distortions and further contributes to impoverished, one-dimensional thinking on various characteristics. These characteristics include ethnicity, socioeconomic status, language, education, immigration patterns, political differences, traditions, variations of certain cultural values, skin color, experiences with discrimination, prejudice and racism, and level of acculturation and/or assimilation (García & Marotta, 1997).

Through the voices of diverse Latino/Hispanic scholars, the compilation of articles included in this volume attempts to dispel pervasive historical and contemporary misconceptions and inaccuracies about Latino/Hispanic experiences. The integration of these articles compliment recent studies that are successfully challenging previous notions of Latino/Hispanic family life as "deviant, deficient, and disorganized" (Baca Zinn & Wells, 2000, p. 253). This compilation of articles further presents a process for generating hope for Latinos/Hispanics whose quiet presence has been embarrassingly invisible, and neglected (Vega, 1990).

Contrary to various myths, Latinos/Hispanics reflect a population that is relatively, a young population with large families, urban, and diverse. In addition, the Census Bureau's report on Latinos/Hispanics further highlights several predisposing socioeconomic characteristics that differentiate them from non-Latino/Hispanic Whites and which influence their health care. These characteristics indicate that Latinos/Hispanics are (1) less likely to have a high school diploma, (2) more likely to be unemployed, (3) less likely to be married, (4) more likely to have a female householder with no spouse present, (5) affected by poverty three times as much (with poverty rates ranging from 30.9 percent among Puerto Ricans to 13.6 percent among Cubans), (6) that Latino/Hispanic children are more likely to be living in poverty, and (7) that Latino/Hispanic families are more likely to be living below the poverty level U.S. Bureau of the Census, 1999).

Although Latinos/Hispanics share a common cultural bond and various socioeconomic characteristics, their heterogeneity may affect individuals and families differently. Differences may depend on their location in the class structures (i.e., unemployed, poor, working class, or professional); their location in the gender structures as male or female, and their location in the sexual orientation system as heterosexual, gay, lesbian, or bisexual (Baca Zinn & Dill, 1996). Furthermore, Latino/Hispanic family life is also affected by age, generation living in the U.S., citizenship status, and geographical location of the different groups throughout the U.S.

Literature on the Latino/Hispanic culture and its relationship to the provision of competent mental health services has broadly emphasized common value characteristics associated with the various Latino/Hispanic groups. Among the frequently discussed themes are family, including *familismo* (a reliance on extended family for support and kinship) and culturally shared values such as *personalismo* (importance of personal ties), *respeto* (respect as the core of relationships, especially intergenerationally), *dignidad* (dignity), and *machismo* and *marianismo* (sex related patterns of behaviors). Guarnaccia and Rodriguez (1996) caution that a general knowledge of these cultural value orientations and other Latino/Hispanic cultural information is insufficient given the diversity within and between each of the different Latino/Hispanic groups.

In the context of the reported Latino/Hispanic increasing growth over the twenty-first century, and their devastating socioeconomic characteristics, this population is of great importance to the American society as well as to politicians and other policy makers, educators and health and social service providers. Social workers in particular can no longer ignore the presence of Latinos/Hispanics, their fundamental contributions to the United States, and the challenges emanating from the emerging demographic trends that affect the demand for and provision of competent health, social, and psychological services. Some of the challenges reflect the presentation of a people with a different language, cultural values, serious health issues, social problems, and different patterns of communication.

As we move into the 21st century, the changing demographics among Latinos/Hispanics necessitates that we move on beyond the established body of knowledge and expand our research to more problem-solution orientations in a contemporary environment. As the editors of this volume, we have attempted to include a range of conceptualizations relevant to Latino/Hispanic experiences that are currently being discussed and will unquestionably receive increased attention among our people. In the broadest sense, a goal of this edition is to fill a gap in the education and training of social workers serving this population. The nine articles included in this edition presents a candid and honest perspective on how Latinos/Hispanics and non-Latinos/Hispanics must move beyond the level of exclusiveness and instead promote the richness of inclusion among Latinos/Hispanics. Each of the articles represents a synthesis of the scholarship and experience of the authors, complimenting each other to varying degrees.

Yolanda Padilla presents a comprehensive profile of the social ecology of Mexican American child development by integrating the most current theoretical and empirical evidence on the influence of various socio-cultural contexts. Padilla further discusses the implications of disadvantagement on other environmental influences impacting on the child's development, and opportunities for social service delivery to the child and his/her family.

Sandra Magaña, Marsha Mailick Seltzer, Marty Wyngaarden Krauss, Mark Rubert and José Szapocznick's article provides an intriguing small area of study relevant to Latinos/Hispanics, but minimally published in the social science literature. The authors focus on the caregiving context of Cuban and Puerto Rican mothers of an adult child with mental retardation in order to better understand the influence of culture on the stress and coping process. They specifically examine predictors of caregiver well-being among these two Latino groups, identifying similarities and differences in the effects of the caregiving context and cultural characteristics among the study participants. Magaña and her colleagues argue that social workers must take into account the Latino/Hispanic heterogeneity as well as assessing the social environment and the ability of the family with non-normative caregiving responsibilities to conform to cultural expectations.

Raul Quiñones Rosado and Esterla Barreto present an integral model of well-being and development, developed and implemented by the authors with Latinos/Hispanics on the mainland and in Puerto Rico, over a ten year period. Their integrative model, presents various cultural influences (i.e., Indigenous, African, Asian, European, Anglos, and Latino/Hispanic American), and other social science models; theories and philosophies that move beyond an individual perspective to a collective dimension including the social, political, economic and cultural forces that affects all individuals and communities.

Maria Elena Puig examines the immigration and adjustment of Cuban refugee families who migrated to the U.S. from the 1994-1995 Guantanamo wave of immigrants. Her study specifically explores the social and emotional adjustment of adultified Cuban refugee children, particularly the effects of changing family roles on intergenerational relations and family well-being.

Flavio Francisco Marsiglia and John Michael Daley present a case study of a Southwestern communitys' efforts to create a multiethnic neighborhood coalition with the intent to develop a substance abuse prevention program. The neighborhood is separated by a school based parents association including younger Latino/Hispanic neighbors, focused on strengthening community efforts towards substance abuse prevention among local youth. The authors discuss challenges and guidelines for developing multiethnic urban coalitions.

Cultural competence is a theme that has received much professional attention in recent years. Juan Paz presents a conceptualization of key elements necessary to training culturally competent health care providers in substance abuse treatment programs and other social services to Latino/Hispanic populations.

Noting that Latino immigrants rank second to Asians as the largest documented immigrant group in the U.S., Maria E. Zuniga discusses the stresses and adaptive mechanisms of the large percentage of immigrants from Mexico and Central America who also enter the U.S. as undocumented immigrants. Zuniga delineates immigrants from refugees, their varied challenges in an often-hostile environment, and recommendations for sensitive social service intervention.

Nilsa M. Burgos presents the findings of a qualitative study focused on examining changes in Caribbean women's lives in response to their experiences with migration, family and work, ten or more years after migrating to the United States. Burgos argues that although Dominican, Cuban and Puerto Rican women experience numerous personal and social problems adapting to their new environment, they also make significant contributions to the U.S. As a growing component of the changing society, Burgos presents their needs, aspirations and sense of identity through the voices and expressions of the women themselves.

Recognizing current arguments suggesting that *race,* as an analytical category, has become a meaningless concept, Maria Vidal de Haymes, Keith Kilty, and Stephen Haymes, discuss this concept as well as ethnicity, culture, and language. In the context of their application to the current situation of Latinos/Hispanics by contemporary scholars. The examination of these concepts focuses on the context of their application to the current situation of Latinos/Hispanics by contemporary scholars. The authors highlight points of disagreement and consensus, as well as emerging theories.

José B. Torres encourages Latinos/Hispanics to think beyond their traditional group specific dynamics and recognize the potential of a more inclusive coalition, particularly in the context of the nation's growing Latino/Hispanic population. Acknowledging the frustrating, painful, and misleading misconceptions that exist about Latinos/Hispanics, Torres argues for Latinos/Hispanics to enter into coalition (i.e., collective) politics that allow for an expansion of community power and boundaries instead of a narrow, ethnocentric or racial (i.e., color) based view.

CONCLUSION

The panoply of articles in this special collection presents a challenge to those working with Latino/Hispanic communities. The authors and editors have presented empirical and conceptual evidence helping to eliminate the insidious myths and stereotypes victimizing our people. However, this is but a beginning. To bring about change in our communities is a Herculean task, but one that must be done.

Our mandate is clear. We need to challenge practitioners, social planners, policy experts, community organizers, and researchers. They must continue developing efficacious intervention strategies, comprehensive programs that are not only culturally sensitive but also address the basic structural issues of oppression and racism, and, also continue supporting research activities that may be used in developing ways of social work that are innovative and daring in their conceptualizations.

José B. Torres
Felix G. Rivera

REFERENCES

Baca Zinn, M. & Wells, B. (2000). Diversity within Latino families: New lessons for family social science. In D. H. Demo, K. R. Allen, & M. A. Fine (Eds.), *Handbook of family diversity* (pp. 252-273). New York: Oxford.

De la Garza, R. O. (1993). Researchers must heed new realities when they study Latinos in the U.S. The Chronical of Higher Education, (June 2, 1993), 39, pp. B1-2.

García, J. G. & Marotta S. (1997). *Psychological interventions and research with Latino populations*. Needham Heights, MA: Allyn & Bacon.

Guarnaccia, P. J. & Rodriguez. O. (1996). Concept of culture and their role in the development of culturally competent mental health services. *Journal of Behavioral Sciences*, 18, 419-433.

Massey, D. S., Zambrana, R. E., & Bells, S. A. (1995). Contemporary issues for Latino families: Future directions for research, policy, and practice. In R. E. Zambrana (Ed.), *Understanding Latino families* (pp. 190-204). Thousand Oaks, CA: Sage.

U.S. Bureau of the Census (1992). *1990 Census of the population and housing summary: Tape file 3A*. Washington, DC: Department of Commerce, Data User service Division.

U.S. Bureau of the Census (1997). *1997 Population Profile of the United States*. Current Population Reports, Series P23-194. U.S. Government Printing Office, Washington, D.C.

U.S. Bureau of the Census (1999). *The Hispanic Population in the United States: Population Characteristics*. March 1999. Current Population Reports, P20-527. U.S. Government Printing Office, Washington, D.C.

Vega, W. A. (1990). Hispanic families in the 1980s: A decade of research. *Journal of Marriage and the Family*, 52, 1015-1024.

The Social Ecology of Child Development in the Mexican American Population: Current Theoretical and Empirical Perspectives

Yolanda C. Padilla

SUMMARY. This article explores the influence of contextual factors on the developmental outcomes of Mexican American children. The contextual structure of child development is conceptualized as a complex system of environments, including the socio-demographic, social service, academic, and parental home environments. Based on an extensive review of the current theoretical and empirical literature, we find that the disadvantaged social position of Mexican American children has detrimental implications for all other aspects of their environment, thus hindering their development. In addition, although Mexican American parents are highly competent in providing a nurturing and culturally-rich

Yolanda C. Padilla, PhD, LMSW-AP, is Associate Professor at the School of Social Work and Research Affiliate at the Population Research Center, University of Texas at Austin. She holds a joint doctoral degree in social work and sociology from the University of Michigan. She is currently involved in two socio-demographic studies of child development in the Latino population. Her major areas of interest include Latino studies and social work, immigration, poverty, and social welfare policy.

Address correspondence to: Yolanda C. Padilla, PhD, Associate Professor, School of Social Work, University of Texas at Austin, 1925 San Jacinto, Austin, TX 78712.

The author wishes to thank Robert Hummer and Amy Mizcles.

This study was funded by a grant from the National Institute of Child Health and Development, #1 R01 HD35949-01A1S1.

[Haworth co-indexing entry note]: "The Social Ecology of Child Development in the Mexican American Population: Current Theoretical and Empirical Perspectives." Padilla, Yolanda C. Co-published simultaneously in *Journal of Human Behavior in the Social Environment* (The Haworth Social Work Practice Press, an imprint of The Haworth Press, Inc.) Vol. 5, No. 3/4, 2002, pp. 9-29; and: *Latino/Hispanic Liaisons and Visions for Human Behavior in the Social Environment* (ed: José B. Torres, and Felix G. Rivera) The Haworth Social Work Practice Press, an imprint of The Haworth Press, Inc., 2002, pp. 9-29. Single or multiple copies of this article are available for a fee from The Haworth Document Delivery Service [1-800-HAWORTH, 9:00 a.m. - 5:00 p.m. (EST). E-mail address: getinfo@haworthpressinc.com].

9

environment, there is a often a discontinuity between the home environment and both the academic and the social service environments. *[Article
copies available for a fee from The Haworth Document Delivery Service:
1-800-HAWORTH. E-mail address: <getinfo@haworthpressinc.com> Website:
<http://www.HaworthPress.com> © 2002 by The Haworth Press, Inc. All rights
reserved.]*

KEYWORDS. Child development, Mexican American, Hispanic, academic achievement, social ecological model

Social work assessment of the cognitive, social, and emotional development of Mexican American children requires a culturally-competent
approach. Yet, it is not enough to compare Mexican American children
to children of other ethnic and racial groups and conclude that ethnicity
and culture explains the variation in their outcomes, because that says
nothing of the mechanisms by which culture affects their process of development (Garcia Coll & Magnuson, 1999; Ogbu, 1999). What is essential is to be familiar with the contextual factors and conditions which
determine the developmental outcomes for Mexican American children. This requires a conception of culture that encompasses a holistic
view of their social experience.

As in the case of minority children in general, current theoretical and
empirical literature on Mexican American children stresses the need to
move from an emphasis on whether they perform better or worse than
non-minorities to a greater attention to social context, which has not
been stressed in traditional models of child development (Spencer,
1990). The main argument is not that developmental processes for children of color are inherently different from those of white children (Garcia Coll et al., 1996; Rowe, Vazsonyi, & Flannery, 1995). Rather, that
children of color operate under a unique set of circumstances due to
their disadvantaged social position that often inhibit rather than facilitate development (Garcia Coll et al., 1996, p. 1892). According to Garcia Coll and Magnuson (1999), we cannot assume that universal
processes lead to developmental outcomes devoid of context. It is important to bring context, and specifically cultural context, within which
processes of development vary, to the center of attention.

Given that it is imperative to look at the social and cultural conditions
that influence the Mexican American child, it is useful to organize our
analysis from a social ecological perspective. Thus, the focus is on the

complex system of environments of the child. Clearly, not all the environments that are part of the child's life affect the child at the same level of immediacy, some have a direct and others an indirect influence. Nor are these environments totally separate and distinct from each other. Therefore, we can say that the Mexican American child interfaces with a number of systems, each of which encompasses the other. These systems include, beginning at the broadest level, the socio-demographic environment, the social service environment, the academic environment, and the parental home environment. See Figure 1 for a depiction of the analytical model.

This article attempts to provide a comprehensive profile of the social ecology of Mexican American child development by piecing together the most current theoretical and empirical evidence on the influence of the various socio-cultural contexts. We will first discuss the broader environment of the child, the socio-demographic context, and then move to the child's most immediate environment, the parental home. Using the outer and innermost contexts as a point of departure, we then address two other environments that are present in the child's life at an intermediate level, the academic environment and the social service environment. The social service system is included in the analysis, because in addition to being the point of intersection with human service providers, this system becomes in itself one more context in the process of child development.

The context of child development will be analyzed relative to the various aspects of personality development of Mexican American children; however, the emphasis will be on its effect on one aspect of development, cognitive achievement. This area of study has long dominated research in the field to the neglect of other areas of psychosocial development (Romero, 1983; Solis, 1995). In addition, the focus of the paper is on Mexican American children, but due to the limited number of studies, we also present empirical evidence from studies of Hispanics that did not differentiate between subgroups but that usually included a substantial proportion of Mexican Americans. Studies of the general population in cases for which there is no research on Hispanics, but that are suggestive for this population, are included. In this paper the terms Hispanic and Latino, non-Hispanic white and Anglo, and children of color and minority children are used interchangeably to reflect their use in the literature.

FIGURE 1. Socio-Cultural Context of Mexican American Child Development

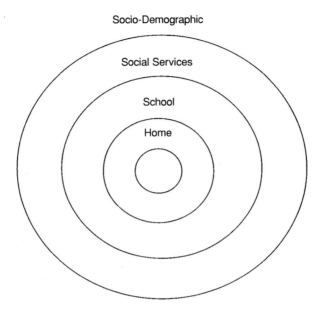

SOCIO-DEMOGRAPHIC CONTEXT

Social position conditions all the other aspects of the child's life: home environment, educational opportunities, and access to social services. Researchers (Garcia Coll et al., 1996; Hernandez, 1997) argue that social demography should be incorporated in all developmental research, but that it must be central in the study of child development among minority populations. How do variables associated with social status influence developmental outcomes? Garcia Coll proposes a conceptual model that is anchored in stratification theory emphasizing the importance of lower status and power (a status characterized by discrimination, oppression, and segregation). In her model, social position has an indirect effect on child development because it determines the probability of living in segregated economic, residential, and social environments. Such environments provide limited access to resources and in turn can influence the availability of supportive environments experienced by children of color within their schools, neighborhoods, and other institutions. In segregated environments, school's classroom instruction is likely to be incompatible with family culture. Neighborhoods are likely to be characterized by violence, which places the children in a position where they are concerned for personal safety. Access to health care is likely to be limited, and thus diseases or other problems that impede normal development are not screened in time. To the extent that these institutional environments are not supportive, they cause psychological stress in the family, often leading to punitive and non-supportive parental behavior toward the child. Finally, in the absence of social support or cultural sources of adaptation (e.g., biculturalism), such stress is conducive to parental interaction with the child that inhibits his or her optimal development.

The socio-demographic context of Mexican American children is significantly disadvantaged. In 1990, 32 percent of Mexican American children were poor compared to 10 percent of non-Hispanic white children (Landale & Lichter, 1997). The poverty rate for all Hispanic children is 30 percent. Economic context significantly influences individual poverty rates among Hispanic children. The probability of living in poverty is the highest for Hispanic children residing in metropolitan areas with high unemployment, low wages, and high segregation (Landale & Lichter, 1997). That geographic area affects poverty is important in light of the fact that 1 in 10 Hispanic children lives in a "severely distressed neighborhood" (areas with extremely high unemployment, poverty, school drop outs, female-headed households, and welfare dependency) compared to 1 in 63 non-Hispanic whites (Zambrana, Dorrington, & Hayes-Bautista, 1995). The trend for Hispanics to be living in highly disadvantaged neighborhoods appears to be increasing (St. John & Miller, 1995).

The socioeconomic environment within the families of Hispanic children also places them in a vulnerable position (Zambrana & Dorrington, 1998). Hispanic adults experience high unemployment rates, 10.5 percent versus 6 percent for non-Hispanics. Only about half of all Hispanics have attained an education beyond high school compared to three-quarters of non-Hispanics. In addition, Hispanics are four times as likely to drop out of school than are non-Hispanics. Hispanic adults tend to be concentrated in service occupations, at a rate twice as high as that of non-Hispanics and are half as likely to occupy professional or managerial positions. Also increasing the vulnerability of Hispanic children is the fact that nearly 60 percent of Hispanics are first or second generation, which increases their probability of being in poverty (Oropesa & Landale, 1997). Despite greater socioeconomic disadvantage, however, the vast majority of Hispanic children (64 percent) live in two-parent families (Lichter & Landale, 1995).

Although there is a great deal of data on the socio-demographic characteristics of Hispanics, the consequences for child development have not been explored. The available research on the general population that shows a relationship between social position and child development outcomes is suggestive. Based on an extensive review of the empirical literature McLoyd (1998) showed that poverty (especially long-term poverty, low socioeconomic status, and residence in poor neighborhoods) has a significant effect on children's cognitive and socioemotional functioning. The causal mechanisms are very complex. Socioeconomic disadvantage hinders child development through: (a) mother's inadequate nutrition and limited prenatal care, (b) fewer resources to counterbalance perinatal complications, such as prematurity, (c) low mother's education, which is related to lower cognitive stimulation for their children, (d) parental stressful life events, which decrease child stimulation in the home environment, and (e) punitive and inconsistent parenting. Similarly, Crooks (1995) found evidence that poverty negatively affects school achievement via cognitive functioning and school behavior outcomes (such as absenteeism, dropout, etc.). The connection between poverty and weak cognitive development are: low birthweight due to poor maternal health care, greater school problems related to low birthweight and poverty, intellectual deficits caused by lead poisoning, and poor cognitive development as a result of hunger.

However, research also shows that certain factors mediate the effects of disadvantaged social position on child development. A study of white and black children between the ages of 1 and 3 (Kiebanov, Brooks-Gunn, McCarton, & McCormick, 1998) revealed that their developmental scores (cognitive functioning) were negatively influenced by family poverty and neighborhood poverty. The effects were complex, with various strengths of association at different ages. However, home environment (i.e., quality of cognitive stimulation and emotional support provided by the child's family) and family cumulative risk (i.e., family structure, and mother's unemployment, teen parent at time of birth, education, low cognitive scores, depression, and social support) both mediated family and neighborhood poverty to a certain extent. However, both home environment and family risks were associated with poverty (both family and neighborhood). That is, higher quality home environments were associated with living in higher income neighborhoods. Still another factor that mediates the effect of poverty is family structure. Children who lived with both natural parents during adolescence received more encouragement and help with school work than did children who lived with single parents or stepparents (Astone & McLanahan, 1991). It is not clear however, what it is about living with both natural parents that leads to better outcomes.

PARENTAL HOME ENVIRONMENT

The most immediate context within which Mexican American child development occurs is the home environment. The home environment encompasses family processes, including general parental perceptions related to child development, child-rearing behaviors, and varying responses to stress. According to Harrison, Wilson, Pine, Chan, and Buriel (1990) given the struggles of power, discrimination, and social position, the family context of minority children is different than that of majority children. Thus, they argue that the mechanisms that characterize minority families, such as family extendedness and biculturalism, are "adaptive strategies" to societal pressures. Such mechanisms shape parental perceptions and socialization of children, and thus influence child development outcomes. Family extendedness arises from the necessity to deal with transitions and crises faced as a result of societal tensions. Biculturalism is adopted in order to deal with the pressure for acculturation and the devaluing of immigrant cultures. For Mexican Americans, the immigration experience is considered at the center of family processes and developmental outcomes. Siantz (1999) proposes a model of the adaptation of Hispanic immigrant children that incorporates risk factors (family stress), protective factors (individual characteristics of children and parents that mediate risk factors), and child outcomes (adaptation level). She hypothesizes that the risks for the child include (a) loss due to separation from part of their immediate or extended family, (b) trauma, especially for children who came from situations in their countries of origin that were characterized by violence, and (c) low self-esteem, due to a societal devaluation of cultural diversity. Protective factors include social and cultural support, a strong ethnic identity and self-concept, and coping ability. The consequences of the immigration experience for Mexican American children, however, have not been extensively studied, and available literature generally reports on anecdotal data (see for example, Partida, 1996).

The social, economic, and cultural context of Mexican American and Hispanic families affect the home environment by defining parental perceptions of child development. Research shows that Mexican American mothers tend to attribute developmental outcomes to a complex interaction of factors rather than to singular causes (Gutierrez & Sameroff, 1990). This is especially evident among more acculturated and bicultural mothers, in comparison to less acculturated and Anglo-American mothers. Moreover, Mexican American parents place a very high emphasis on helping their children develop social skills, teaching their children to be *bien educados*, as the foundation for development, according to an in-depth ethnographic study of low-income families (Delgado & Ford, 1998). In addition, parents value maintaining a strong connection with extended family (e.g., grandparents) for their children. Finally, parents place a strong emphasis on the importance of their children learning English, so that they can have a better life than they do, but this is viewed as something occurring separately from family life.

Passing on culturally-relevant skills is considered important to Mexican American parents. A study of Mexican American children and their mothers (Knight, Cota, & Bernal, 1993) showed that regardless of generation, mothers tended to teach their children about their culture. This is especially true of mothers who reported a greater degree of knowledge and identification with their ethnic culture. Furthermore, these mothers had children who have a stronger ethnic identification. Finally, children with a stronger ethnic identification tended to conform to what are considered Mexican American cultural values by displaying greater cooperative and less competitive tendencies, when compared to children with a lower sense of ethnic identification. Furthermore, for a large proportion of Latino families, part of the home context of children includes bilingualism. The findings from a study of 10 Hispanic families who maintained bilingualism illustrates the rationale for maintaining bilingualism. Hispanic parents believed that knowing two languages would provide their children with an advantage both at school and in future employment. Other reasons center around providing a connection with family and their roots and taking advantage of a resource that is readily available in the home.

Research shows that Mexican American parents use a range of teaching strategies in their everyday interactions with their children, and that these strategies are demonstrate effective instruction. Mexican American children tend to favor "collaborative" learning styles in the home. For example, children tend to engage their parents by asking questions and observing and imitating siblings (Perez-Granados & Callanan, 1997). Mothers are responsive to their children's learning styles. A study by Moreno and Cisneros-Cohenour (1999) found that mothers provided structure for the child, continually engaged the child, displayed sensitivity toward their child's needs, and recognized the child's growing competence and allowed for independence.

Level of acculturation and generation are significantly associated with child-rearing practices. Child-rearing behavior of parents of first and second generation children (i.e., immigrant parents) reflects an emphasis on earlier autonomy, productive use of time, strictness, and permissiveness to a greater extent than is evident for third generation parents (Buriel, 1993). The child-rearing behavior of parents of third generation children varies by gender. Third generation mothers express more concern and support relative to first and second generation mothers. Fathers stress autonomy for their daughters and less strictness for their sons. All groups have similar outlooks concerning the level of equality that they encourage in parent-child relationships. On the other hand, research demonstrates that less acculturated Hispanic parents believe that their children's ability to plan and participate in various home, school, and social activities emerges at an older age than do more acculturated Hispanic parents and non-Hispanic white parents (Savage & Gauvain, 1998). Child-rearing practices of Hispanic fathers have received much less attention in the literature. However, a recent study based on a nationally-representative survey (Toth & Ku, 1999) showed that consistent with more recent research on Hispanic families, Hispanic fathers maintained high involvement in parental and family roles than may be expected given the assumption that they hold more traditional ideologies. Fathers tended to monitor and enforce their children's routines, including the amount of television viewed, types of programs viewed, and responsibility for chores, to a greater extent than did non-Hispanic white fathers.

Stress and other risk factors associated with minority status affect child-rearing practices among Mexican American parents and in turn the developmental outcomes of their children. A study of 50 Mexican American and 50 white non-Hispanic teen mothers with young children revealed that Mexican American mothers reported less nurturing and more punitive behaviors than did white mothers (Uno, Florsheim, & Uchino, 1998). However, a significant proportion of the variance between the parenting behaviors of Mexican American and white mothers is explained by the presence of greater levels of parental and financial stress among Mexican American mothers. Of course not all mothers who experience stress engage in negative parenting practices. A study of low-income Mexican American mothers showed that the effects of maternal stress on children's adjustment (conduct disorders and depression) were exacerbated by the mothers' inconsistent discipline (Dumka,

Roosa, & Jackson, 1997). However, mothers' supportive parenting decreased the negative effects. Indeed, parental competence (confidence in parenting skills) appeared to be more important than the presence of social networks in determining child rearing practices. A comparative study of Hispanics, American Indians, and Anglo caregivers found that although Hispanic social networks are large and close-knit, parental self-efficacy was more important in determining parental child rearing behaviors than was the effect of social support (MacPhee, Fritz, & Miller-Heyl, 1996).

ACADEMIC ENVIRONMENT

One reason that knowledge about parenting practices in Mexican Americans families is important to understanding the context of child development is that it allows us to assess the continuity between the home and social institutions. As stated earlier, the social interaction between Mexican American families with other systems, such as the academic and social service environments, can promote or inhibit healthy development. Smith-Maddox (1998) proposes that academic achievement occurs in the context of home, community, and school cultures, but more precisely at the point where the three intersect. Nevertheless, the perspective that a disparity, a "mismatch," between home and other social institutions is a major cause of less than optimal developmental outcomes for Mexican American children is nowhere stronger than when it comes to the educational system. Even more problematic is that the approach to cognitive achievement among minority children that has been prevalent is one that points to individual deficits of Hispanic children and their families (Solarzano & Solarzano, 1995). An extensive review of the literature by Trueba (1999) shows that the main theoretical orientation to explain the low academic achievement of Hispanics has been the deficit model, that is, deficits in Hispanic culture have been used to explain academic problems.

What characterizes the academic context of Mexican American children? First, what are the academic expectations among Mexican American students and their families? A highly comprehensive and rigorous study of a large sample of elementary school students across 20 schools covering a range of racial and ethnic and socioeconomic populations showed puzzling results (Stevenson, Chuansheng, & Uttal, 1990). It showed that in elementary school the academic expectations of Hispanic children were not substantially different than those of white children, even when controlling for socioeconomic status. Furthermore, the belief system of Hispanic children, their parents, and their teachers were consistent with what is associated with success in school: a commitment and interest in school, a belief in the value of education, and high academic expectations. Yet, what is not clear is why the ultimate educational outcomes of Hispanics are far more disadvantaged than that of whites, that is, why they are more likely to drop out of school or obtain a lower level of education than non-Hispanic whites.

To some degree, schools in fact fail to integrate the home and school context of Mexican American children, as in the case of teaching styles. For example, Stevenson, Chuansheng, and Uttal (1990) found that Hispanic mothers, regardless of socioeconomic status, considered themselves less competent than whites and black mothers to provide the type of help that their children needed in order to achieve academically in elementary school. Yet, when observing Hispanic mothers more closely, it is clear that that they are highly competent in teaching their children. An in-depth study of 12 Hispanic low-income parent-child dyads compared the parental teaching strategies on a *home* task versus a *school* task, as well as the child responses (Kermani & Janes, 1999). The findings indicated that when teaching their children a specific culturally-based self-directed task, mothers showed a higher level of teaching competence in approaching their children's learning than they did when teaching a school-like task. Furthermore, both parents and children displayed more formal and less interactive behavior in the school-like task. In general, teaching strategies of low-income Hispanic parents were characterized by hands-on modeling and guidance. At least one demonstration study showed that, in fact, when home and school literacy contexts are connected by involving parents in culturally-relevant activities with their children, children have higher levels of achievement and motivation (Morrow & Young, 1997). From the student's perspective, Hispanic children appear to favor a more cooperative learning school environment. Compared to African American students, in addition to defining a positive school climate as one that emphasizes obeying rules, doing well, and caring teacher-student relationships, Mexican American students were also more sensitive to how kids get along with each other and their level of comfort at school (Slaughter-Defoe & Carlson, 1996).

Failing to integrate the home and school contexts may be counterproductive for the performance of Mexican American children, because there is evidence to suggest that sociocultural aspects of Mexican American students may serve as resources within the academic environment (Valenzuela, 1999). One such socio-cultural characteristic is ethnic identification. A study of fourth and fifth graders of low-and middle-income Mexican American families revealed that identification with their own ethnic group lead to more positive self-perceptions concerning their social competence, behavioral competence, and self-worth (Okagaki, Frensch, & Dodson, 1996). Although it did not influence academic achievement, such positive self-concept also lead to positive attitudes toward school, including school engagement and motivation for learning. Another socio-cultural perspective that characterizes the Mexican American family and that affects school competency among Mexican American students is familism (proximity and a positive attitude toward drawing on relatives for support). Valenzuela and Dornbusch (1994) found that familism has an impact of the school grades of Mexican American, but not on Anglo youth. However, the positive effect of familism were evident only for youth of parents who had higher levels of education and who were not from immigrant families. Thus, familism is more than a cultural norm, it is a form of social capital, a resource for Mexican American youth. Bilingualism also represents a socio-cultural attitude that serves as a resource for Mexican American youth in the academic environment. Mexican American bilingual students who have gained English proficiency outperform Mexican American students of English-only backgrounds (Rumberger & Larson, 1998).

SOCIAL SERVICE ENVIRONMENT

According to Garcia Coll and Magnuson (1999), social policy designed specifically for children of color is virtually non-existent. However, policies created for low-income families disproportionately affect minority children because minority children tend to be poor. Although there is an understanding of the great economic disparities between minority and mainstream families and of the heavy negative consequences on child development, policy does not address this fundamental problem. A detailed analysis by Garcia Coll and Magnuson shows that social policy is based on a deficit perspective of minority children and their families, and that this has lead to the creation of programs seeking to remediate their personal limitations. Early childhood programs have been created to compensate for early childhood experiences that are considered lacking and disadvantaged. Parenting education programs have been designed to re-educate parents because their parenting practices have been considered ineffective. Policy that does simply provide limited relief but does not help children get out of poverty. Indeed, based on early evaluations of the current welfare program, it is clear that addressing the well-being of children in welfare families is not a priority (Padilla, 1999). All in all, Garcia Coll and Magnuson propose a re-conceptualization of social policy, such that its' goals incorporate contextual and macro-structural influences on the development of minority children, including culture, social position, discrimination, prejudicial treatment, and neighborhood and community involvement.

Thus, the social service context bears many similarities to the educational context of Mexican American children. Not only are both driven by a deficit perspective, but both are characterized by a discontinuity between home and institutional values. Curtis (1990) takes a closer look at some of the assumptions concerning Hispanic culture that have dominated social service delivery. The authors note that the literature has tended to offer guidelines concerning how to work with Latinos that are not empirically based. Based on an evaluation of a program providing mental health services in a predominantly Hispanic neighborhood in Chicago, the authors investigated four assumptions dealing with acculturation, language, folk healers, and "personalismo." Fifty Hispanic children and their families were assessed. First, he found that although issues of acculturation are considered a major source of family problems in the professional literature, there was no relationship between issues of ethnic identity and scores on the children's behavioral problems scale, nor did parents attribute their problems to cultural clashes between themselves and their children. What parents were more concerned about was their children's academic achievement. In fact, one study (Knight, Virdin, & Roosa, 1994) showed that although Latino and Anglo families varied significantly in terms of socialization styles, there was no difference in the mental health of their children.

Second, Curtis's study found that service providers cannot assume that Hispanic clients wish to speak Spanish with them in cases when clients are bilingual. This is especially true of second generation children who identify with the Hispanic culture, but who are fluent in English. Third, the study provided evidence that the significance of folk healing among Hispanics has been exaggerated. When asked if they had received services from folk healers, 76 percent of the children did not even know what that term meant, although the vast majority came from immigrant families. That Hispanic families did not believe or rely on alternative medicine, such as folk medicine or religious rites, has been supported by more recent research. A study of Hispanic parents of children with disabilities showed that only 1.5 percent of families used a combination of alternative medicine and bio-medical treatments (Bailey, Skinner, Rodrigues, Gut, & Correa, 1999). Instead they reported relying on doctors and service providers to obtain treatment for their children. The final area explored in Curtis's study concerned the expectation that Hispanics want a personal relationship with their service providers because of the value of "personalismo" (an emphasis on closer more informal rather than formal connections with people). However, the study found that although Hispanics described their relationship with their service providers in very personal terms, their overall assessment of the service provision focused on the effectiveness of the services in helping their families in very concrete terms (e.g., behavioral change in their children).

All in all, research on the continuity between Mexican American or Hispanic family context and that of social service organizations is quite limited. However, recent research is indicative of the types of issues that are important. A study by Fuller, Eggers-Pierola, Holloway, Liang, and Rambaud (1996) asked, "why do Latino parents forgo preschooling?" Based on analyses of the National Household Education Survey, the authors found that Latino families use preschool or other formal child care centers at a much lower rate (59 percent) than do African American (75 percent) or white families (69 percent). However, the lower use is not completely explained by their income, job status, education, and parenting practices. In combination with the quantitative analysis, an in-depth qualitative study of four women across a three-year period was conducted. Interviews indicated that the perception of cultural incongruences between the home and the child care facilities may help explain the lower use of formal care by Latino families. These include incongruence in terms of language (concern with the children's loss of Spanish if children are placed in these settings), relationship expectations (a preference for a personal relationship with caregivers), and socialization styles (a priority on children receiving an *educación* social skills that focus on learning respect).

Thus, although there is a growing awareness that socio-cultural factors need to be incorporated in the service delivery to Hispanic and other minority children and their families (Altarriba & Santiago Rivera, 1994; Dumas & Rollock, 1999; Ridley, Li & Hill, 1998; Rosado & Elias, 1993), problems remain. A study of social workers, counselors, psychologists, and medical professionals who provide mental health services showed that the vast majority perceived that cultural factors need to be considered when evaluating Hispanic children (Ramirez,

Wassef, Paniagua, Linskey, & Oboyle, 1994). However, the majority of professionals did not consider themselves highly capable of assessing acculturation levels, and nearly three quarters did not consider that they had adequate levels of training related to cultural background. Nevertheless, there is some evidence to show that counselors who have received training are perceived to be more effective by their clients, but the research that examines the relationship between training and therapy outcomes is limited (Yutrzenka, 1995).

Likewise, the issue of assessment and measurement tools has been foremost in the discussion concerning the social service delivery context of Mexican American children. There has been some research testing the validity and reliability of diagnostic tools for mental disorders (Chavez, Moran, Reid, & Lopez, 1997; Knight, Virdin, & Roosa, 1994), but it is very limited. Cervantes and Arroyo (1994) conducted a detailed analysis of the Diagnostic and Statistical Manual of Mental Disorders (DSM-IV) to determine problems that may arise when using it with Hispanic children. They concluded that several DSM-IV disorders are more likely to be culturally biased. For example, some sources of bias in cognitively-based diagnoses may include the failure to accurately assess language fluency in the presence of bilingualism. The potential inability of clinicians to understand language patterns may lead to errors in diagnosing psychotic disorders and other language disorders. Socialization and communication disorders may also be misdiagnosed if clinicians do not take into account cultural norms, such as the tendency of some Hispanic clients not to make eye contact as a sign of respect toward authority.

Adequacy of assessment tools for use with Mexican American children is important, not only for proper diagnosis and treatment, but to better investigate the dynamics of child development that may otherwise go unexplained. For example, a recent study by Gonzalez (1994) demonstrated that standardized testing has underestimated the positive effects of bilingualism on children's cognitive development. The reason is that standard language proficiency tests do not adequately measure both nonverbal and verbal concepts formation. Another example is the adaptation of the Societal, Attitudinal, Familial, and Environmental Stress Scale to children (Chavez, Moran, Reid, & Lopez, 1997). By using the modified version, researchers showed that despite being US-born, later generation Latino children experienced a variety of stressors and perceptions of discrimination not evident in Anglo children.

CONCLUSION

In summary, the contextual structure of child development in the Mexican American population can be conceptualized as a series of concentric circles. At the center is the immediate parental home environment surrounded by the academic, the social service, and the socio-demographic environments. Each of these environments play a role in fostering or hindering healthy development. The socio-demographic context of Mexican children is characterized by high levels of poverty and unemployment, low occupational and educational status, and residence in distressed neighborhoods. This places children in a vulnerable position because both directly and indirectly low socioeconomic status is associated with poor developmental outcomes. At the center of the social ecology of development is the parental home environment. In response to the pressures associated with a disadvantaged social position, Mexican American families draw on their cultural resources. These resources include placing a high value on bilingualism and maintaining a connection with extended family. Nevertheless, Mexican American parents display a high degree of competence in terms of their perceptions of child development and their child rearing practices.

Beyond the influence of the home, the most important milieu for Mexican American children is the academic environment. Mexican American families place a high value on education, and children in their early years in school have high educational expectations for themselves. However, there is evidence that schools fail to integrate the home and school contexts. Ethnic identification, bilingualism, and familism, important cultural values in Mexican American families, increase children's motivation and achievement in school. Yet, rather than drawing on their cultural capital, the educational system has viewed culture as the source of deficits in Mexican American children and their families and the cause of poor academic achievement. The social service system is the point of intervention for social programs. This environment mirrors the academic environment of Mexican American children in terms of its discontinuity with the family environment. In addition, social policy does not address the socioeconomic disadvantage of Mexican Americans, although the research demonstrates the detrimental consequence of such disadvantage on Mexican American child development. Furthermore, assumptions concerning Mexican Americans that have guided social service delivery have generally not been empirically tested.

A major limitation to our understanding of the development of child development in the Mexican American population is the dearth of research on children of color in general. According to the *Proceedings of the Second Society for Research on Child Development Round Table: Children of Color* (Fitzgerald, Lester, & Zuckerman, 1999), although there is advanced knowledge about cultural diversity, knowledge about how children develop within different cultures is extremely limited. Available research continues to primarily rely on deficit models of child and family functioning and has failed to advance integrative approaches, thus ignoring the influence of structural factors (Garcia Coll et al., 1996). In addition, according to Ogbu (1999), developmental research on minority children has been very problematic because it has been guided by a white middle class perspective, the focus of the research has been on children with problems, and there has been a poor understanding about the meaning of culture.

REFERENCES

Altarriba, J. & Santiago Rivera, A.L. (1994). Current perspectives on using linguistic and cultural-factors in counseling the Hispanic client. *Professional Psychology-Research and Practice, 25*(4), 388-397.

Astone, N.M. & McLanahan, 5.5. (1991). Family structure, parental practices and high School completion. *American Sociological Review, 56*(3), 309-320.

Bailey, Jr., D.B., Skinner, D., Rodriguez, P., Gut, D. & Correa, V. (1999). Awareness, use, and satisfaction with services for Latino parents of young children with disabilities. *Exceptional Children, 65*(3), 367.

Buriel, R. (1993). Child-rearing orientations in Mexican-American families: The influence of generation and socio-cultural factors. *Journal of Marriage and the Family, 5*(4), 987-1000.

Cervantes, R.C. & Arroyo, W. (1994). DSM-IV-Implications for Hispanic children and adolescents. *Hispanic Journal of Behavioral Sciences, 16*(1), 8-27.

Chavez, D.V., Moran, V.R., Reid, S.L., & Lopez, M. (1997). Acculturative stress in children: a modification of the SAPE Scale. (Societal, Attitudinal, Familial and Environmental Acculturative Stress Scale). *Hispanic Journal of Behavioral Sciences. 19*(1), 34-45.

Crooks, D.L. (1995). American children at risk: Poverty and its consequences for children's health, growth, and school achievement. *Yearbook of Physical Anthropology, 38*, 57-86.

Curtis, P.A. (1990). The consequences of acculturation to service delivery and research with Hispanic families. *Child and Adolescent Social Work, 7*(2), 147-159.

Delgado, B.M. & Ford, L. (1998). Parental perceptions of child development among low-income Mexican-American families. *Journal of Child and Family Studies, 7*(4), 469-481.

Dumka, L.E., Roosa, M.W. & Jackson, K.M. (1997). Risk, conflict, mothers' parenting, and children's adjustment in low-income, Mexican immigrant, and Mexican American families. *Journal of Marriage and the Family, 59*(2), 309-323.

Dumas, J.E. & Rollock, D. (1999). Cultural sensitivity: Problems and solutions in applied and preventive intervention. *Applied & Preventive Psychology, 8*(3), 175-196.

Fitzgerald, H.E., Lester, B.M., & Zuckerman, B.S. (1999). *Children of Color: Research, Health & Policy Issues.* New York: Garland Publishing Co.

Fuller, B., Eggers-Peirola, C., Holloway, S.D., Liang, x. & Rambaud, M.F. (1996). Rich culture, poor markets: Why do Latino parents forgo preschooling? *Teachers College Record, 97*(3), 400-419.

Garcia Coll, C., Lamberty, G., Jenkins, R., McAdoo, H.P., Crnic, K., Wasik, B.H. & Garcia, H.V. (1996). An integrative model for the study of developmental competencies in minority children. *Child Development, 67*(5), 891-1914.

Garcia Coll, C. & Magnuson, K. (1999). Cultural influences on child development: Are we ready for a paradigm shift? *Cultural Processes in Child Development,* 29,1-24.

Gonzales, V. (1994). A model of cognitive, cultural, and linguistic variables affecting bilingual Hispanic children's development of concepts and language. *Hispanic Journal of Behavioral Sciences, 16*(4), 396-421.

Gutierrez, J. & Sameroff, A. (1990). Determinants of complexity in Mexican-American and Anglo-American mothers. *Child Development, 61*(2), 384-394.

Harrison, A.O., Wilson, M.N., Pine, C.J., Chan, S.Q., & Buriel, R. (1990) Family ecologies of ethnic minority children. *Child Development, 6*(2) 347-363.

Hernandez, D.I. (1997). Child development and the social demography of childhood. *Child Development, 68*(1), 149-169.

Kermani, H. & lanes, H.A. (1999). Adjustment across task in maternal scaffolding in low-income Latino immigrant families. *Hispanic Journal of Behavioral Sciences, 21*(2), 134-135.

Knight, G.P., Cota, M.K. & Bernal, M.E. (1993). The socialization of cooperative, competitive, and individualistic preferences among Mexican American children: The mediating role of ethnic identity. *Hispanic Journal of Behavioral Sciences, 15*(3), 291-309.

Knight, G.P., Virdin, L.M. & Roosa, M. (1994). Socialization and family correlates of mental-health outcomes among Hispanic and Anglo-American children-Consideration of crossethnic scalar equivalence. *Child Development, 65*(1), 212-224.

Landale, N.S. & Lichter, D.T. (1997). Geography and the etiology of poverty among Latino children. *Social Science Quarterly, 78*(4), 874-894.

Lebanon, P.K., Brooks-Gun, J., Carton, C. & McCormick, M.C. (1998). The contribution of neighborhood and family income to developmental test scores over the first three years of life. *Child Development, 69*(5), 1420-1436.

Lichter, D.T. & Landale, N.S. (1995). Parental work, family-structure, and poverty among Latino children. *Journal of Marriage and the Family, 57*(2), 346-354.

MacPhee, D., Fritz, J. & Miller-Heyl, J. (1996). Ethnic variations in personal social networks and parenting. *Child Development, 67*(6), 3278-3295.

McLoyd, V.C. (1998). Socioeconomic disadvantage and child development. *American Psychologist*, *53*(2), 185-204.

Moreno R.P. & Cisneros0Cohernour, E.J. (1999). Strategies for effective instruction: Mexican American mothers and everyday instruction. *Latino Studies Journal*, *10*(2), 56.

Morrow, L.M. & Young, J. (1997). A family literacy program connecting school and home: Effects on attitude, motivation, and literacy achievement. *Journal of Educational Psychology*, *89*(4), 736-773.

Ogubu, J.V. (1999). Cultural context of children's development. *Children of Color: Research, Health & Policy Issues*. (pp. 73-92). New York: Garland Publishing Co.

Okagaki, L., Frensch, P.A. & Dodson, N.E. (1996). Mexican American children's perceptions of self and school achievement. *Hispanic Journal of Behavioral Sciences*, *18*(4), 469-474.

Oropesa, R.S. & Landale, N.S. (1997). Immigrant legacies: Ethnicity, generation, and children's familial and economic lives. *Social Science Quarterly*, *78*(2), 399-416.

Padilla, Y.C. (1999, September). Discussions of paper entitled: Early findings from two large studies on the consequences of welfare reform. Paper presented at the meeting of the Joint Center on Poverty Research (For better and for worse: State welfare reform and the well-being of low-income families and children), Washington, D.C.

Partida, J. (1996). The effects of immigration on children in the Mexican-American community. *Child & Adolescent Social Work Journal*, *13*(3), 241-254.

Perez-Granados, D.R. & Callahan, M.A. (1997). Parents and siblings as early resources for young children's learning in Mexican-descent families. *Hispanic Journal of Behavioral Sciences*. *19*(1) 3-34.

Ramirez, S.Z., Wassef, A., Paniagua, F.A., Linskey, A.O. & Oboyle, M. (1994). Perceptions of mental-health providers concerning cultural-factors in the evaluation of Hispanica children and adolescents. *Hispanic Journal of Behavioral Sciences*, *16*(1), 28-42.

Ridley, C.R., Li, L.C. & Hill, C.L. (1998). Multicultural assessment: Reexamination, reconceptualization, and practical application. *Counseling Psychologist*. *26*(6), 827-910.

Romero, A. (1983). The Mexican-American child: A Socioecological approach to research. *The Psychological Development of Minority Group Children*. 538-570.

Rosado, J.W. & Elias, M.J. (1993). Ecological and psychocultural mediators in the delivery of services for urban, culturally diverse Hispanic clients. *Professional Psychology Research and Practice*, *24*(4), 450-459.

Rowe, D.C., Vazsonyi, A.T. & Flannery, D.J. (1995). Ethnic and racial similarity in developmental process. *Psychological Science*. *6*(1), 33-38.

Rumberger, R.W. & Larson, K.A. (1998) Toward explaining differences in educational achievement among Mexican American language-minority students. *Sociology of Education*, *71*(1), 68-93.

Savage, S.L. & Gauvain, M. (1998). Parental beliefs and children's' everyday planning in European-American and Latino families. *Journal of Applied Developmental Psychology*, *19*(3), 319-340.

Schecter, S.R., Sharken-Taboada, D. & Bayley, R. (1996) Bilingual by choice: Latino parents' rationales and strategies for raising children with two languages. *Bilingual Research Journal, 20*(2), 261-282.

Siantz, M.D. (1999). Children in crisis: The mental health status of immigrant and migrant Hispanic children. *Children of Color: Research, Health, and Policy Issues*, (pp. 95-120). New York: Garland Publishing Co.

Slaughter-Defoe, D.T. & Carlson, K.G. (1996). Young African American and Latino children in high-poverty urban schools: How they perceive school climate. *Journal of Negro Education, 65*(1), 60-70.

Smith-Maddox, R. (1998). Defining culture as a dimension of academic achievement: Implications for culturally responsive curriculum, instruction, and assessment. *Journal of Negro Education, 67*(3), 302-317.

Solis, J. (1995) The status of Latino children and youth: Challenges and prospects. In Zambrana, R.E. (Ed.). *Understanding Latino Families: Scholarship, Policy, and Practice*, (pp. 62-80). Thousand Oaks, CA: Sage Publications.

Solorzano, D.G. & Solorzano, R.W. (1995). The Chicano educational experience–A framework of effective schools in Chicano communities. *Educational Policy, 9*(3), 293-314.

Spencer, M.B. (1990). Development of minority children: An introduction. *Child Development, 61*(2), 267-269.

St. John, C. & Miller, S. (1995). The exposure of Black and Hispanic children to urban: ghettos: Evidence from Chicago and the Southwest. *Social Science Quarterly, 76*(3), 562-576.

Stevenson, H.W., Chen, C. & Uttal, D.H. (1990). Beliefs and achievement: A study of black, white, and Hispanic children. *Child Development, 61*(2), 508-523.

Tharp, R.G. (1991). Cultural-diversity and treatment of children. *Journal of Consulting and Clinical Psychology, 59*(6), 799-812.

Toth, J. F. & Ku, X. (1999). Ethnic and cultural diversity in fathers' involvement: A racial/ethnic comparison of African American, Hispanic, and white fathers. *Youth & Society*, 31, 76-77.

Trueba, E.T. (1999). *Latinos Unidos: From Cultural Diversity to the Politics of Solidarity*. Lanham, MA: Rowman & Littlefield Publisher.

Uno, D., Florsheim, P., & Uchino, B. (1998). Psychosocial mechanisms underlying quality of parenting among Mexican-American and White adolescent mothers. *Journal of Youth and Adolescence, 27*(5), 585-589.

Valenzuela, A. (1999). Subtractive schooling: US-Mexican youth and the politics of caring. *Reflexiones 1998: New directions in Mexican American Studies*, 123-146.

Valenzuela, A. & Dornbusch, S.M. (1994). Familism and social capital in the academic achievement of Mexican origin and Anglo adolescents. Social Science Quarterly, 75(1), 18-36.

Yutrzenka, B.A. (1995). Making a case for training in ethnic and cultural-diversity in increasing treatment efficacy. *Journal of Consulting and Clinical Psychology, 63*(2), 197-206.

Zambrana, R.E. & Dorrington, C. (1998). Economic and social vulnerability of Latino children and families by subgroup: Implications for child welfare. *Child Welfare*, *77*(1), 5-27.

Zambrana, R.E., Dorrington, C., & Hayes-Bautista, D. (1995). Family and child health: A neglected vision. In Zambrana, R.E. (Ed.). *Understanding Latino Families: Scholarship, Policy, and Practice*, (pp. 157-174). Thousand Oaks, CA: Sage Publications.

Well-Being and Family Role Strains Among Cuban American and Puerto Rican Mothers of Adults with Mental Retardation

Sandra Magaña
Marsha Mailick Seltzer
Marty Wyngaarden Krauss
Mark Rubert
José Szapocznik

Sandra Magaña, PhD, is Assistant Professor at the University of Wisconsin-Madison School of Social Work and the Waisman Center on Mental Retardation and Human Development. Her research centers on Latino families who have a child or relative with a developmental disability or mental illness.

Marsha Mailick Seltzer, PhD, is Professor at the University of Wisconsin-Madison with appointments at the School of Social Work and the Waisman Center on Mental Retardation and Human Development. Her research focuses on the well-being of caregiving families across the life course.

Marty Wyngaarden Krauss, PhD, is Professor of Social Welfare and Associate Dean of the Heller School, Brandeis University. Her research investigates how families with young children and those who have reached adulthood adapt to the challenges of disability.

Mark Rubert, PhD, is a faculty member in the Department of Psychiatry and Behavioral Sciences at the University of Miami School of Medicine. His research examines aging and caregiving.

José Szapocznik, PhD, is Professor of Psychiatry and Behavioral Sciences, Psychology and Counseling Psychology at the University of Miami. Dr. Szapocznik is Director of the Center for Family Studies and the Spanish Family Guidance Center, at the University of Miami School of Medicine. His research has cut across a range of mental health issues for Hispanic and minority families including families and HIV, family therapy and family based prevention, families and substance abuse, and families and developmental disabilities.

[Haworth co-indexing entry note]: "Well-Being and Family Role Strains Among Cuban American and Puerto Rican Mothers of Adults with Mental Retardation." Magaña, Sandra et al. Co-published simultaneously in *Journal of Human Behavior in the Social Environment* (The Haworth Social Work Practice Press, an imprint of The Haworth Press, Inc.) Vol. 5, No. 3/4, 2002, pp. 31-55; and: *Latino/Hispanic Liaisons and Visions for Human Behavior in the Social Environment* (ed: José B. Torres, and Felix G. Rivera) The Haworth Social Work Practice Press, an imprint of The Haworth Press, Inc., 2002, pp.31-55. Single or multiple copies of this article are available for a fee from The Haworth Document Delivery Service [1-800-HAWORTH, 9:00 a.m. - 5:00 p.m. (EST). E-mail address: getinfo@haworthpressinc.com].

SUMMARY. This article examines predictors of depressive symptoms and caregiving burden in a sample of Cuban American and Puerto Rican caregivers of an adult child with mental retardation. Using a stress process model of caregiving, the focus of this analysis was on family role strains that result from the caregiving process, which were hypothesized to be particularly strong predictors of maternal well-being in Latino families. Findings indicate that Cuban American mothers of adults with mental retardation had higher socioeconomic status than Puerto Rican mothers, yet there was a substantial amount of within-group heterogeneity in family socio-demographic characteristics, linked closely with immigration patterns for the Cuban American mothers. However, taking into account socio-demographic diversity and ethnicity, findings demonstrate that mothers whose family had more problems had higher levels of burden and depressive symptoms, supporting the hypothesized importance of family functioning to Latina mothers with a non-normative parenting challenge. *[Article copies available for a fee from The Haworth Document Delivery Service: 1-800-HAWORTH. E-mail address: <getinfo@haworthpressinc.com> Website: <http://www.HaworthPress.com> © 2002 by The Haworth Press, Inc. All rights reserved.]*

KEYWORDS. Well-being, role strains, Cuban, Puerto Rican, mental retardation

INTRODUCTION

This article examines the caregiving context of Cuban American and Puerto Rican mothers of an adult child with mental retardation in order to better understand the influence of culture on the stress and coping process. We investigated the predictors of caregiver well-being among these Latino samples to identify both similarities and differences in the effects of important aspects of the caregiving context and cultural characteristics for Cuban American and Puerto Rican mothers.

Recent family research on mental retardation has been based on a life course perspective, which examines caregiving across different life stages (Seltzer & Heller, 1997). As a result, mental retardation family research has expanded beyond studying families with young children to include families at different stages of the family life course (Seltzer & Ryff, 1994). Findings from Seltzer and Krauss' (1994) longitudinal study of older mothers of adult children with mental retardation were surprising. Although these mothers were expected to exhibit more psychological and health problems than parents of young children with mental retardation, the aging mothers were in fact less stressed and less burdened than parents of young children, in better health than other women their age, and had better morale than caregivers of elderly persons (Krauss & Seltzer, 1999; Seltzer & Krauss, 1994). Other studies have emphasized the unique service needs of older families caring for an adult with mental retardation (Fullmer, Tobin, & Smith, 1997; Heller & Factor, 1994; Smith, Fullmer & Tobin, 1994).

The conceptual framework utilized in much research about older adults with mental retardation and their families is based on stress process models that have been adapted from life course and caregiving studies (Lazarus & Folkman, 1984; McCubbin & Patterson, 1983; Pearlin, Mullan, Semple, & Skaff, 1990). One such model has been specified by Pearlin and his colleagues (1990) which has had a considerable influence on research on stress and coping among caregivers of older adults. An important domain in this model is the social context (i.e., age, gender, marital status, and socio-economic status), which is expected to have an important influence on the stress process because these characteristics may indicate where people stand in the social order and what resources they may have available to them. Other domains include primary stressors (e.g., maladaptive behaviors and functional limitations of the person receiving care) which determine the nature and magnitude of care required, and secondary stressors (e.g., family and job conflict) which are conceptualized as strains that potentially result from the primary stressors.

The role of the social and cultural context on individual family members is receiving attention in the theoretical, research and practice literatures (Szapocznik & Kurtines, 1989; Szapocznik & Coatsworth, 1999, Szapocznik & Williams, 2000). There is a growing literature on Latinos as caregivers for the elderly (Aranda & Knight, 1997; Cox & Monk, 1993; Delgado & Tennstedt, 1997; Mintzer et al., 1992; Mintzer, Rubert, & Herman, 1994; Sotomayor & Randolph, 1988) and some studies of Latino caregivers of young children with mental retardation (Bailey et al., 1999; Blacher, Shapiro, Lopez, Diaz, & Fusco, 1997; Harry, 1992; Heller, Markwardt, Rowitz, & Farber, 1994). However, virtually no published research has been focused on family caregivers of adult Latinos with mental retardation, with the exception of a study of Puerto Rican families (Magaña, 1999).

Only a few studies have been published on families of color who have an adult son or daughter with mental retardation (Chen & Tang,

1997; Magaña, 1999; McCallion, Janicki, & Grant-Griffin, 1997; Pruchno, Patrick, & Burant, 1997). Chen and Tang (1997) conducted a study of thirty Chinese mothers of adults with mental retardation living in Hong Kong, and found that the most common stressors were similar to those found in Western studies: behavior problems of the son or daughter and the need for future planning. Another recent study, which explored cultural values and beliefs in the context of caregiving, described older families from various ethnic groups caring for persons with developmental disabilities in the US, including African American, Chinese American, Haitian American, Latino/Latina American, Korean American, and Native American communities (McCallion et al., 1997). Using focus group methodology, researchers in this study found that adherence to cultural values varied based on differing levels of acculturation. Virtually all of the participants valued family involvement and expected family participation in caregiving, even though economic and social realities interfered with the ability of some families to maintain this cultural value (McCallion et al., 1997).

Socioeconomic limitations were common in other studies of samples of color who cared for an adult with mental retardation. For example, Pruchno et al. (1997) found that African American mothers of adults with mental retardation were of lower socioeconomic status, were more likely to live with their adult with the disability, and experienced less caregiving burden and reported greater satisfaction than White mothers. In contrast, in a study of Puerto Rican mothers of an adult with mental retardation, Magaña (1999) found that in addition to extremely low socio-economic status, these mothers were in very poor health, which, in turn, was associated with elevations in both caregiving burden and depressive symptoms.

The current study focuses on two groups of Latina mothers in the US (Cuban Americans and Puerto Ricans) who have an adult son or daughter with mental retardation. In this study we test an adaptation of the stress process model of Pearlin and his colleagues (1990) by investigating the relationship of family problems to the mothers' psychological well-being. Family is an important institution for most cultural groups, particularly in the caregiving process. Pearlin et al. (1990) incorporate the importance of family into the stress process model by including family conflict in the domain of secondary role strain. The significance of the family for Latinos has been well documented, although there has been some criticism that more research is needed to understand its unique significance (Aranda & Knight, 1997; Baca Zinn & Wells, 2000). In this article we build on the concept of family strain put forth by Pearlin et al. (1990) by examining problems in family functioning that result from the caregiving process. Because of the importance of family for Latinos, we hypothesize that mothers' own psychological well-being will be more strongly affected by the functioning of their family than by the other factors measured in our study.

Research on Latino families with a child with mental retardation has confirmed the importance of the family (Bailey et al., 1999; Blacher et al., 1997; Harry, 1992; Heller et al., 1994; Magaña, 1999). For example, Blacher et al. (1997) found that high family cohesion was associated with low maternal depression among a primarily Mexican-American sample of mothers with a child with mental retardation. In a qualitative study of Puerto Rican mothers with a child in special education, Harry (1992) found that mothers made many references indicating the importance of family. For example, some parents described the strengths and weaknesses of their child as family characteristics (rather than child characteristics), which served to protect the child by shifting the responsibility for these characteristics from the child to the family. In a study of Puerto Rican mothers of adults with mental retardation, Magaña (1999) found that various family members provided instrumental caregiving support to their relative with mental retardation, but this type of support was not predictive of the mothers' emotional well-being. Instead, having larger social support networks (which were composed primarily of family members) and greater satisfaction with support were predictive of lower levels of depressive symptoms for these mothers. In a study of Mexican American and Puerto Rican families of preschool age children with developmental disabilities, Bailey et al. (1999) found that parents reported receiving equally high levels of support from the family and the formal support system, but significantly less support from friends. On the other hand, there is evidence that support from the family may be no different for Latinos than for other groups. Heller et al. (1994) found that Latino and non-Latino White mothers of an adult with mental retardation had similar degrees of family support, although Latino mothers had less support from friends. However, when controlling for SES, this difference in support from friends was no longer significant.

It is important to recognize that US Latinos are a very diverse group with different countries of origin, migration patterns to the US, and political histories. Although most research on Latinos has been conducted on Mexican-Americans, findings have been over-generalized to other Latino groups (Baca Zinn & Wells, 2000). The current study adds to the literature by examining two distinct US Latino groups, Cuban Americans and Puerto Ricans, to determine differences and similarities they report in the stress and coping process.

Political history and migration patterns are two factors that are distinct between Cuban Americans and Puerto Ricans. Cuban migration to the US was initially precipitated by the 1959 Castro revolution and is frequently characterized by three waves. The first wave began in the early 1960s with the former Cuban economic and political elite. The second began in the mid-1960s and continued until the late 1970s, and was representative of all socioeconomic levels in the Cuban population. The third wave started in 1980 and continued through the 1990s with Cubans of low socio-economic status (Baca Zinn & Wells, 2000; Bernal & Shapiro, 1996; Garcia-Preto, 1996a). The combination of support provided by the US government and the already economically advantaged status of the first wave of Cuban immigrants resulted in a strong and economically viable Latin ethnic enclave in the Miami area. This enclave sustains itself economically and politically through Cuban American ownership of businesses, professional services, and institutions (Baca Zinn & Wells, 2000). It also provides a unique context that may itself influence the caregiving experience for those Cuban Americans who live in the Miami area. How caregiving fits within that social context is in question. Are there natural supports within this community available to caregivers, or alternatively, do caregivers struggle with balancing multiple roles that are unique to their culture and social structure?

In contrast, mainland Puerto Ricans are among the most economically disadvantaged of all Latino groups (Baca Zinn & Wells; 2000; Garcia-Preto, 1996a). Puerto Rican migration, although politically influenced, is more economically based. In 1898, the US colonized Puerto Rico. Since the early 1900s, Puerto Ricans have been migrating to Northeastern US cities in search of jobs, education and new opportunities. Migration increased after World War II due to greater economic opportunities. The period after World War II to about 1965 is referred to as the "Great Migration." Since that time there has been a "revolving door migration" in which Puerto Ricans migrate back and forth depending on economics and employment opportunities on the Mainland and the Island. Some families migrate to solve problems including obtaining help from relatives who already migrated, resolving marital problems, or obtaining help for a sick or disabled relative (Garcia-Preto, 1996b).

Most studies that make comparisons across Latino groups report socio-demographic differences. For example, analyses based on the

1988 National Survey of Hispanic Elderly People (NSHEP) found that in comparison to Cuban American elders (N = 714), Puerto Rican elders (N = 368) were more likely to live in poverty, and were less likely to be married or to have a high school education (Burnette & Mui, 1995; Dietz, John, & Roy, 1998; Tran & Dhooper, 1996; Tran & Williams, 1998). Puerto Rican elders were also found to be in worse health and had more daily living impairments than Cuban American elders in the NSHEP (Burnette & Mui, 1995).

Other studies investigated adherence to cultural values such as familism among specific Latino groups, including Mexican Americans (Keefe, Padilla, & Carlos, 1979), Puerto Ricans (Cortes, 1995; Rodríguez & Kosloski, 1998), and Cuban Americans (Szapocznik, Scopetta, Aranalde, & Kurtines, 1978). However, only one published study has made direct comparisons about cultural values across Latino groups (Sabogal, Marin, Otero-Sabogal, Marín, & Perez-Stable, 1987). Sabogal et al. (1987) compared Mexican-, Cuban- and Central Americans on three attitudinal factors of familism: perceived family support, familial obligations, and family as referents. The researchers found that all three Latino groups reported agreement with these attitudinal factors and, in comparison to a White non-Latino sample, the combined Latino sample showed stronger endorsement of these factors. The present study extends this line of research to investigate how problems in the family might influence the stress process for two groups of Latinos caring for an adult with mental retardation.

The research questions and hypotheses for this study are:

1. To what extent do Cuban Americans and Puerto Ricans caring for a son or daughter with mental retardation differ with respect to socio-demographic characteristics? Based on the literature cited above, it is hypothesized that the Cuban American mothers in this study will be more likely to be married, have higher socio-economic status (as measured by income, home ownership, and years of education), and to be in better health than Puerto Rican mothers of adults with mental retardation.

2. Do Puerto Rican and Cuban American caregivers differ in family functioning and emotional well-being, as measured by level of family problems, depressive symptoms and subjective caregiving burden? It is hypothesized that because Puerto Rican mothers are expected to be in poorer health and of lower SES, they will have higher levels of family problems, depressive symptoms and more caregiving burden than Cuban American mothers.

3. What are the predictors of depressive symptoms and burden among Latina mothers of adults with mental retardation? It is hypothesized that because of the theorized importance of family functioning to maternal well-being among Latinas, family problems will be the strongest predictor of depressive symptoms and caregiving burden for both Cuban American and Puerto Rican mothers.
4. To what extent are the predictors of caregiving burden and depressive symptoms different for the two groups? We do not include a hypothesis for this question as it is an exploratory analysis.

METHOD

Sample

Participants included in this study were 44 Puerto Rican mothers from Massachusetts and 49 Cuban American mothers from Miami-Dade County, all of whom had an adult child with mental retardation who lived at home. Puerto Rican mothers were recruited with the help of personnel from 14 area offices of the Massachusetts Department of Mental Retardation and community organizations in Massachusetts that serve Latino families who have a family member with mental retardation. In addition, eight families were identified by participating sample. Service providers were asked to refer all families who met the three criteria: the mother was the main caregiver for a son or daughter with mental retardation, the son or daughter lived at home, and the mother and/or the son or daughter were of Puerto Rican descent.

A key element of sample recruitment in this study was a reliance on personal contact of service providers with potential sample members. Service providers presented information written in Spanish or English to the families and reviewed it with them. They then asked families if they would be interested in being contacted by the study staff. There was a 97% response rate of those families who were approached about the study, which resulted in the participation of 73 Puerto Rican mothers. Only those mothers who were age 55 and over ($N = 45$) were included in the present analysis in order to sharpen the focus on older mothers caring for an adult with mental retardation. However, one mother had substantial amounts of incomplete data, so this family was not included, leaving 44 Puerto Rican families in this analysis.

Names for the Cuban American sample were obtained from the State of Florida Department of Children and Families–Developmental Services (CFS-DS) in Dade County that serves clients with developmental disabilities. All families of CFS-DS who were identified as Latino and whose son or daughter was not living in an institutional setting or group home were sent letters describing the project and given a number to call if they were interested in participating. Of those families who were in contact with the study, 83% participated. Families who participated met the following criteria: the adult with the developmental disability was living with a family member; the primary caregiver was a relative and Latino; and the primary caregiver provided the majority of assistance with activities of daily living to the adult with a developmental disability. Only those families in which primary caregiver was a mother aged 55 or older who self-identified as Cuban or Cuban American were included in the present analysis (N = 49).

Measures

Characteristics of the mother included ethnicity, marital status, age, years of education, years in the US, and self-reported physical health status. Dummy variables were constructed for ethnicity (1 = Cuban American, 0 = Puerto Rican) and marital status (1 = married, 0 = widowed, divorced, separated or single). Physical health was measured by a question taken from the Older Americans' Resources and Services Multidimensional Functional Assessment which asks the mother to rate her own health from excellent (4) to poor (1). The criterion-related validity of this item with a physical examination was reported to be .70 (Multidimensional Functional Assessment Manual, 1978).

Characteristics of the son or daughter with mental retardation included level of mental retardation, the number and severity of maladaptive behaviors, and the number of services received. Level of mental retardation was measured by mother's reports ranging from (3) mild to (0) profound retardation. Number and severity of maladaptive behaviors were measured by a scale from the ICAP (Inventory for Clients in Agency Planning; Bruininks et al., 1986). There were eight items in which the mother was asked whether her son or daughter had the maladaptive behavior, and if so, with what severity, ranging from (1) not serious to (5) extremely serious. To determine the number of maladaptive behaviors, researchers counted the maladaptive behaviors of the son or daughter. To determine severity of maladaptive behaviors, the severity ratings for the eight items were added together.

Items in which the son or daughter did not exhibit the behavior were coded as 0. In addition, each study site (Miami and Massachusetts) included a measure listing services that are typically received by persons with mental retardation. Mothers were asked if their son or daughter received the service. Services that both studies had in common were counted. Services included in this measure were: case management, therapy services, psychological services, legal services, transportation, self-care services, respite, income support, and social/recreational activities.

Family problems were measured by a subscale of the revised version of the Questionnaire on Resources and Stress-F (Friedrich, Greenberg, & Crnic, 1983). This subscale consists of 20 items answered yes (score of 1) or no (score of 0) reflecting family well-being and functioning. Sample items are: "Other members of the family have to do without things because of (son or daughter)." "The constant demands for care for (son or daughter) limit growth and development of someone else in our family." The scale's alpha reliability was .74 for the present sample.

Outcome variables for this study included two measures: depressive symptoms and caregiver burden. Depressive symptoms were measured by the Center for Epidemiologic Studies Depression (CES-D) Scale (Radloff, 1977). This is a measure of the frequency of 20 depressive symptoms that had occurred over the last week, each rated on a 4-point scale. The CES-D has been shown to be valid and reliable with many populations and is often used in cross-cultural research (Blacher et al., 1997). Some researchers have cautioned against making cross-cultural comparisons between Latinos and non-Latino cultural groups, because Latinos are more likely to report elevated symptoms (Coelho, Strauss & Jenkins, 1998; Guarnaccia, Angel & Lowe Worebey, 1989; Kolody, Vega, Meinhardt & Bensussen, 1986; Stroup-Benham, Lawrence & Treviño, 1992). Loss is known about the validity of using the CES-D to compare different Latino groups to each other. The scale's alpha reliability was .88 for the present sample.

Caregiver burden was assessed by an adaptation of the Zarit Burden Scale (Zarit, Reever & Bach-Peterson, 1980). Twelve items that both studies had in common were used in this analysis, each answered on a 3-point scale, ranging from 0 (not at all true) to 2 (extremely true). Examples of items we used are, "I feel that my son or daughter makes requests which I perceive to be over and above what she needs," "Because of my involvement with my son or daughter, I don't have enough time for myself, " and "I feel embarrassed over my son or daughter's behavior." The scales' alpha reliability was .73 for the present sample.

Data Collection Procedures

In both research sites, families who expressed interest in the study were contacted by telephone by bilingual, bicultural interviewers who explained the study in more detail and confirmed that recruitment criteria were met. Demographic information was also obtained in the telephone call. Bilingual, bicultural interviewers with two days of training in survey interview techniques administered structured interviews at the participants' homes. Measures not already available in Spanish were translated in Miami using the translation, back translation-method (Kurtines & Szapocznik, 1995). For the Puerto Rican sample, all items were read aloud to the mothers even though some measures are typically self-administered because it was recognized that some mothers may not have been able to read or may not have felt comfortable with a reading and writing component. For the Cuban American sample, most items were read to the mothers with the exception of the Family Problems scale and the CES-D. These measures were self-administered by those who were able to complete the questionnaire, and read to those who were not. Mothers in both research sites were paid $20 for the interview at the end of the visit as a gesture of respect for their time. Interviews lasted an average of three hours.

RESULTS

Ethnic Differences in Demographic Characteristics

Our first research question asked, to what extent do the two Latino groups differ on sociodemographic characteristics? Consistent with our hypothesis, Cuban Americans had higher socioeconomic status, were in better health, and were more likely to be married (see Table 1).

With respect to socioeconomic status, Table 1 shows that the median income of Cuban American families was slightly higher, but the difference not significant. However, Cuban Americans were significantly more likely to own their home and had more years of education. Additional findings shown in Table 1 are that Puerto Rican mothers had significantly more children, and the Puerto Rican adults with mental retardation received more services. Differences in service systems between Miami and Massachusetts may account for differences in receipt of services. Because the number of services correlated with outcomes

TABLE 1. Comparison of Demographic Characteristics

Variable	Puerto Rican (N = 44)	Cuban (N = 49)	Test
Mother Characteristics			
Mean age	63.6 (8.5)	63.7 (8.3)	t = .1
Mean years of education	6.6 (4.6)	10.7 (4.5)	t = 4.3***
Percent who own home	11.4	66.7[1]	χ^2 = 29.2***
Median income	10,000-14,999	15,000-15,999[2]	t = 1.7+
Mean years in the US	25.4 (14.7)	26.3(10.6)	t = .4
Percent in poor/fair health	79.5	53.1	χ^2 = 7.2**
Percent married	25.0	83.7	χ^2 = 32.4***
Mean number of children	6.7 (3.9)	2.3 (1.7)	t = −7.0***
Household size	3.0 (1.1)	3.4 (1.0)	t = 1.8+
Child Characteristics			
Percent male	47.7	55.1	χ^2 = .5
Mean age	33.0 (9.3)	34.1 (10.0)	t = .6
Percent with profound or severe mental retardation	52.5[3]	47.0	χ^2 = .3
Percent in day program	54.5	53.1	χ^2 = .0
Mean # of behavior problems	2.4 (1.8)	1.9 (2.0)	t = −1.2
Mean behavior problem severity	5.0 (5.0)	5.9 (6.9)	t = .7
number of services received	4.3 (1.6)	1.9 (1.4)	t = −77***

+p < .10, *p < .05, ** p < .01, *** p < .001
Standard deviations in parentheses; [1]N = 48, [2]N = 46, [3]N = 40

(see Table 2), the number of services was used as a control variable in the multivariate analysis.

Because the Cuban American sample was not expected to be homogeneous in socioeconomic status due to the varying waves of migration discussed earlier, a comparison was made among the three migration waves to determine differences in socio-demographic variables. A categorical variable was constructed in which Wave 1 included all Cuban American mothers who migrated before 1965 (N = 17), Wave 2 included Cuban American mothers who migrated between 1965 and 1979 (N = 21), and Wave 3 included Cuban American mothers who migrated from 1980 on (N = 11). As expected, there were differences among the three groups in socioeconomic status. Cuban American mothers who migrated early had the most education (*M* = 12.5, *SD* = 2.9) and the most recently arrived mothers had the lowest level of education *(M* = 8.8,

TABLE 2. Correlations of Study Variables (n = 93)

	1	2	3	4	5	6	7	8	9	10	11
1. CES-D											
2. Burden	.32**										
3. Family problems	.30**	.66***									
4. Mother's age	−.08	−.15	−.04								
5. Mothers' health status	−.42***	−.16	−.19+	−.01							
6. Years of education	−.24*	.07	.16	−.27**	.20+						
7. Marital status (married = 1)	−.10	.44***	.36***	−.21*	.11	.35**					
8. Ethnicity (Cuban = 1)	−.08	.46***	.55***	.01	.22*	.41***	.59***				
9. Years in the US	−.31**	−.05	−.16	.17	.14	.10	.01	.04			
10. Severity of behaviors	−.18+	.29**	.25*	−.10	−.16	.09	.04	.07	−.02		
11. Number of services	.03	−.25*	−.32**	.04	−.11	−.14	−.42**	−.63***	−.07	−.02	

+p < .10, *p < .05, **p < .01, ***p < .001

$SD = 4.5$), F (2, 49) = 2.7, P = .08. Likewise, 87.5% of Cuban American mothers who migrated early owned their own homes, while only 36.4% of Cuban American mothers who arrived most recently owned their own homes, χ^2 (2, $N = 49$) = 7.7, $p = .02$.

We also examined differences in the demographic variables in Table 1 between Puerto Rican mothers who migrated in two different periods (the Great Migration period, those who migrated before 1964; and the revolving door period, those who migrated from 1965 on) but found no significant differences.

Ethnic Differences in Family Problems and Emotional Well-Being

Our second research question asked, to what extent do Cuban American and Puerto Rican caregivers differ in family functioning and emotional well-being, as measured by the level of family problems, depressive symptoms, and subjective caregiving burden? We hypothesized that because Puerto Ricans are in poorer health and of lower SES, they would have higher depressive symptoms and more family problems and caregiving burden. These hypotheses were not supported. There was no significant difference between the two groups with respect to depressive symptoms, (M Cubans = 16.7, SD = 11.6; M Puerto Ricans = 18.5, SD = 12.2), t (93) = $-.75$, p = .454. However, contrary to the hypothesis, the Cuban American mothers (M = 10.4, SD = 3.2) were significantly more burdened than the Puerto Rican mothers M = 6.2, SD = 4.9), t (93) = 4.9, p = .000, and had significantly more family problems (M = *101 SD* = 2.8) than the Puerto Rican mothers (M = 66 SD = 3.5), t (93) = 6.2, p = .000.

We also examined differences in family problems and emotional well-being within the two ethnic groups according to migration patterns, and found differences in the level of depressive symptoms only within the Cuban American group. Cuban American mothers who migrated early had lower levels of depressive symptoms (M = 11.4, SD = 10.9), while Cuban American mothers who migrated most recently had considerably higher levels of depressive symptoms (M = 21.3, SD = 11.6), F (2, 49) = 3.1, p = .05. When years of education and home ownership were controlled for, however, this difference was no longer significant.

Predictors of Depressive Symptoms and Burden

Our third research question asked, what are the predictors of depressive symptoms and burden among Latina mothers of adults with mental retardation? To examine patterns predictive of the outcome variables, hierarchical multiple regressions were conducted. Three domains of independent variables were entered into the regression models: mother characteristics, which represent the social context domain of Pearlin et al.'s model (1990); child characteristics, which represent the primary stressors domain; and family problems which represent the secondary stressor/role strain domain. Because of sample size, the total number of variables used in the model was limited. Variables were chosen based on theoretical importance, their correlation with the dependent variables, and variables that needed to be taken into account because they were significantly different between the two groups. In addition, ethnicity was used as dummy variable (Cuban American = 1, Puerto Rican = 0). Because of the importance of timing of migration, at least for the Cuban American sample, years in the US was included in the regression model.

Table 2 shows the bivariate relations among the study variables of the combined sample. More depressive symptoms were correlated with more family problems, mothers' poor health, fewer years of education, and fewer years in the United States. More caregiving burden was correlated with more family problems, being married, being Cuban American, having a son or daughter with more severe behavior problems, and receiving fewer services. Table 3 shows the multiple regression results. As in the bivariate analysis, poor health of the mother, fewer years of education and fewer years in the US were predictive of higher levels of depressive symptoms (step 1). The addition of child characteristics (step 2) did not explain any additional variance in maternal depressive symptoms. In step 3, the family problems variable was entered into the model, and consistent with our hypothesis, a higher score on family problems was predictive of more depressive symptoms. The final model accounted for 27% of the variance in depressive symptoms, with 4% of the explained variance associated with family problems.

In examining the predictors of burden, poor maternal health, being married and ethnicity were predictive of higher burden, with Cuban Americans having higher burden scores (see Table 3, step 1). There were weak effects for younger mothers and those with fewer years of education to be more burdened. Additionally, more severe behavior problems of the son or daughter was predictive of more burden (step 2). Family problems were a major predictor of burden (step 3), accounting for 14% of the total variance explained ($R^2 = .50$).

When the family problems variable was entered into the model for predicting burden, ethnicity was no longer a significant predictor. This finding suggests that family problems mediate the main effect of ethnicity on burden. The correlation matrix (Table 2) shows three bivariate correlations relevant to this mediation effect: ethnicity with family problems (with Cuban Americans having higher family problems than Puerto Ricans: $r = .55$, $p < .001$), family problems with burden ($r = 66$, $p < .001$), and ethnicity with burden (with Cuban Americans having higher burden scores than Puerto Ricans: $r = .46$, $p < .001$). Figure 1 shows the mediation effect, namely that when controlling for family problems, ethnicity is no longer predictive of burden, but family problems still are. Thus, one reason why Cuban Americans appear to be more burdened by caregiving is their elevated level of family problems.

Differences in Predictors Between Cuban Americans and Puerto Ricans

Our fourth research question asked to what extent the predictors of depressive symptoms and caregiving burden are different for the two

TABLE 3. Hierarchical Regression of Maternal Emotional Well-Being

Mother Characteristics	Depressive Symptoms						Caregiver Burden					
	Step 1		Step 2		Step 3		Step 1		Step 2		Step 3	
Age	−.13	(.14)	−.12	(.14)	−.12	(.14)	−.16+	(.05)	−.14	(.05)	−.13+	(.05)
Health status	−.37***	(1.15)	−.35**	(1.17)	−27**	(1.21)	−.25**	(.42)	−.21*	(.42)	−.08	(.39)
Years of education	−.21*	(.26)	−.22*	(.26)	−.20+	(.25)	−.20+	(.09)	−.23*	(.09)	.20*	(.08)
Years in the US	−.22*	(.09)	−.23*	(.09)	−.19*	(.09)	.01	(.03)	.01	(.03)	.08	(.03)
Marital status (married = 1, other = 0)	−.11	(2.79)	−.11	(2.81)	−.12	(2.74)	.24*	(1.02)	.25*	(.99)	.23*	(.88)
Ehnicity (1 = Cuban, 0 = Puerto Rican)	.17	(2.89)	.14	(3.43)	−.03	(3.78)	.46***	(1.06)	.51***	(1.21)	.20	(1.21)
Child Characteristics												
Severity of maladaptive behaviors			.12	(.18)	.08	(.18)			.22*	(.07)	.14+	(.06)
Number of services received			−.02	(.75)	−.03	(.73)			.12	(.27)	.10	(.24)
Family Role Strain												
Family problems					.28*	(.38)					.49***	(.12)
Adjusted R²	.24		.23		.27		.32		.36		.50	
F statistic	5.7***		4.5***		4.8***		8.2***		7.5***		11.2***	

Standardized beta coefficients are reported, standard errors in parentheses
+p < .10, *p < .05, **p < .01, ***p < .001

groups? To determine whether there were any differences in predictors across the two groups, interaction terms between ethnicity and each of the eight other independent variables in the regression models were constructed and tested in preliminary exploratory analyses. For caregiving burden, we did not find any differences in predictors between the two groups when interaction terms were entered into the model. For depressive symptoms, we found only one significant interaction, namely that maternal health was a stronger predictor of depressive symptoms for Puerto Rican mothers than for Cuban American mothers (see step 2 of Table 4 and Figure 2). Figure 2 shows that Puerto Rican mothers who are in poor health have very high levels of depressive symptoms, whereas those in excellent health have no depressive symptoms. For the Cuban American mothers depressive symptoms were elevated regardless of health status. Note that the health variable was centered (the mean of maternal health was subtracted from the value in each case) in the interaction term to minimize the correlation with other variables.

FIGURE 1. Relationship of ethnicity to burden when controlling for family problems

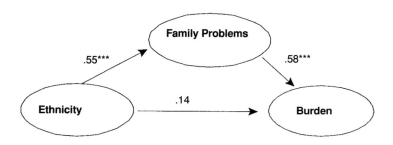

DISCUSSION

The Latina mothers in our study share two very important common characteristics: they have cared for a son or daughter with mental retardation over the course of most of their adult lives and their families were members of a Latino ethnic minority group. At the same time, we recognized that the cultural context of caregiving may be different for each group. Overall, we found that, consistent with other studies that have compared Latino groups, Puerto Rican mothers were more disadvantaged than the Cuban American mothers in socioeconomic status and demographic characteristics such as health and marital status. In contrast, Cuban American mothers had higher levels of distress than Puerto Rican mothers as measured by family problems and burden. We argue below that the social structure of the Cuban American enclave in Miami may contribute to this elevated level of family problems, despite their socioeconomic advantage.

Another difference between the two groups concerned the relation of maternal health to depressive symptoms, reflected in Figure 2. Poor health was more strongly related to depressive symptoms among Puerto Rican mothers than for Cuban American mothers. The strong relation of health to depression among Puerto Rican women has been documented in other studies (Angel & Guarnaccia, 1989; Guarnaccia, Good & Kleinman, 1990). For example, a study comparing the relation of self-rated health and depressive symptoms between Puerto Ricans and Mexican Americans found that Puerto Ricans who reported themselves to be in fair and poor health had higher CES-D scores than Mexican-Americans with similar levels of health problems (Angel & Guarnaccia, 1989).

TABLE 4. Regression of Depressive Symptoms with Interaction Term

	Step 1		Step 2	
Mother Characteristics				
Age	−.12	(.14)	−.08	(.14)
Health status	−.27**	(1.21)	−.58***	(1.80)
Years of education	−.20+	(.25)	−.17	(.25)
Years in the US	−.19*	(.09)	−.20	(.09)
Marital status	−.12	(2.74)	−.14	(2.65)
Ethnicity	−.03	(3.78)	.00	(3.66)
Child Characteristics				
Severity of maladaptive behaviors	.08	(.18)	.15	(.18)
Number of services received	−.03	(.73)	−.06	(.71)
Family Role Strain				
Family problems	.28*	(.38)	.20	(.38)
Interaction Term				
Mothers' health X ethnicity			.38**	(2.32)
Adjusted R²	.27		.32	
F statistic	4.8***		5.4***	

Standardized beta coefficients are reported, standard errors in parentheses
+$p < .10$, *$p < .05$, **$p < .01$, ***$p < .001$

More research is needed to determine why Puerto Rican mothers are particularly vulnerable emotionally to health problems. On the other hand, the level of distress of Cuban American mothers was not a function of their health.

We found that there was variability among the three waves of Cuban migration with respect to depressive symptoms. Mothers who migrated during the first wave were comparable in their average CES-D score to a similar sample of Anglo-American caregivers (Seltzer, Krauss, & Greenberg, 1995), while the CES-D score of Cuban mothers who migrated more recently were similar to the Puerto Rican mothers in the current study. This suggests substantial within-ethnic group heterogeneity, which underscores the importance of socioeconomic status and, for Cuban Americans, historical time of migration, for maternal well-being. Vidal de Haymes (1997) refutes the so-called Cuban American success story by describing differential poverty rates, social class positions, and occupational roles for later wave immigrants who are often Black or of mixed race origin. Our findings corroborate Vidal de Hayme's assertion: Cuban American mothers who have lived in Miami the longest are more economically and psy-

FIGURE 2. Interaction between ethnicity and maternal health

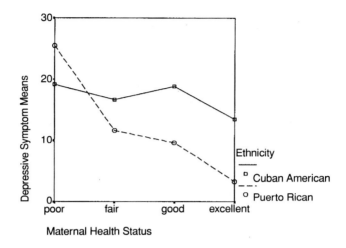

chologically advantaged, while those who migrated later are poorer and more distressed. In contrast, Puerto Ricans on the mainland have remained a minority group that is poor, and in poor physical and emotional health.

A finding of interest related to both Puerto Ricans and Cuban Americans was that married mothers were more burdened by caregiving than unmarried mothers, a pattern not characteristic of Anglo-American mothers who care for an adult with mental retardation (Seltzer, Greenberg, Krauss, & Hong, 1997). Unique gender roles among Latino groups may account for this relationship. Although the gender terms often attributed to Latinos, "machismo" and "marianismo," may be overgeneralized and contribute to negative stereotypes, some understanding of these terms may help in interpreting the findings. "Marianismo" is based on the Catholic belief in the Virgin Mary, and denotes that women are morally and spiritually superior to men, and as a result, better able to endure suffering (Comaz-Diaz, 1982; Sanchez-Ayendez, 1989; Torres, 1998). The cultural expectation is that women will demonstrate self-sacrifice in favor of their children and husbands, and consequently will be more involved in child rearing and maintaining the household. In contrast, the expectations of "machismo" are that the men will protect and provide for the family and maintain self-respect (Torres, 1998) and not do housework or child care. In the context of caregiving, women who are married may be more burdened because they not only are providing care for the adult child with mental retardation, probably without direct day-to-day help with caregiving from their husband, but are also expected to cook, clean, and defer to their husband. This is not to say that the husband does not contribute to the well-being of the family and the son or daughter with mental retardation, but he probably does not contribute much in day-to-day caregiving, which is what the burden scale reflects. Findings from this study do not indicate that being married is negatively associated with the mothers' overall well-being, as this relationship is not found with depressive symptoms.

Initially, we found that Cuban American mothers were more burdened than Puerto Rican mothers, but when taking into account the extent of family problems, this difference was no longer significant (as shown in Figure 1). Understanding the social context of the ethnic enclave in the Miami area may shed some light on why Cuban Americans report more family problems and as a result are more burdened. Both Puerto Rican and Cuban American mothers may be expected to be self sacrificing, and may expect little help from their spouses, but the Cuban American families have the added cultural expectations of the Miami Cuban American community, including a hierarchical social and economic structure. This may create an environment in which culturally prescribed social roles are important, but difficult to maintain for mothers who are providing full time care for a son or daughter with mental retardation. For example, family participation in community activities may be important for those striving to maintain or gain social status within the Cuban American community, but difficult to accomplish for mothers who care for a son or daughter with mental retardation. We looked more closely at the differences between Cuban American and Puerto Rican mothers on each of the family problem scale items and we found some evidence to support this explanation. We found that the Cuban American mothers were substantially less likely than Puerto Rican mothers to "enjoy going places with the family when their son or daughter comes along," visit friends whenever they want," to feel that "the family can do things together as always," and to feel that "the family can do the same kinds of things as other families." Social pressure for conformity and culturally related stigma toward mental retardation warrants more research as a possible secondary role strain among Cuban American caregivers.

Limitations of this study are that the convenience samples used may not be representative of the larger population of Latina mothers caring for an adult with mental retardation, cross sectional analysis does not allow for causal inferences, different geographical locales may present comparison problems, and the small sample size may not allow for detection of all significant relationships and differences between groups.

Implications for practice are that assessing the social environment and the ability of the family to conform to cultural expectations are essential to the provision of culturally competent services to Latinos with non-normative caregiving responsibilities. Using interventions that take into account Latino cultural values and gender roles, and that teach families how to adapt to stressful situations within the context of acculturative change is valuable (Szapocznik, Kurtines, Santisteban, & Rio, 1990; Szapocznik, Rio, Perez-Vidal, Kurtines, & Hervis, 1986; Szapocznik, Santisteban, Kurtines, Perez-Vidal, & Hervis, 1984). It is also important to take into account how Latino groups may differ as well as in what ways they may be similar. For example, Puerto Rican mothers tend to be in poorer health, which is a threat to their emotional well-being. Ensuring that mothers who are providing care to adults with mental retardation have adequate health care is especially important for Puerto Rican families. It is equally important not to assume homogeneity within Latino groups, as demonstrated by the diversity within the sample of Cuban American mothers. Many of the later-wave immigrants in this population may need help with income and housing supports, as do many mothers from the Puerto Rican sample.

In summary, although overall, Cuban American mothers of adults with mental retardation had higher socioeconomic status than Puerto Rican mothers, we found that there was a substantial amount of within group heterogeneity in family socio-demographic characteristics, linked closely with immigration patterns for the Cuban American mothers. While Puerto Rican mothers had poorer health, Cuban American mothers had more caregiving burden and family problems. However, cutting across socio-demographic diversity and ethnicity was the importance of the family and family problems for maternal well-being. We found that mothers whose families had more problems had higher levels of burden and depressive symptoms, supporting the hypothesized significance of family functioning to Latina mothers who have a non-normative parenting challenge.

AUTHOR NOTE

Support for the preparation of this manuscript was provided by grants from the National Institute on Aging (R01 AG08728-Seltzer & Krauss, supplemented with funds from the NIH Office of Research on Minority Health), the National Institute of Child Health and Human Development (732 HD07194-Abbeduto & Seltzer, 732 HDO7489-Krauss, R01 HD31849-Szapocznik) and the Merck Scholars H Program. Support was also provided by the Starr Center on Mental Retardation, Heller Graduate School at Brandeis University; the Waisman Center at the University of Wisconsin-Madison; and the Center for Family Studies at the University of Miami.

REFERENCES

Angel, R., & Guarnaccia, P. (1989). Mind body and culture: Somatization among Hispanics. *Social Science and Medicine*, 28, 1229-1238.

Aranda, M., & Knight, B. (1997). The influence of ethnicity and culture on the caregiver stress and coping process: A sociocultural review and analysis. *The Gerontologist*, 37, 342-354.

Baca Zinn, M., & Wells, B. (2000). Diversity within Latino families: New lessons for family social science. In D.H. Demo, K.R. Allen, & M.A. Fine (Eds.). *Handbook of family diversity* (pp. 252-273). London: Oxford.

Bailey, D., Skinner, D., Correa, V., Arcia E., Reyes-Blanes, M., Rodriguez, P., Vásquez-Montilla, & Skinner, M. (1999). Needs and supports reported by Latino families of young children with developmental disabilities. *American Journal on Mental Retardation*, 104, 437-451.

Bernal, G., & Shapiro, E. (1996). Cuban families. In M. McGoldrick, J. Giordano, & J. Pearce (Eds.) *Ethnicity and family therapy* (pp. 155-168). New York: Guilford.

Blacher J., Shapiro, J., Lopez, S., Diaz, L., & Fusco, J. (1997). Depression in Latina mothers of children with mental retardation: A neglected concern. *American Journal on Mental Retardation*, 101, 483-496.

Bruininks, R. H., Hill, B.K., Weatherman, R.F., & Woodcock, R.W. (1986). *Inventory for client and agency planning* (ICAP). Allen, TX: DLM Teaching Resources.

Burnette, D., & Mui, A. (1995). In-home and community-based service utilization by three groups of elderly Hispanics: A national perspective. *Social Work Research*, 19, 197-206.

Chen, T. Y., & Tang, C. S. (1997). Stress, appraisal, and social support of Chinese mothers of adult children with mental retardation. *American Journal on Mental Retardation*, 101, 473-482.

Coelho, V., Strauss, M., & Hunter Jenkins, J. (1998). Expression of symptomatic distress by Puerto Rican and European-American patients with depression and schizophrenia. *Journal of Nervous and Mental Disease*, 186, 477-483.

Comas-Diaz, L. (1982). Mental health needs of Puerto Rican women in the United States. In R. Zambrana (Ed.). *Work, family and health: Latina women in transition*, Monograph No. 7. NY: Hispanic Research Center, Fordham University.

Cortes, D. (1995). Variations in familism in two generations of Puerto Ricans. *Hispanic Journal of Behavioral Sciences*, 17, 249-255.

Cox, C., & Monk, A. (1993). Hispanic culture and family care of Alzheimer's patients. *Health and Social Work*, 18, 92-99.

Delgado, M., & Tennstedt, (1997). Making the case for culturally appropriate community services: Puerto Rican elders and their caregivers. *Health and Social Work*, 22, 246-255.

Dietz, T., John, R., & Roy, L. 1998). Exploring intra-ethnic diversity among four groups of Hispanic elderly: Patterns and levels of service utilization. *International Aging and Human Development*, 46, 247-266.

Friedrich, W., Greenberg, M., & Crnic, K. (1983). A short form of the Questionnaire on Resources and Stress. *American Journal of Mental Deficiency*, 88, 345-351.

Fullmer, E., Tobin, S., & Smith, G. (1997). The effects of offspring gender on older mothers caring for their sons and daughters. *The Gerontologist*, 37, 795-803.

Garcia-Preto, N. (1996a). Latino families: An overview. In M. McGoldrick, J. Giordano, & J. Pearce (Eds.). *Ethnicity and family therapy* (pp. 141-154). New York: Guilford

Garcia-Preto, N. (1996b). Puerto Rican families. In M. McGoldrick, J. Giordano, & J. Pearce (Eds.). *Ethnicity and family therapy* (pp. 183-199). New York: Guilford.

Guamaccia, P., Angel, R., & Lowe Worobey, J. (1989). The factor structure of the CES-D in the Hispanic Health and Nutrition Examination Survey: The influences of ethnicity, gender and language. *Social Science and Medicine*, 29, 85-94.

Guarnaccia, P., Good, B., & Kleinman, A. (1990). A critical review of epidemiological studies of Puerto Rican health. *American Journal of Psychiatry*, 147, 1449-1456.

Harry, B. (1992). Making sense of disability: Low-income, Puerto Rican parents' theory of the problem. *Exceptional Children*, 59, 27-40.

Heller, T., & Factor, A. (1994). Facilitating future planning and transitions out of the home. In M. M. Seltzer, M.W. Krauss & M.P. Janicki (Eds.). *Life course perspectives on adulthood and old age* (pp. 39-50). Washington D. C.: AAMR.

Heller, T., Markwardt, R., Rowitz, L. & Farber, B. (1994). Adaptation of Hispanic families to a member with mental retardation. *American Journal of Mental Retardation*, 99, 289-300.

Keefe, S., Padilla, A., & Carlos, M. (1979). The Mexican-American extended family as an emotional support system. *Human Organization*, 38, 144-152.

Kolody, B., Vega, W., Meinhardt, K., & Bensussen, G. (1986). The correspondence of health complaints and depressive symptoms among Anglos and Mexican-Americans. *The Journal of Nervous and Mental Disease*, 174, 221-228.

Krauss, M.W., & Seltzer, M.M. (1999). An unanticipated life: The impact of lifelong caregiving. In H. Bersani (Ed.). *Responding to the challenge: International trends and current issues in developmental disabilities* (pp. 173-188). Brookline, MA: Brookline.

Kurtines, W.M., & Szapocznik, J. (1995). Cultural competence in assessing Hispanic youths and families: Challenges in the assessment of treatment needs and treatment evaluation for Hispanic drug abusing adolescents. In E. Rahdert & D. Czechowicz (Eds.) *Adolescent drug abuse: Clinical assessment and therapeutic interventions* (NIDA Research 23 Monograph No. 156, NIDA Publication No. 95-3908, pp. 172-189). Rockville, Maryland: NIDA.

Lazarus, R.S. & Folkman, S. (1984). *Stress, appraisal and coping.* New York: Springer.

Magaña, S. (1999). Puerto Rican families caring for an adult with mental retardation: The role of familism. *American Journal on Mental Retardation,* 104, 466-482.

McCallion, P., Janicki, M., & Grant-Griffin, L. (1997). Exploring the impact of culture and acculturation on older families caregiving for persons with developmental disabilities. *Family Relations,* 46, 347-358.

McCubbin, H. I. & Patterson, J.M. (1983). The family stress process: The double ABCX model of adjustment and adaptation. In H. I. McCubbin, M.B. Sussman, & J.M. Patterson (Eds.). *Social stress and the family: Advances and developments in family stress theory and research* (pp. 7-37). New York: Haworth.

Mintzer, J., Rubert, M., & Herman, K. (1994). Caregiving for Hispanic Alzheimer's disease patients: Understanding the problem. *American Journal of Geriatric Psychiatry,* 2, 32-38.

Mintzer, J., Rubert, M., Loewenstein, D., Gamez, E., Millor, A., Quinteros, R., Flores, L., Miller, M., Rainerman, A., & Eisdorfer, C. (1992). Daughters caregiving for Hispanic and non-Hispanic Alzheimer's patients: Does ethnicity make a difference? *Community Mental Health Journal,* 28, 293-303.

Multidimensional Functional Assessment: The OARS Methodology. A Manual. 2nd edition (1978). Durham: Duke University, Center for the Study of Aging and Human Development.

Pearlin, L., Mullan, J., Semple, S., & Skaff, M. (1990). Caregiving and the stress process: An overview of concepts and their measures. The Gerontologist, 30, 583-594.

Pruchno, R., Hicks P. J. & Burant, C. (1997). African American and White mothers of adults with chronic disabilities: Caregiving burden and satisfaction. *Family Relations,* 46, 335-346.

Radloff, L. (1977). The CES-D scale: A self-report depression scale for research in the general population. *Applied Psychological Measurement,* 1, 385-401.

Rodnguez, J., & Kosloske, J. (1998). The impact of acculturation on attitudinal familism in a community of Puerto Rican Americans. *Hispanic Journal of Behavioral Sciences,* 20, 375-390.

Sabogal, F., Marin, G., Otero-Sabogal, R., Marin, B.V. & Perez-Stable, E.J. (1987). Hispanic familism and acculturation: What changes and what doesn't. *Hispanic Journal of Behavioral Science,* 9, 397-412.

Sanchez-Ayendez, M. (1989). Puerto Rican elderly women: The cultural dimension of social support networks. *Women and Health,* 14(3-4), 239-252.

Seltzer, M. M., Greenberg, J. S., & Krauss, M. W. (1995). A comparison of coping strategies of aging mothers of adults with mental illness or mental retardation. *Psychology and Aging,* 10, 64-75.

Seltzer, M. M., Greenberg, J. S., Krauss, M. W., & Hong, J. (1997). Predictors and outcomes of the end of co-resident caregiving in aging families of adults with mental retardation or mental illness. *Family Relations,* 46, 13-22.

Seltzer M. M., & Heller T. (1997). Families and caregiving across the life course: Research advances on the influence of context. *Family Relations,* 46, 321-323.

Seltzer M. M., & Krauss, M. W., (1994). Aging parents with coresident adult children: The impact of lifelong caregiving. In M. M. Seltzer, M.W. Krauss & M.P. Janicki (Eds.). *Life course perspectives on adulthood and old age* (pp. 3-18). Washington D. C.: AAMR.

Seltzer M. M., & Ryff, C. D. (1994). Parenting across the life span: The normative and nonnormative cases. In D. L. Featherman & R. Lorner (Eds.). *Life-span development and behavior* (pp. 1-40). New Jersey: Lawrence Erlbaum Associates, Inc.

Smith, G., Fullmer, M., & Tobin, S. (1994). Living outside the system: An exploration of older families who do not use day programs. In M. M. Seltzer, M.W. Krauss & M.P. Janicki (Eds.). *Life course perspectives on adulthood and old age* (pp. 19-38). Washington D.C.: AAMR.

Sotomayor, M., & Randolph, S. (1988). A preliminary review of caregiving issues and the Hispanic family. In M. Sotomayer & H. Curiel (Eds.). *Hispanic elderly: A cultural signature* (pp. 137-160). Edingburg, TX: Pan American University Press.

Stroup-Benham, C., Lawrence, R., & Trevino, F. (1992). CES-D factor structure among Mexican American and Puerto Rican women from single- and couple-headed households. *Hispanic Journal of Behavioral Sciences*, 14, 310-326.

Szapocznik, J., & Coatsworth, J. D. (1999). An ecodevelopmental framework for organizing the influences on drug abuse: A developmental model of risk and protection. In M. Glantz & C. R. Hartel (Eds.) *Drug abuse: Origins and interventions* (pp. 331-366). Washington, D.C: American Psychological Association.

Szapocznik, J., & Kurtines, W.M. (1989). *Breakthroughs in family therapy with drug abusing problem youth.* New York: Springer.

Szapocznik, J., Kurtines, W.M., Santisteban, D., & Rio, A. (1990). Interplay of advances in treatment interventions aimed at behavior problem children and adolescents. *Journal of Consulting and Clinical Psychology*, 58, 696-703.

Szapoczrtik, J., Santisteban, D., Kurtines, W.M., Perez-Vidal, a., & Hervis, O.E. (1984). Bicultural effectiveness training: A treatment intervention for erhancing intercultural adjustment. *Hispanic Journal of Behavioral Sciences*, 6, 317-344.

Szapoczrik, J., Santisteban, D., Rio, A., Perez-Vidal, A., Kurtines, W.M., & Hervis, O.E.(1986). Bicultural effectiveness training (BET): An intervention modality for families experiencing intergenerational/intercultural conflict. *Hispanic Journal of Behavioral Sciences*, 8, 303-330.

Szapoczrik, J., Scopetta, A., Aranalde, M., & Kurtines, W. (1978). Cuban value structure: Treatment implications. *Journal of Consulting and Clinical Psychology*, 46, 961-970.

Szapocznik, J., & Williams, R.A. (2000). Brief strategic family therapy: Twenty-five years of interplay among theory, research and practice in adolescent problem behavior and drug abuse. Manuscript submitted for publication [Article invited by the Editor, *Clinical Child and Family Psychology Review*], University of Miami, Center for Family Studies.

Torres, J. B. (1998). Masculinity and gender roles among Puerto Rican men: Machismo on the U.S. mainland. *American Journal of Orthopsychiatry*, 68, 16-26.

Tran, T., & Dhooper, S. (1996). Ethnic and gender differences in perceived needs for social services among three elderly Hispanic groups. *Journal of Gerontological Social Work*, 25, 121-147.

Tran, T., & Williams, L. (1998). Poverty and impairment in activities of living among elderly Hispanics. *Social Work in Health Care*, 26, 59-78.

Vidal de Haymes, M. (1997). The golden exile: The social construction of the Cuban American success story. *Journal of Poverty*, 1, 65-80.

Zarit, S.H., Reever, K.E., & Bach-Peterson, J. (1980). Relatives of the impaired elderly: correlates of feelings of burden. *The Gerontologist*, 26, 260-266.

An Integral Model of Well-Being and Development and Its Implications for Helping Professions

Raúl Quiñones Rosado
Esterla Barreto

SUMMARY. This article describes a theoretical construct that serves as a framework for anti-oppression social transformation work in Latino communities. The authors present an integral model that considers the structures and processes of individual well-being within the context of and in relationship to collective development. With this model as a baseline for a critical analysis of current realities, the authors also examine the forces that hinder individual and collective well-being, particularly, institutional oppression: racism, colonialism, classism, and other "isms." Based on the belief that institutional oppression robs both oppressor and

Raúl Quiñones Rosado, MEd, is Founder, Co-Director, and Senior Trainer of ILÉ: Institute for Latino Empowerment, an anti-oppression education, organizing, and leadership development entity. He is also a founding member of the Undoing Racism Organizing Committee in western Massachusetts, and of Taller Coaí: Circulo de Trabajo para la Conciencia y Acción in Puerto Rico.

Esterla Barreto, PhD, is Co-Director of Taller Coaí: Circulo de Trabajo para la Conciencia y Acción in Puerto Rico, a collective of anti-oppression community educators and organizers based in Puerto Rico which is currently involved in the struggles against racism, sexism, heterosexism, and militarism. She is also a faculty member of the Beatriz Lasalle Graduate School of Social Work at the University of Puerto Rico, and a trainer of ILÉ: Institute for Latino Empowerment.

[Haworth co-indexing entry note]: "An Integral Model of Well-Being and Development and Its Implications for Helping Professions." Rosado, Raúl Quiñones, and Esterla Barreto. Co-published simultaneously in *Journal of Human Behavior in the Social Environment* (The Haworth Social Work Practice Press, an imprint of The Haworth Press, Inc.) Vol. 5, No. 3/4, 2002, pp. 57-84; and: *Latino/Hispanic Liaisons and Visions for Human Behavior in the Social Environment* (ed: José B. Torres, and Felix G. Rivera) The Haworth Social Work Practice Press, an imprint of The Haworth Press, Inc., 2002, pp. 57-84. Single or multiple copies of this article are available for a fee from The Haworth Document Delivery Service [1-800-HAWORTH, 9:00 a.m. - 5:00 p.m. (EST). E-mail address: getinfo@haworthpressinc.com].

57

the oppressed of their humanity, the authors provide an overview of a transformative process model. Implications of the model for the development of professional selves among social workers, counselors, and other helping professionals in relationship to the communities they serve are discussed. Broader applications of the model to other practices of the helping professions are also presented. *[Article copies available for a fee from The Haworth Document Delivery Service: 1-800-HAWORTH. E-mail address: <getinfo@haworthpressinc.com> Website: <http://www.HaworthPress.com> © 2002 by The Haworth Press, Inc. All rights reserved.]*

KEYWORDS. Well-being, development, culture, Latinos

INTRODUCTION

What is life like for Latinos (i.e., Puerto Ricans, Mexican Americans, Cubans, Central and South Americans), as a community, as a people, in the United States? Are individual Latinos experiencing satisfying levels of emotional and physical health, social and spiritual lives? Collectively, are we as Latinos adequately developing our economic potential, political influence, social participation, and cultural influence as contributing members of the U.S. society? Are we individually and collectively experiencing a path of evolution in which we exercise our cultural way of life, including our spirits, our reality? Do those of us committed to the well-being and development of Latinos and Latinas have a clear understanding about what true well-being and development are? Do we understand what conditions are necessary to move in that direction?

The integral model of well-being and development that we share here, we believe, may be a valuable resource to helping professionals, educators, organizers, and others who work within Latino communities in the U.S. The model offers a broad conceptual framework that provides a way of understanding the context for social transformation work, and a vision of an ideal state of well-being. Unlike humanistic and transpersonal models of well-being and human development that focus primarily on the individual (Maslow, 1968; Wilbur, 1977), this model uniformity considers our collective dimension, and the social, political, economic, and cultural forces that effect most human beings. By expanding the scope of what is often called "holistic" or "integral," this model allows us to engage in a more complete assessment of well-being and development, at both the individual and collective levels. In this manner, this model facilitates a critical analysis of the particular dynamics and circumstances–in ourselves *and* in our society–that hinder the attainment, or even the pursuit, of our well-being and evolution.

In this article we describe a model we are using in our Latino leadership development and community organizing work, mainly through ILÉ: Institute for Latino Empowerment, and *Taller Coaí: Círculo de Trabajo para la Conciencia y Acción*. These two organizations, of which we are active members, are committed to individual and group empowerment (*concienciación*) from an anti-oppression perspective. ILÉ does its work in Latino communities in the U.S., while *Taller Coaí* works in Puerto Rico. Both organizations offer workshops, presentations, consultation, mentoring and counseling, geared mostly to the development of oppressed individuals, groups, organizations and communities. Their members are personally active in community organizing, and are currently involved in local, national and international struggles against racism, sexism, classism, homophobia, colonialism and militarism.

This integral model of well-being and development is in itself an integration of various cultural influences (Indigenous, African, Asian, European, Anglo-, Anglo-, African-, and Latino-American), and numerous social science models, theories, and philosophies (Akbar, 1996; Am, 1994; Assagioli, 1973; Fanon, 1963; Freire, 1970; Martín-Baró, 1994; Memmi, 2000; Montero, 1997; Quiñones-Rosado, 1995; Wilbur, 1977; among others), and continues to be a work-in-progress. For the purpose of this discussion, the authors present a brief overview of the model including its most basic concepts.

Central to the model of well-being and development are three key components:

- The Medicine Wheel
- The Cyclone of Oppression
- The Spiral of Transformation

Before we look at the Medicine Wheel, let us consider the two primal elements at the core of our being. Located at the center of the model are: *consciousness*–our capacity to be aware, and our ability to focus our awareness, or attention; and *will*–our ability to act with intent, to direct our volition.

Consciousness and will, or awareness and volition, are essential to our being, in both senses of the word: they are *absolutely necessary* to our existence, and therefore, they are *intrinsic to our essence* as humans. Like the Taoist *ying/yang*, or the Yoruba *ibeji* (twins), consciousness and will are complementary aspects of our essential selves, of our core being. These elements work in concert, one with the other, as they are inextricably linked in our human form. One cannot exist without the other (Assagioli, 1976; Wilber, 1977). Together, consciousness and will enable us to make sense of our experience, our existence, and the world around us. They allow us to consider options, make decisions, and take action, thus, giving us the ability to use and mediate between the different, and sometime competing, aspects of both the individual and collective dimensions of life. As we will see, consciousness and will are what allow us to utilize the resources necessary for our personal well-being and collective development.

THE MEDICINE WHEEL

The conceptualization of *The Medicine Wheel* comes to us from the Lakota people of North America.[1] The concepts of "medicine," or that which brings, enhances and restores life, and the "wheel," the all-encompassing circle of life, are concepts shared by ancient cultures around the world (Bopp, Bopp, Lane, & Brown, 1988; Lörler, 1991). These concepts offer us a worldview that is significantly broader and more relevant to our reality than contemporary models of health, well-being, and development of European origin. The Medicine Wheel points to both our individual and collective dimensions. These two dimensions coexist in a dynamic, interdependent relationship in which the individual exists and develops within the collective, while the collective is created and nurtured by the individuals who comprise it. See Graphic 1.

The Individual Dimension

Four aspects are included in the individual dimension of the Medicine Wheel. These are: (1) the *mental*–refers to the logical mind, the ability to reason, to seek and to find solutions to problems. It also refers to the creative mind, the capacity to imagine, wonder, and to create new things. It is the mind that allows us to shape and name reality; (2) the *spiritual*–refers to our capacity for intuition, to sense an intimate relatedness and/or connection to other beings, the planet, and a universal

GRAPHIC 1. The Medicine Wheel

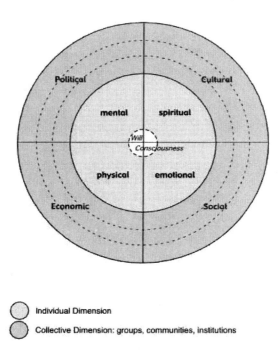

Individual Dimension

Collective Dimension: groups, communities, institutions

Adapted by Raúl Quiñones Rosado, ILÉ: Institute for Latino Empowerment, from the Four Worlds Development Project.

transcendental consciousness. Our values, principles, convictions and life purpose are also associated with this aspect; (3) the *emotional*–refers to our affect, our feelings and desires. Our emotions are what allow us to effectively interact with other individuals, and are key to learning and survival itself and (4) the *physical*–refers to the body and all its physiological functions, which allow us to interact directly in the world.

These four aspects are intimately related and inseparable. Like any conceptual model, the divisions represented here ("elements," "aspects" or "dimensions") are, in fact, artificial and arbitrary. These aspects coexist holographically, one aspect intrinsically tied to and contained within the other. For example, a human being's mind and emotions do not exist independently of the biochemical and electromagnetic processes in the brain, which in turn, depend on other many and complex functions of the body. And as many would affirm, corporal life, with mind and feelings, simply cannot exist without spirit.

The Collective Dimension

Well-being is not limited to the individual dimension, nor is development limited to individuals. After all, we individuals live in communities, and belong to groups that organize, and develop structures, policies, processes, and shared purposes that, over time, become institutionalized. So, if we focus our attention on the collective dimension of The Medicine Wheel, we will see its four aspects. *First*, the *political*–refers to the rules and laws by which societies are governed. It encompasses all groups, organizations and institutions in charge of adopting and implementing these rules and laws. Among these are the government and all its agencies and dependencies, and, of course, political parties and other political groups (i.e., think tanks, lobbyists, etc.); *second, cultural*–refers to the values, beliefs, attitudes and behaviors shared by members of particular social groups and/or communities, and by the members of society at large. Among the main institutions responsible for teaching and (re)enforcing these values, beliefs, etc., are the school system, religious institutions, and the media; *third, social*–refers to the norms and ways in which people relate as members of families, neighborhoods, communities, organizations, and interact between distinct identity groups (by race, gender, class, ethnicity, etc.); and *fourth, economic*–refers to the production, management and distribution of the material resources of a society. Obviously, it includes banking, industry, commerce, and other forces within our economic system, including labor, and consumers.

Well-Being

According to the Medicine Wheel, a person's well-being and development are attained through the on-going process of nurturing and fostering each and all of the aspects of both the individual and collective dimensions. At the individual level, well-being is attained to the extent that a person nurtures his or her mind, body, feelings, *and* spirit. In order for integral well-being, to occur through one's life, there must be *balance*, in which every aspect is given the necessary attention and care. There can be no well-being in a person whose main activity and focus is, for example, his or her professional training; a person who, in the process, abuses their body with drugs or inadequate exercise and diet, neglects their personal (i.e., loving) relationships, and betrays their own core values of service, honor and justice. The person committed to his or her well-being cares for their body, engages their loved ones, and honors their principles, while also attending to their own intellectual and professional development.

Equally important in the process of integral well-being is the principle of *harmony*. This refers to *congruency* between the four aspects of this dimension. This principle affirms the need for consistency between our ideas and beliefs (mental aspect), our values (the spiritual), our feelings (the emotional) and our behaviors (the physical). It is the principle captured in the popular phrases, "Practicing what you preach," or "Walking the talk." It is embodied in the ongoing struggle to resolve contradictions, conflicts or *dissonance* between what we think, feel, believe and do.

Together, the principles of *balance and harmony* lead us to another key principle in the process of well-being, *integrity*. The concept of integrity includes several connotations. One of these alludes to the mathematical concept of *oneness* (i.e., unity, the union of potentially fragmented parts). A second connotation is one that is commonly used to refer to a person of flawless personal character, and of high moral standing. Yet another refers to the architectural concept of "structural integrity," which refers to the synergistic strength obtained by the strategic and precise placement of the different elements of construction.

Integrity, a unity free of fragmentation and flawless character, gives a person the ability, capacity–a psychological, physical, and spiritual strength, to increase the potential to lead their life with enhanced levels of well-being and development. In this broader sense, *integrity* is the basis of what we call *personal power*, *authentic power* or *transformative power*. It is the source of what we refer to as true *empowerment* that may become authentic or transformative leadership.

Consciousness and will play a key role in this process, since it is through our capacity of self-awareness and the ability to direct our actions that we can create change in our lives. Our *consciousness* allows us to become aware of the internal conflicts and contradictions as they arise; our *will* permits us to take the necessary corrective action. This way, we mobilize and utilize the internal resources of each of the four aspects of our being for the purpose of enhancing our personal well-being and development.

Through our consciousness and will, we can identify, and seek to mobilize and utilize the external resources we may need to further our survival, growth and beyond. This leads us to the collective dimension of the Medicine Wheel. Similar to well-being at the individual level, *balance and harmony*, and the resulting *integrity*, are also essential to the well-being of the collective and to its on-going development. In a similar manner, a society (or a particular community or group within a society) must use its *collective consciousness and will* to address its political, economic, social and cultural needs.

Collective consciousness and will refers not only the sum of the personal self-awareness of individuals and their particular capacities to direct their own actions, but also the synergistic, group-level awareness and volition attained through people's shared experience in addition to a common history, identity, and purpose. It is this *synergy* that enables a society, community or group to identify, mobilize and utilize all of their resources to meet the needs of the entire collective. *Collective consciousness for* example, gives a society a sense of national identity on the basis of a shared history and a present experience. *Collective will* is what would have the people of that nation rally together to defend that shared identity, and seek and protect their national sovereignty.

In keeping true to the principle of integrity, collective well-being and development are attained and maintained by continually striving for congruence between the shared ideas, values, feelings and behaviors of the group, and between the potentially competing interests of its political, cultural, social, and economic institutions. This, we believe, enables a society, community or group to consciously and skillfully direct its future development, allowing it to be truly self-determining. Therefore, a, fundamental key to this model is: the greater the level of well-being and development of a society, *the greater the level of well-being, development and empowerment of the individuals that comprise it.* Naturally, the inseparable "twin" of this principle is that: *the greater the level of well-being of individuals within a society, the greater the level of collective well-being, the greater its potential for full development, and the greater its ability to be self-determining.*

The Forces that Hinder Well-Being and Development in Latino Communities

In an ideal world, and in accordance with the Medicine Wheel of Well-Being, individuals and communities should be able to grow and develop to their fullest potential, in the individual as well as the collective dimensions of their life experience. However, we understand that in the real world there are societal forces that negatively impact, and moreover, hinder our ability as people, communities, and nations to fully develop our potential. This is particularly true in Latino and other diverse ethnic minority communities across the U.S.

A critical analysis of societal forces in the U.S. allows us to recognize and understand a discernable pattern, an observable dynamic that is present in every sphere of human activity. This is the dynamic by which members of dominant social groups systematically subordinate members of other groups for the purpose of maintaining access to, and control of the resources of this society. This historical pattern of control and power is known as *institutional oppression*.[2] See Graphic 2.

In our integral model of well-being and development, these forces are represented as a vortex surrounding and encompassing the collective dimension of the Medicine Wheel. We alternately refer to this phenomenon the "wheel," the "circle," or the *cyclone of oppression*.

GRAPHIC 2. The Cyclone of Oppression

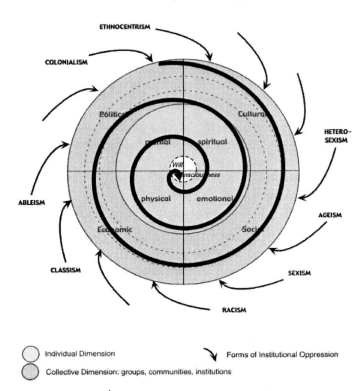

© 2000 Raúl Quiñones Rosado, ILÉ: Institute for Latino Empowerment

As we can see in the graphic, oppression takes on many forms, since it impacts subordinated members of each of the major social identity groups in a society. While the major social identity groups may vary from one society to another, in the U.S.[3] the primary groups include: ethnicity, religion, sexual orientation, age, gender, race, class, mental and physical ability, and nationality.[4] Racism, classism, Eurocentrism, sexism and the other "isms" illustrated here are specific forms of *institutional oppression*.

Among anti-oppression educators and organizers, *institutional oppression* is often defined as: *prejudice + power = institutional oppression*. This definition serves to make sure that *institutional oppression* is not confused with *prejudice* or *discrimination*. *Prejudice*, in this context, is a set of beliefs, positive and negative, about members of a social group based on stereotypes, myths, misinformation and/or lies. It is a *belief system*, not a behavior. When a prejudiced belief system is acted upon and becomes a *behavior* used to hurt, harm or otherwise exclude others based on their membership of a different group (i.e., race, gender, etc.), it then becomes *discrimination*. When discriminatory behavior is legally sanctioned by the state, through its political, economic, and social institutions, reflecting the interests of the dominant cultural group, such activity is then referred too as *institutional oppression. Institutional* oppression then, symbolizes the ideology, behaviors, beliefs, attitudes and values of the dominant society, that have been *institutionalized* throughout the history of the United States. By creating all the major institutions of the society (i.e., governmental, economic, religious, educational, military, etc.), this dominant, albeit relatively small, group has managed to systematically impose their way of life upon all groups in this society. To ensure the inheritance of membership, leadership, and control of these institutions by their descendants, this dominant group's "culture" became and remains the cultural norm, the standard by which everyone else is expected to adopt.

INTERNALIZED DOMINANCE AND OPPRESSION

The process of socialization in the dominant culture impacts everyone in a society. We are all thoroughly socialized in the ideas, behaviors, feelings, attitudes, beliefs and values of those who retain control and power. Early in life we all learn that "Pink is for girls" and "Real men don't cry," that "White is right," and that "I want to live in America" ("America" meaning the United States, of course) since it is only here that "All men are created equal." However, these and other messages about our different social identities do not impact us all the same way. From these messages, dominant group members internalize a sense of superiority and dominance, and learn to, consciously or unconsciously, exercise their power and privilege in the pursuit of their well-being and development. This is what we refer too as *internalized dominance*. In contrast to the dominant group's internalized dominance, the same messages resulted in subordinated group members internalizing feelings of inferiority, powerlessness, limited ability to access resources needed for their well-being, if not for their very survival. This is what is then referred to as *internalized oppression.*

Given the daily assault of negative messages carried out by teachers, ministers, entertainers and reporters, judges, merchants, bankers and bosses, who continue to communicate untruths, half-truths or no information at all about our groups, it is understandable how subordinated group members are influenced to believe these negative characteristics about themselves. In concert with the violent impact of blatant negative expressions of institutional oppression (i.e., poverty, police profiling and brutality, violence against women, continued *de facto* segregation in housing, education and health care delivery, etc.), internalized oppression leads oppressed people to doubt their very selves, their inherent worth as human beings. In this context, to say that oppression undermines its victims' self-image and self-esteem is a gross understatement. The unmitigated internalization of racist, sexist and other oppressive messages and experiences, in fact, leads to self-hatred and self-destruction among oppressed people (Akbar, 1996; Bulhan, 1985; Fanon, 1963; hooks, 1995, 1993).

The assaults, previously noted, upon people who are oppressed, is represented by the inward spiral in the "cyclone of oppression" graphic, with its powerful "winds" impacting each of the aspects of the individual dimension of being. Furthermore, the massive and persistent assault of institutional oppression impacts the very essential core–consciousness and will–to the point where the oppressed person's awareness and volition are also severely impaired. This inevitably results in mental, physical, emotional and spiritual unbalance and disharmony, "disease," and all too often, death (Bulhan, 1985).

This internal state is often externalized toward others, most often toward those of the same social identity group or toward members of other similarly oppressed groups. Colorism, the negative dynamic between diverse ethnic and racial minority individuals (i.e., People of Color), due to the relative privilege granted to, or assumed by, those that are lighter-skinned, is one manifestation of this *cross-group and intra-group hostility*. Other expressions observed between and within these diverse groups include non-cooperation, distrust, competition, aggression and violence.

A similar dynamic of intra-group hostility is also witnessed among women, gays and lesbians, poor people, and virtually all oppressed groups, as they, too, are socialized to uphold the societal norms of the dominant culture. Similar to racially and ethnically oppressed groups, members of these groups also find themselves competing against each other for access to resources, such as opportunities in employment, pay raises, promotions, and political positions. Other circumstances may include seeking favors from those in power and/or by *assimilating* to the dominant culture.

It is also important to understand that the internalization of institutional oppression impacts negatively on members of the dominant group. In the context of the principles that inform this integral model of well-being and development, we propose the following: (1) to the extent that a man must rely primarily on the privileges bestowed upon him merely by virtue of his maleness, he is, ultimately, weak; (2) to the extent that a white person can enjoy a higher social status based on the long history of institutional violence perpetrated by their ancestors against Indigenous Peoples, Africans, Latin Americans, Asians, and Arabs, their socially-constructed sense of superiority is, ultimately, false; (3) to the extent that a millionaire may obtain his or her sense of worth at the expense of exploited workers and on the backs of those left without any employment, he or she is, ultimately, poor; and (4) to the extent that any dominant group member gains his or her sense of power, status, worth, and identity merely on the basis of their dominant group membership, he or she is, ultimately devoid of truth, *integrity*, and lacks the *authentic power* attained only from true *integral well-being and development*.

These principles are mutually applicable at individual and group levels in our society. It applies to men, *as a group*, whites, *as a group*, the owning class, *as a group*, heterosexuals, Christians, and to each and every dominant group in this society. This is why we clearly understand that: *institutional oppression also hinders the well-being and development of those who wield institutional power over others, as it ultimately robs them of their own humanity.*

FROM OPPRESSION TO TRANSFORMATION

Clearly, transformation works at both the personal and collective dimensions, with both oppressors and oppressed, is essential if we are to seriously seek our integral well-being and development as a society. By *transformation* we mean change that is radical (at the root) as it positively alters the foundation of the person, of the group, of the organization, of society. Transformation cannot be realized if it does not end institutional oppression. Otherwise, all changes will remain superficial, limited to reforming or reorganizing the same institutional structures and dynamics without fundamentally changing the outcome: i.e., that dominant group members maintain their continued advantage in the pursuit of their well-being and development at the expense of those subordinated.

We further understand that revolution (i.e., merely shifting the center of power from the oppressor to the oppressed), does not fundamentally transform society, as it leaves intact the undesired oppressive power dynamics. Like reform, revolution simply does not facilitate the *integral* well-being and development to which we aspire. After all, the vast majority of people are members of one or more dominant groups, even those of us whose primary social identity is that of a targeted, oppressed group member. In the U.S., a person such as a foreign-born, poor, unemployed, uneducated, lesbian, atheist, women of color with severe psychological and/or physical disabilities would find it difficult to claim any dominant group membership. The rest of us, even most white men, are in one way or another subordinated by virtue of one or more of our multiple group memberships.

Each of us has the difficult task of identifying both those situations in which we are dominant and those in which we are subordinated. We must be clear about the privileges we obtain, consider the disadvantages of our subordinated group memberships, and evaluate the overall impact these memberships have on our lives in terms of our well-being. The key point here, again, is that institutional oppression, and the internalization of the culture of oppression, negatively impacts everyone–including those who control our society. This is why both oppressors and the oppressed must work together toward their well-being and development by struggling together to undo or dismantle institutional oppression. See Graphic 3.

How do we go about transforming our selves, our communities, our society? The model suggests a process that applies to both personal and collective transformation. In essence, the process of transformation begins by interrupting the cycle or cyclone of oppression. First, we need to *perceive* (recognize) oppression: to see it, to hear it, to feel it. To consciously acknowledge that "something" just happened to me, to my child, to my neighbor. . . ; to become aware that "something" is "wrong," because somewhere in our mind, body, feeling, or spirit we "know" that whatever just happened (or was said, or done), is sensed as

GRAPHIC 3. The Spiral of Transformation

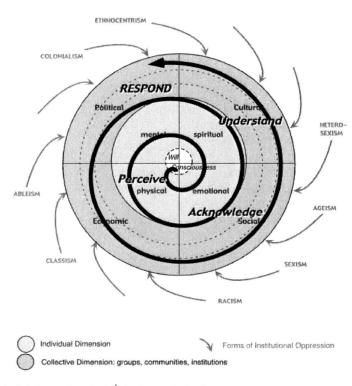

© 2000 Raúl Quiñones Rosado, ILÉ: Institute for Latino Empowerment

disharmonious or out of synch with our being, our true nature, our group, our identity. Clearly, the more in touch we are with our true nature, and the different aspects of our personal and group identity, the more likely we will quickly be in touch with this perception.

This ability to perceive is what leads us to *acknowledge* oppression, and to name it. When we acknowledge what we see, hear, feel, or otherwise notice in our field of awareness, we stop denying that oppression exists. Then we can begin to observe more skillfully, and recognize patterns of behaviors and power dynamics, beyond those isolated instances of misuse or abuse of power. We may notice, for example, how men at work tend to get heard more often than women; that almost all Black/African Americans on TV are in comedy shows, and Latinos are rarely seen at all;

that the majority of all people in political office are relatively wealthy; how most social service organizations and agencies are run by people who are not from the communities they serve. We begin to notice, and even predict, patterns of behaviors and outcomes affecting others like us, and those that are different from us by social group and rank.

As we become more skillful at observing and noticing oppression, and become more honest in acknowledging and recognizing the lack of balance and harmony in us and in our society, we begin to better *understand* it. We are then in a position to engage in a critical analysis of the meaning of these patterns. We are able to see and understand just how we are an integral part of this reality. Through our understanding, we gain increased consciousness, whether as dominant or subordinated members of the society, that we are active participants, and that it is impossible for us, to be neutral.

This consciousness is what leads us to engage our will, to *respond* to oppression. This *consciousness-in-action* is the essence of *empowerment*. Empowerment (*concienciación*) therefore, is to recognize, acknowledge, and understand oppression, so that we may then *respond* effectively, in spite of it, in order to overcome it. When we can clearly perceive, acknowledge, and comprehend our situation, we no longer remain condemned to merely *react* unconsciously in fear and pain. Therefore, true empowerment, according to this model, begins the moment we consciously choose our response to the oppression with which we are confronted.

The process of empowerment is the process of transformation. Transformation takes place as we move toward the attainment of balance and harmony, of integrity and authentic power, of individuals, groups, and society at large. Empowerment and transformation is living in accordance to the Medicine Wheel of Well-Being. This transformative process, represented in Graphic 3 by an outward-directed spiral, is on-gong and never-ending. As noted previously, this process occurs simultaneously at the individual and collective dimensions. Unlike classical Marxist theory or contemporary transpersonal perspectives, this integral model does not presuppose that-development at one dimension is a prerequisite for development of the other. Social change and transformation is not a linear process requiring that individuals first attain well-being and develop their potential so that they may then influence group and societal change. However, this may be a useful strategy for change. Transformation happens anywhere in "the circle," in every "sphere" of life.

IMPLICATIONS OF THE INTEGRAL MODEL
OF WELL-BEING AND DEVELOPMENT
TO THE HELPING PROFESSIONS

The majority of mission statements included in the codes of ethics of most helping professional associations, refer to the association and professions' commitment to the well-being of human beings. National Association of Social Workers' Code of Ethics (1996), for example, goes even further by affirming their commitment to fight for social justice. However, these commitments have been easier to declare in a document than to exercise in practice. There have been multiple conceptual approaches and interventions that helping professionals have developed with the good intention of promoting and maintaining the well-being of individuals and collectives. Nevertheless, there are numerous examples where our approaches and interventions in practice contradict the mission expressed in our declarations and professional oaths.

It is in this process that we can generally identify deficit models that emphasize deficiencies among individuals and collectives, in contrast to those that do have these elements (i.e., a lack of capacities, conditions, genes, abilities, defenses, capital, resources, etc.). Generally, in the Americas, "comparison" or "control" groups (i.e., those who have what others lack), tend to be white, heterosexual, middle/upper class males, of European descent, Christian, relatively physically and psychologically healthy, and with all the other privileges associated with an oppressive system. Practice models and interventions are those that we usually refer to when we speak of traditional models in the different professional areas of the helping relationships. For example, in social work, the assistance models; in psychology, the therapies of adaptive and behavioral change; and in medicine, the emphasis on medications to combat symptoms and not the source of the illness. These models are based on a paternalistic view that promotes charity among those who are socio-economically well-to do, toward others who are less well off, without addressing the root causes of problems of inequality. Other characteristics of the noted models include: the fragmentation and array of specializations among the disciplines; the professionalization and distancing of professionals from those who are in need of help; and the conceptualization and treatment of individuals as objects (Wallerstain, 1998; Ani, 1996; Maguire, 1987).

On the other hand, subsequent to the impact of historical materialism, conflict theories, and other theories in the social sciences, we find a peak in the development of alternative models attempting to focus on revolution or social change as the basis for the work of helping professionals. From this conceptualization then, our professional work identifies us as change agents, rather than help agents. In contrast to traditional models of the helping professions, contemporary models of social change are characterized by their promotion of interdisciplinary collaborations, encouraging increased proximity between practitioners and their clients, acknowledging clients as individuals with strengths and resources, and understanding individual and community problems from the clients' perspectives. In spite of increased efforts to develop intervention models to promote change among individuals and collectives, there remains a lack of integral models that practitioners could use to study, analyze, and evaluate our realities and the interaction among individuals, collectives, and structures. Also missing is the perspective by which we visualize and project ourselves toward the creation of a vision for individual and collective well-being.

Traditional models of helping as well as alternative models developed in Western societies have been influenced by European cultural thought. As a result, some authors argue that when the latter are intended to denounce systematic oppression and offer alternatives to this reality, both lack an understanding of the interaction between different forms of oppression and their influence on the social identity of different group members. They also fail to identify an integrated vision acknowledging different aspects of our individual and collective being. As a result, feminists as well as anti-racist workers have criticized the limitations of historical materialism, conflict theories and dialectics from Marx to Freire, as explanations to the reality of different oppressed groups (Ani, 1994; hooks, 1994; Maguire, 1987; Martinez, 1999; McLaren, 1993).

Marimba Ani (1994), in an African-American centered criticism of European thought, explains how the dichotomous and lineal thinking characteristic of this cultural element has influenced the works of the best alternative thinkers of European background in trying to eradicate oppression. According to Ani (1994), traditional and alternative models of helping influenced by Eurocentric perspectives, are products of a similar paradigm since to a great extent social thinkers of European descent have not been able to overcome their own ideology of supremacy. This in turn explains the emphasis placed on rational thinking above considerations of emotional and spiritual character, a factor that negatively impacts on our integrity as human beings and further dehumanizing the individual. Ani's criticisms affirm the need for a transformation to the interior of the ideology of European supremacy in the development of models of well-being and health with which we are more familiarized with in Western societies.

The model of integral well-being and development presented here is in fact nurtured by a range of models from multiple disciplines with European based philosophical perspectives as well as in models of Native American, African, and Asian origin. The influences of Marx and Weber, conflict theory, the relationship between knowledge and power of Foucault and the synergy of Covey are evident in these models. One can also identify the presence of Freires' (1970) conscientization work, the Native American medicine wheel, the Taíno hurricane (cyclone), and the Asian *ying/yang* among others previously mentioned. The importance of any technique, intervention, or approach to reach our full development and well-being is in its effectiveness to facilitate healing processes, transformation, and liberation in an integrated vision of the human being. As a result, those of us using this model have incorporated a wide variety of "interventions," such as relaxation techniques, meditation and visualization, interpretation of dreams, goals setting, confrontations, recognition of feelings and fears, role playing, modeling, self-assessments; processes of participatory education, popular theater, community organizing, and oratorical presentations. We also capitalize on integrating other cultural elements into our work, including music, incense, rituals, altars, retirements, art projects, medicinal herbs, doll making, preparation of foods, among others. From the integration of these tools into our community work, a dynamic and creative model of interventions has been developed that is in turn a tool for analysis and evaluation; a guide for a process of individual and collective transformation; and a goal and vision for an integrated human being. As such, the model is graphically intellectually stimulating, and the opportunity to elaborate a three-dimensional graphic perspective, its theoretical possibilities, and implications may be of a physical/metaphysical character.

The implications of this model to the practice of helping professionals are varied and apply to multiple disciplines in the fields of psychology, social work, and health care. We also believe that they are of relevance to the multiple roles that we play in the helping professions as healers, consultants, facilitators, researchers, advocates, lobbyists, educators, organizers, mentors and agents of change and transformation. The following are a few of those transformations we consider most relevant.

The Sphere

There Is No Beginning–There Is No End

What seems to be this model's most evident contribution is its circular form which forces us to re-conceptualize our basic human needs not in a lineal or pyramidal[5] form, but with the same distance from its center and in accordance with the values of non-European cultures. On the one hand, this implies that all human needs are of equal importance and interrelated. The only division made is between the individual dimension and the collective, which supposes a relative distance between the range of the individual's influence with self and the collectives in which she or he interacts (i.e., family, community, institutions, nation, etc.). On the other hand, this leads us to question if the transformation processes have a beginning place and an end. Or, if we can begin where the circumstances and interests allow us to, and leave with the faith that we will arrive at the place we need to be at, knowing that where we are going is not the end of the road. This is not to imply that the transformation toward a state of integral well-being is not reachable, but that once it is reached, maintaining it will require a continued walking together, integrated, or what Freire (1970) called a permanent culture of revolution or transformation (p. 139). We then are encouraged to re-evaluate the concept of *revolution*, a term emerging from a mechanical conception of society and indicating a change in the hierarchal structure. The change would reflect a restructuring of those who are on top of the pyramid, with those below, without altering the original pyramida in hierarchical structure that maintains the oppression.

Finally, the sphere gives us a sense of connection among all the parts, among one and the other, among our individual and collective dimensions of being, among all our struggles. For this reason, the sphere forces us to affirm ourselves as spiritual beings connected to each other. As helping professionals it forces us to include ourselves inside the model, not outside of it, as facilitators of a process *with* others but *for all*. This in turn implies that in our practice we have to be willing to be held accountable for our own personal contradictions and the inadequate use of our privileges to maintain positions of power as gatekeepers, specially in relation to knowledge and information. For example, if as helping professionals we believe in the power of personal transformation, then we have to respond to our alcohol and tobacco addictions, as well as to our access and control to institutional resources and information. It also requires that we be more inclusive in the variety of communities and people we work with. From working with or without indigent clients in poor neighborhoods, to our work settings, the nice suburbs and urban areas we live in, the professional organizations, social groups, political parties, and health insurance organizations we belong too. Others may include individuals involved in acts of corruption, organized crime, violence (e.g., batterers/abusers of women and children), students, an so on. Too often helping professionals go in search of helping those who live in poor communities, however it seems to be less the times that we use our influence in our nearest circles; as with family, friends, co-workers and members of our own socially dominant groups.

Well-Being

The Well-Being of One Is the Well-Being of All

An individual's well-being is the well-being of the collective, and vice-versa. The model does not lend itself to justify that the well-being of a person could be contrary to that of the other, or that this is a world for the survival of the fittest. Neither does it imply that for practical reasons the owning class has to live off the surplus of the poorest, or where an individual's needs have to be sacrificed for the needs of the collective or vice-versa. The model's spherical and integral design requires a conceptualization of well-being as a potential for all individuals. In this way it becomes a vision to guide our personal transformation and to aspire for the well-being of all members of the community.

The model also forces us to re-focus our professional practices with individuals and collectives. First, it requires that we think about refocusing our interventions (i.e., medications or therapies) as healing processes and the effects of years of internalized multiple manifestations of oppression. Thus, if a practitioner is presented a young, poor, black, Latina, with a problem of a drug addiction, the practitioner should avoid focusing automatically on the client's addiction problem. The practitioner could instead attempt to understand that the addiction problem may be one manifestation of years of socialization (including those of her ancestors), internalizing fears and negative messages, and dehumanization of her as a person in relation to her gender, class status, race, and colonization. Within this context of the client's reality, it is her ability to respond with consciousness and critical action to these messages that she will help herself to heal and overcome the effects of these multiple oppressions. The range of interventions that we can use to facilitate the healing process can be varied and creative as is necessary. This may vary from prescribing methadone to firewalking[6] provided they are compatible with the principles of integrity and transformation of the model.

According to the model, transformation work is not complete once we deal with her immediate drug problem or we help her raise her elf-esteem. Effective treatment is more complete when the client can al from her multiple oppressions, increase her self-efficacy (Bandura,

1986), and see herself as part of a collective of people, who united can transform their political, economic, social, and cultural conditions. This also means that in our interventions we need to rediscover, recover and regain healing processes of non-European origin. This does not mean to recover ancient healing practices as a cliche or new age fashion for personal power, but as part of a conscious effort that these are vital processes in our individual and collective healing, and ultimately the recovery of our humanity. Dealing with, or healing, internalized oppression through the process of social transformation is perhaps the greatest challenge for helping professionals, second only to the challenge of healing internalized dominance.

Second, it is necessary to practice and actively promote our collective consciousness and action since the transformation process cannot be achieved if institutional oppression is not dismantled. This requires the awareness that existent structures of power have not been built by chance neither are they maintained by pure coincidence and innocence. They were built and are maintained to satisfy the interests of the groups' agents of oppression. For many, it is clear that the creation of our political, social, cultural, and economic institutions are class oriented, racists, sexist, heterosexist, and so on. Furthermore, they were created with full conscience to perpetuate the power of the dominant groups. It is imperative however, to recognize that everyone who is identified as a member of an oppressive group cannot give up privileges that she or he enjoys within that system whenever they would like too. We, the authors, as people of lighter skin complexion in our country, must also acknowledge and take responsibility for unearned white privilege(s) we enjoy and benefit from, despite our commitment to dismantle racism in Puerto Rico and the United States.

Finally, the model offers a clear vision of what integral well-being is, and if accepted, would set forth a challenge to our professional practice. It would also provide us an opportunity to do our work with more direction and sense of purpose.

Development

Development Is a Continuous and Interactive Process

Development in this model is not a lineal process where there is a continuum or progression that goes from savage to civilized, sub-developed to developed, or from naïve conscience to critical consciousness. It requires a re-conceptualizing of development as a dynamic, multidimensional, and interactive process that evolves from the constant interaction among the individual and collective dimension. It also requires an understanding and appreciation of those aspects that compose each one of these elements, including the hurricane or cyclonic effects of oppression. Describing the developmental process as an interaction among multiple development spirals in the individual and collective dimensions, spiraling from the center of the sphere toward the outside, maintaining balance and harmony in a unified force, empowers us to challenge and move toward dismantling institutional oppression. Therefore, depending on available resources and needs, individuals and communities can develop different aspects from each dimension at different levels in relation to different forms of oppression. However, transformation will be attained only when these different components are unified. This development is not exclusive of those who are targets of different forms of institutional oppression, for example, the poor, black/African Americans and Latinos, women, and children. Members of oppressive groups also require healing processes, development, and a recovery of their humanity. In order for helping professionals to effectively facilitate healing and transformation processes, they must aspire for their own personal integrity and participate in the struggle for transformation. They must recognize that they (we) are not alone, but that we are all a part of a larger movement.

As an evaluation or diagnosis process of our individual or collective development, the proposed model could be used to assess the needs and resources of different aspects and levels of development. This process can help us identify specific areas requiring healing and strengthening in the development of our authentic transformative power. The process can also help us identify specific responses-abilities to confront institutional oppression in order to regain the humanity denied us through a system of institutionalized oppression. It could also be used as an analysis framework for the development and formulation of social welfare policies and programs since every aspect of our individual and collective well-being is identified in the model. The evaluation criteria could include: a measure by which social policies contribute in the promotion of balance and harmony among the different aspects of the individual and collective dimensions of well-being.

Integrity

The Authentic Power Emerges from the Integration of All the Parts, but Never of Any of Them Separately.

We cannot assume or believe that the acquisition of economic, political, social, or cultural powers, separately, will solve all our collective problems. Obviously, each one of these aspects of collective power has as much of a decisive role in our dehumanization as in our survival. However, our collective transformation cannot be achieved until a harmonious balance is achieved among all these four aspects of power. Harmony is vital in this transformation process since it would be ineffective and inefficient if the elements contradict each other.

Equally false is the illusion of individual power based on privileges granted to each of us by virtue of our membership to an oppression group or to our positions in the structures or systems of institutional oppression. In other words, the power associated with the privilege is not an authentic power since it has been earned from personal integrity, but is granted as a benefit of institutionalized oppression. A man who violates and mistreats women, or harasses female coworkers in the work place, does so because institutions grant him that privilege, and allow him to act as agent of oppression despite laws and policies prohibiting such behavior. This power is so illusive that it could turn against him if the special interests of other dominant groups with institutional power are present. Furthermore, individual oppression could not exist without institutional oppression, a condition that is true for all forms of oppression. Therefore, in our interventions, we must integrate psychological, social, and structural theories. It is not a matter of which one is best, but rather that they are all necessary for understanding the interactions between individual and collective needs, and in confronting the impact of a structure of oppression on those needs. Thus, in the previous case, the man's problem as an abuser/violator or harasser cannot be resolved individually without dismantling the structural root of institutional sexism. Nor can it be solved without providing an individual intervention that addresses his psychological and social needs.

Given the choice in the use of empowerment as a tool to create interventions for individuals and different communities (i.e., public health and community development projects), we must discuss other implications of *integrity* as used in our empowerment work. It is erroneous to think that the problem of marginalization faced by these communities will be resolved through community development or social capital projects, without considering the fundamental importance of balance and harmony in relationship to the political, social, and cultural aspects of community development. Ideally, work in community development or health promotion, for example, could be provided at the same time that the community is politically organized to demand resources; have a strong and cohesive group membership; and critically analyze the values and principles that guide the work in their community. It is equally important to adequately address specific needs of the individual such as the emotional, physical, and spiritual. Consequently, we need to seriously consider, beyond rhetoric proclaims, the need to create spaces and processes for multidisciplinary work in our commitment to the process of transformation. There is no reason why committed social workers, psychologists, doctors, artists, and economists, to name a few, cannot work collaboratively in a common mission for social justice.

As much as integrity requires a balance and harmony among all the aspects of the individual and collective dimensions, it also requires recognition of our own multiple identities including those of agents as well as targets of oppression. Therefore, it is indispensable that we analyze for ourselves and facilitate for others a process of self-assessment focused on the effects of our internalized oppression privileges. Therefore, we promote that people in all types of groups must acknowledge their privileges in relation to each group member, as well as the group behaviors that are products of their internalized oppression. In a community group organized for the purpose of promoting community development, for example, it is as necessary that the men of the group reflect upon the impact their male privileges has on the women in the group. It is equally important that the women work with their internalization of sexist values. Similar considerations are necessary in family therapy or in understanding the relationship between doctor and patient. In order to do this, a greater level of trust must exist between individuals and an appropriate process needs to be offered to acknowledge and promote these connections. It is also imperative that helping professionals' acknowledge their own privileges (internalized dominance), and the impact internalized oppression has upon them.

The dynamics of oppression indicate a need to recognize the limitations and counteractive effects that exist when fragmentally working with different forms of oppression and the false notion that if we successfully fight against one form, we can subsequently challenge and take care of other forms. Three forms of oppression with significant impact are: colorism, sexism, and homophobia present in anti-racist organizations; racism and sexism in the anti-colonization movements in Puerto Rico; and, the lack of effective intervention strategies against child abuse, racism, and classism in the feminist movement that leads the fight against domestic violence. In all three cases we are guilty of ignoring different forms of oppression that are interrelated. We have refused to understand the difficulty this poses in our capacity and ability to effectively work to dismantle any form of oppression. This may be due to our lack of understanding the connections among the different forms of oppression and our avoidance to promote the dismantling of all forms of oppression, including that which exists within our own organizations and movements. For example, sexist actions by fellow community organizers and educators in anti-racist or anti-colonial movements must be dealt with at the institutional levels in these organizations and not left up to the individuals directly involved to deal with it themselves. The same is true for racist, homophobic, and/or nationalistic behaviors in any organization working to end oppression.

Finally, the concept of authentic transformative power can help us in the reconceptualization of *integrity*. This can take place by *first*, recognizing that authentic transformative power develops from the balance and harmony among all its components, and *secondly*, that this balance and harmony can only be achieved through our individual, collective and divine consciousness and will. The latter is identified in the model the spiritual character of humanity. Subsequently, integrity occupies a central place as much in our personal development as in our professional practice and in what we aspire for all. Living with integrity will become the force, the power that will propel our individual and collective transformation. Fulfilling our professional roles with integrity should lead to our becoming more effective practitioners, organizers, and agents of transformation.

The previously noted implications for practitioners are not exclusive of this model. Neither are they new discussions in the fields of health and social sciences. They have previously been presented in relation to new conceptualizations and research of the varied disciplines in the helping professions. This discussion has addressed practice and policy implications as they relate to a model of well-being and development and a rethinking of the concept of integrity. More in-depth dialogues should focus on other implications for the field of social research, leadership development, issues of accountability, and the helping professional's role as gate keepers in the area of human services.

CONCLUSION

As social workers, community psychologists, educators, and other health and helping professionals, we attempt to promote a positive influence in the lives of people we seek to assist. Therefore, it is incumbent upon us to be clear in our analysis about the impact that institutional oppression has upon the communities we work in. After all, not all practitioners work with society's most wealthy, most educated, healthy or otherwise well-to-do citizens. Many of us, for the most part, work with society's most oppressed populations, primarily women, children, ethnic minority groups, and people in poverty.

Furthermore, it is particularly important that we gain consciousness of our own ideas, beliefs, feelings, attitudes and values, of how we ourselves have been socialized in the dominant cultural worldview. We must be mindful of the conflicts and contradictions–lack of integrity and authentic power–in all aspects of our lives. It is especially important that as social workers, educators and other helping professionals, we apply our critical awareness and responsibility as we work on behalf of oppressed people.

NOTES

1. It is with great appreciation and gratitude that we acknowledge Dr. Lenore Stiffarm, the Four Worlds Development Project, University of Lethbridge, Alberta, Canada, and the Lakota people for sharing the wisdom of their Medicine Wheel with us.

2. In addition to the vast literature on oppression, primary sources of information include numerous professional training programs and anti-oppression workshops attended by the authors presented by groups including. Equity Institute, Amherst, MA; The People's Institute for Survival and Beyond, New Orleans, LA; Elsie Y. Cross Associates, Inc., Philadelphia, PA.

3. In Puerto Rico and elsewhere in Latin America, political affiliation is considered a major social group identity, since the livelihood and even the lives of subordinated political group members are often at stake.

4. The nationality (or national identity) of an entire Latin American country itself may be considered a major identity group, as the people of that nation may be subordinated in a colonial or neo-colonial relationship to an imperialistic foreign national power. This subordinated relationship is a very important, and a most overlooked, aspect of the social group identity of Latinos in the US.

5. Pyramids are used in African cultures but not in the same way as in Western philosophy. In African thought it is used as a symbol of equality since all sides of the pyramid are equal, and of integrity between thesis and antithesis which results in a synthesis. In European cultural thought it is has been used to symbolize a hierarchy of power and dominance.

6. Firewalking is a ritual or technique that is used to facilitate the process of recognizing our personal power to overcome fear and confront difficult situations.

REFERENCES

Akbar, N. (1996). *Breaking the Chains of Psychological Slavery*. New Jersey: Mind Productions.

Ani, M. (1994). *Yurugu: An Afrikan-Centered Critique of European Cultural Thought and Behavior*. New Jersey: Africa World Press, Inc.

Assagioli, R. (1976). *Psychosynthesis*. New York: Penguin Books.

Assagioli, R. (1973). *The Act of Will*. New York: Penguin Books.
Bopp, J., Bopp, M., Lane, P., Brown, L. (1988). *The Sacred Tree. Reflections on Native American Spirituality*. Alberta, Canada: Four Worlds Development Press.
Bulhan, H. A. (1985). *Frantz Fanon and the Psychology of Oppression*. NY: Plenum.
Chisom, R. & Washington, M. (1997). *Undoing Racism A Philosophy for Social International Change*. Louisiana: The People's Institute Press.
Fanon, F. (1963). *The Wretched of the Earth*. New York: Grove Weidenfeld.
Freire, P. (1970). *Pedagogla del oprimido*. Mexico: Siglo Veitiuno Editores.
Freire, P. (1970). Cultural Action and Conscientization. *Harvard Educational Review*, 40, pp. 452-477. 1970.
Gil, D. (1992). *Social Unravelling Policy*. (5th Edition). Vermont: Schenkman Books.
Gil, D. (1993). *Confronting Oppression Social and Injustice*. In F. Reamer (Ed.). The Foundation Social of Work knowledge (pp.). New York: Colombia University Press.
Gordon, L. R., Sharpley-Whiting, T. D., & White, R.T. (1996). *Fanon: A Critical Reader*. Cambridge, MA: Blackwell.
hooks, b. (1995). *Killing Rage: Ending Racism*. New York: Hemy Holt & Co.
hooks, b. (1993). *Sisters of the Yam: Black Women and Self-Recovery*. Boston, MA: South End Press, 1993.
hooks, b. (1984). *Feminist Theory. From Margin to Center*. Boston, MA: South End Press.
Lorler, M. L. (1991). *Shamanic Healing within the Medicine Wheel*. Albuquerque, NM: Brotherhood of Life.
Maguire, P. (1987). *Doing Participatory Research. A Feminist Approach*. The Center for International Education, School of Education, University of Massachusetts.
Martín-Baró, 1. (1994). *Writings for a Liberation Psychology*. (Adrianne Aron and Shawn Corne, eds.) Cambridge, MA: Harvard University Press.
Martinez, L. M. (1999). *La pedagogía de la liberación desde unaperspectiva de género. Diálogo,* diciembre, p.22. Río Piedras, PR.
Maslow, A. H. (1962). *Toward a psychology of being*. Princeton, NJ: Van Nostrand.
Maslow, A. H. (1968). *Toward a Psychology of Being*. New York: Van Nostrand Reinhold.
McLaren, P. & Leonard, P. (2000). (Eds.). *Paulo Freire a Critical Encounter*. London: Routledge.
Memmi, A. (2000). *Racism*. Minneapolis, MN: University of Minnesota Press.
Montero, M. (1997). *Ideologlía, alienación e identidad nacional*. Caracas, Venezuela Universidad Central de Venezuela, Ediciones de la Biblioteca.
Quiñones-Rosado, R. (1995). *Latino & African-American Male Mentors Training Manual*. Springfield, MA: Gandara Mental Health Center & Dunbar Community Center.
Quiñones-Rosado, R. & Barreto-Cortéz, E. (in press). Un modelo de bienestar integral y sus implicaciones a la practica de profesionales de ayuda. *Análisis*. Rio Piedras, PR: Universidad de Puerto Rico.

Schipani, D. S. & Freire, P. (1992). *Educación, libertady creatividad. Encuentroy diálogo con Paulo Freire.* Universidad Interamericana de Puerto Rico.

Wallerstain, I. (1998). *Abrir las Ciencias Sociales. Informe ante la Comisión Culbenkianpara la reestructuracion de las ciencias sociales. Siglo Veintiuno Editores.* S.A. de C.V., Mexico.

Wilber, K. (1977). *The Spectrum of Consciousness.* Wheaton, IL: The Theosophical Publishing House.

The Adultification of Refugee Children: Implications for Cross-Cultural Social Work Practice

Maria Elena Puig

SUMMARY. This paper presents the findings of a study that examines the social and emotional adjustment of adultified Cuban refugee children from the 1994-1995 Guantanamo wave. It also discusses how changes in family roles affect intergenerational relations and family well-being, and how the migration and resettlement experience affects parent/child roles and disrupts the refugee family. *[Article copies available for a fee from The Haworth Document Delivery Service: 1-800-HAWORTH. E-mail address: <getinfo@haworthpressinc.com> Website: <http://www.HaworthPress.com> © 2002 by The Haworth Press, Inc. All rights reserved.]*

KEYWORDS. Migration, refugees, adultification, Cubans

My daughter openly defies us. I believe it is because we are busy working and because we don't speak English. We always have to ask her for help. (Excerpt from an interview with a Cuban refugee family)

Maria Elena Puig, PhD, is Assistant Professor in the Department of Social Work at Colorado State University in Fort Collins, CO. She is the former Refugee and Entrant Director for the State of Florida, Department of Health and Rehabilitative Services' Office of Refugee Affairs. Dr. Puig's research focuses primarily on Cuban refugee issues.

[Haworth co-indexing entry note]: "The Adultification of Refugee Children: Implications for Cross-Cultural Social Work Practice." Puig, Maria Elena. Co-published simultaneously in *Journal of Human Behavior in the Social Environment* (The Haworth Social Work Practice Press, an imprint of The Haworth Press, Inc.) Vol. 5, No. 3/4, 2002, pp. 85-95; and: *Latino/Hispanic Liaisons and Visions for Human Behavior in the Social Environment* (ed: José B. Torres, and Felix G. Rivera) The Haworth Social Work Practice Press, an imprint of The Haworth Press, Inc., 2002, pp. 85-95. Single or multiple copies of this article are available for a fee from The Haworth Document Delivery Service [1-800-HAWORTH, 9:00 a.m. - 5:00 p.m. (EST). E-mail address: getinfo@haworthpressinc.com].

85

INTRODUCTION

Since 1959, when the first group of Cubans arrived in the United States as political refugees, two aspects of this migration have remained the same. First, Cuban refugees have come in waves, and second, each wave has brought Cubans with distinct cultural beliefs, cultural values, norms, and behaviors. As a result, each refugee's reaction to living in the U.S. has varied and added to the diversity of Cubans' migration and resettlement experiences.

Often, the Cuban migration experience has involved the unsettling of families, as the difficulty of maintaining the culture of origin, combined with the effects of assimilation and acculturation, render parents powerless to deal with the new environment. Oftentimes, as parents struggle to keep traditions and resist cultural norms from the country of settlement, refugee children quickly learn to adjust and adapt to the new conditions and environment. The roles of parents and children are usually disrupted and, unwittingly, responsibilities shift as refugee children assume obligations that do not correspond to their chronological, emotional, or psychological age. The adjustment of the refugee family is frequently agitated by this differential process of assimilation (Canino, Earley, & Rogler, 1980).

For social work practitioners working with refugees from any country, the need to understand the emotional, psychological, and cultural consequences of displacement and differential assimilation is critical. First, practitioners need to appreciate that what happens to individual refugees and their families depends on a myriad of factors, including why and how they left their country and culture of origin, and how resettlement efforts were effected. Second, because migration and resettlement automatically disrupt family life, social workers must help refugee families deal with the trauma and stress of the displacement experience. Issues surrounding loss and bereavement must be explored, because these families have lost contact with relatives, friends, communities, and parts of their cultural self-identity. Third, social workers should assist refugee parents and children in dealing with the dislocation their families experience, as a result of their unfamiliarity with cultural norms and values of the host country (Cervantes, Salgado de Snyder, & Padilla, 1989). The recognition that these families have specific emotional and behavioral reactions to coping and adapting to a different cultural environment, will lead practitioners to have a greater understanding of the psychological reactions of refugee adults and children.

Although this paper presents the findings of a study on Cuban refugee families, the application of these findings, however, are relevant to social work practice with all other refugee populations. This paper explores the social and emotional adjustment of adultified Cuban refugee children from the 1994-1995 Guantanamo wave, and how changes in family roles affects intergenerational relations and family well-being. It also opens the door for further inquiry on the resiliency of refugee children, as there is much to learn about how children and adults cope with their refugee experiences.

BACKGROUND OF THE STUDY POPULATION

In 1994, the existence of *balseros*, or Cubans who left their homeland in rafts, became the focus of both national and international political and media attention. Unlike previous waves of Cuban refugees, the balseros were part of a group of exiles whose departure did not grant them immediate entry into the United States. Instead, these Cubans were intercepted at sea and taken to the U.S. Naval Base in Guantanamo. Eventually, more than 37,000 Cuban balseros were detained in Guantanamo, including 2,833 accompanied minors under the age of 17, and 69 unaccompanied children (U.S. Seventh Coast Guard District, Cuban Rescue Statistics, 1995). On January 26,1996, the last 127 balseros were flown out of Guantanamo and brought to the U.S., ending an 18-month detention period for the majority of these refugees.

Review of the Literature

Research studies on refugee children indicate that these children generally have an easier time with assimilation and acculturation because they are exposed to various socialization systems including the school, teachers, classmates, and friends (Eisenbruch, 1988; Gopaul-McNicol, 1995; Huyck & Fields, 1981; Nikelly, 1997; Szapocznik, Kurtinez, Hervis, & Spencer, 1983). The literature describes how refugee children acculturate and assimilate, and how culture is transmitted, perceived, interpreted, and internalized (Ho, 1995; Okum, 1990; Sue & Sue, 1990; Tarpley, 1993; Triandis, 1994; Wolcott, 1991). Much of this is reported in positive terms, as narratives recount how newly arrived refugee children learn to develop appropriate coping skills and responses that correspond to their new social and cultural environment.

In spite of the number of children who can cope and adjust to their new environment, there is growing concern among mental health practitioners that many of these children are not as irrepressible as the stereotype would suggest (Eisenbruch, 1988; Hulewat, 1996; Roer-Strier, 1997; Thomas, 1995). Studies corroborate that problems among refugee populations, particularly children, are likely to surface during adolescence, or even later in life in second- and third-generation refugee children (Pittman, 1987; Sluski, 1979; Szapocznik et al., 1983).

One of the most significant human problems confronting refugee children is *adultification*, or when a child assumes adult roles before adulthood (Galan, 1992). Adultification usually occurs among this population as a result of parents' inability to cope with the aftermath of the migration experience. Rinsley (1971) sees child adultification as adultomorphization, in which the parent "projects into the child their own reservoir of magic-omnipotence and infantile grandiosity. Such a child becomes, in the parent's mind, a powerful, omniscient being" (p. 11). Much of this child adultification centers parents' relative powerlessness to manage life in a new environment, in a new language, and in a new culture with a different value system (Eisenbruch, 1988). This role reversal has been linked to parents' general inability to function in the new culture and environment (Eisenbruch, 1988).

As refugee children assimilate, studies show that they are more apt to develop bilingual and bicultural skills and coping responses that provide them with greater ability and power to manage social situations (Puig, 1997; Szapocznik et al., 1983). Refugee children are called upon to translate, intervene, and use their dual-frame of reference to help their parents relate and understand the host culture and society. Consequently, they learn sophisticated code-switching responses as well as high levels of social sensitivity, skills that allow these children to develop an acute appreciation of the difficulties their monolingual, monocultural parents experience (Puig, 1997). In addition, the literature on the interrelated problems of separation, loss, coping, and adaptation in childhood points to the fact that human coping and adaptation depends on the interplay between the individual and his or her environment (Berry, 1986; Roer-Strier, 1997; Thomas, 1995). For refugee children, much of this coping and adaptation is brought about as a result of their ability to acculturate and assimilate.

As acculturation occurs, refugee children understand the need to make personal adjustments that allow for the integration of their ethnic identity into the new culture (Puig, 1997; Szapocznik et al., 1983). This integration includes adopting a new value system and developing cultural competence within that system (Puig, 1997). Esquivel and Keitel (1990), Goodstein (1990) and Thomas (1995) further point to the increased amount of conflict among refugee families, as children begin to develop autonomy and differentiation. When refugee children realize they have acquired the ability to manage most social situations, conflict generally occurs with one or both parents lacking bicultural capabilities. These conflicts often contribute to the increased vulnerability of family relationships, as cross-generational, cross-cultural, and interactional problems begin to escalate among refugee families. Threats to family unity, whether real or imagined, are part of the crises with which refugees must contend and social workers must redress. The lack of adequate research on the benefits or drawbacks of assimilation among Cuban refugees, has resulted in mental health professionals assuming that many of these children will be seen as clients in later years, when they are no longer classified as either children or refugees (Eisenbruch, 1988).

PURPOSE OF THE STUDY

This purpose of this exploratory study was to examine whether Cuban refugee children from the Guantanamo immigration wave experienced adultification upon their arrival in the U.S. It also explored how changes in family roles affected intergenerational relations and family well-being, as a result of parents' inability to mediate societal situations in the new environment.

Grounding this study was the work of Karp and Yoels (1993) and McCall and Simmons (1982) concerning the development of self and social interaction. Using social interaction as a theoretical base, this study explored how Cuban refugee children and their parents defined their roles and how these were interpreted in terms of both the expectations others had of them and the expectations they had of themselves.

METHODOLOGY

Using a non-experimental design and qualitative and quantitative methodologies, this study involved the administration of a Spanish language structured questionnaire to collect data concerning the adultification of the children and the parents' perception of this process. Respondents were asked to react in writing to a set of open-ended questions that addressed acculturation and assimilation issues and the family's perception of their well-being.

Sample

A non-probability sampling procedure was used to select 75 Cuban refugee families (n = 50 adults; n = 25 children) who had been part of the balseros/Guantanamo refugee wave. This method was selected because of the nature of the research, the author's knowledge of the population, and the purpose of the study.

Eighty percent of the adult sample population (n = 50) was predominantly White, with Black Cubans and mulattoes, respectively, making up the other twenty percent. The majority of adult respondents were females (82%), with males comprising eighteen percent of the sample. The mean age for adults was 36.8 years, with a mean family income of $12,191. Sixty percent of the adults were married, none spoke English, and all reported having been detained in Guantanamo. The sample for children (n = 25) reflected the same racial make-up as the parents. Fifty-three percent of the children were males, with females comprising forty-seven percent of the sample. The mean age for children was 11.7 years, and all reported attending school and speaking English.

FINDINGS

In relation to the findings concerning the adultification of Cuban refugee children, sixty-four percent of parents reported having to rely on their children to help translate, deal with landlords, and manage situations involving school personnel, government officials, and social services providers. Oftentimes, children paid the bills, dealt with social institutions such as banks and schools, and also did the shopping, particularly if it required going to non-Spanish owned stores. Seventy-two percent of the parents confirmed that when they received a call or written notice from their children's teachers, they relied on the children to translate and/or explain the communication in their native language. Fifty-seven percent of parents acknowledged that the use of their children in this manner "felt wrong." Many believed that it was leading to a lack of trust, cooperation, and respect within the family.

Sixty-nine percent of the parents attributed these changing family dynamics to the constant conflict between the "new ways and traditional

Cuban values." When parents were asked to assess who had more influence and control in the family, the majority (78%) acknowledged that their children had the power because they provided " . . . the connection to the outside world." Language was often cited by a majority of the parents (98%), as the reason for the children's influence and control.

Responses from the children confirmed their having to assume many adult related responsibilities. Seventy-four percent of the children indicated it was their fluency in English that caused them to be given and accept these obligations. The majority of them (89%) admitted being embarrassed about their parents' inability to speak or understand English. One-third indicated their parents "did not exist." Approximately forty-five percent of the children reported feeling frustrated at having to deal with these situations. In their narratives, children often stated they were " . . . tired of always having to explain things to them (parents)." Sixty-six percent asserted that they "just wanted to be left alone."

Examining the parents' and children's perception of their family well-being, adult respondents who were white Cubans rated their family well-being higher than those who were black or mulattoes. Analysis of variance and chi-square tests indicated that race, as a variable, was significantly related to family well-being (see Table 1).

Even though "race" was not a primary construct for evaluation in this study, this finding points to its continued importance in U.S. culture. For recently arrived Cuban refugees of color, the prejudice, racism, and discrimination they confronted provided a rude awakening to American culture and life.

For the children, age was an important variable that helped to modify their perception of personal well-being. Younger children were found to experience greater confusion over their roles and understanding of situations than older children. This sense of uncertainty was alluded to in their narratives and appears to have distorted their sense of self and well-being. For older children, their opinions concerning personal well-being fluctuated. Those who identified with their parents had a higher perception of well-being, in comparison to those who did not. These children generally had withdrawn from the family and appeared anxious. Many wrote about the confusion they experienced between wanting to take care of their parents and wanting to retreat from them altogether.

In their narratives, parents recounted their struggles since coming to the United States and wrote about their realization that life in this country was much more difficult than previously envisioned. Most parents indicated feeling overwhelmed due to a combination of factors, includ-

TABLE 1. Analysis of Variance

Source of Variation	Sum of Squares	DF	Mean Square	F	Sig. of F
Main effects					
Family well-being	3.864	1	3.864	12.208	.001
Explained	3.864	1	3.864	12.208	.001
Residual	13.295	42	.317		
Total	17.159	43	399		

ing nostalgia for their homeland and family, anger and frustration over their inabilities to deal with the culture, their language limitations, and concerns over the changes they were experiencing as a family.

One mother wrote:

> Una nota positiva es que he encontrado libertad y que le he podido dar a mi hijo la oportunidad de ser lo que el quiera. Pero siento much nostalgia por un pasado que se que jamas volvere a tener.

> (On a positive note, I have found liberty and I have been able to give my son the opportunity to become whatever he wishes. But I feel a great sadness for a past that I know I will never have again).

Other parents wrote of their frustrations and disappointment in making the transition from their homeland to their new environment in the U.S. Several mothers shared comparable feelings when they wrote:

> Venir a estepais ha sido muy dificil. Mi familia ha cambiado mucho. Muchas veces me siento oprimida.

> (Coming to this country has been very difficult. My family has changed greatly. Many times I felt have felt depressed and overwhelmed).

> Mi hija se opone abiertamente contra nosotros. Creo que es porque estamos muy ocupados trabajando y por que no hablamos Ingles. Siempre tenemos que pedirle que nos ayude. Tambien tenemos muy poco tiempo para la familia. (My daughter openly defies us. I believe it is because we are very busy working and because we don't speak English. We always have to ask for her help. We also have very little time for the family).

A single-father expressed comparable concerns when he revealed:

> Me he deprimido mucho y estoy ertremadamente frustrado. A veces quisiera morirme. Se que no debo pensar asi porque mis ninos me necesitan. Pero no le puedo explicar lo mal que me siento, siendo un padre solo con tantas necesidades.

> (I have become very depressed and I am extremely frustrated. Sometimes I wish that I would die. I know that I shouldn't think that way because my children need me. But I can't explain how badly I feel being a single father with so many needs).

On a more optimistic note, one mother stated:

> Estoy muy agradecida porque mis ninos son muy inteligente y hablan Ingles. Pero, no quiero depender de ellos.

> (I am very grateful that my children are very smart and can speak English. But I don't want to depend on them).

Similarly, the children wrote about how their parents were living in the past, and how parents spent the majority of their time telling them of their suffering. However, most children did include a few passages about their appreciation for what their parents were going through. Most narratives also contained references about the children's concern over fitting in; many children proudly discussed how they were becoming "American." In spite of expressing this opinion, there were a few entries where the children discussed their fear over losing their Cuban culture. It was, as if unknowingly, they were trying to accommodate their two "selves."

Overall, the narratives provided a glimpse into what family members were experiencing. Most families were bewildered and overwhelmed by their circumstances. There was a palpable tenseness in these families that was captured in their writings. The narratives clearly chronicled the personal, cross-cultural, and intergenerational conflicts among this particular group of Cuban refugees.

DISCUSSION

Though small in scope, this study points to the need for the provision of comprehensive social and mental health services, as primary and secondary prevention, to refugee groups. These support services should be provided as soon as refugee families enter this country, and should continue through their integration into the new culture and society. Social workers need to provide services in the context of rapidly changing situations, since day-to-day life experiences alter the refugees' ability to cope, adjust, and adapt to the changing environment.

In addition, family therapy should be provided to all refugee families to help them deal with the confusion of living in a new environment, and to address the disorientation members feel over role reversal and divided loyalties. Socio-educational groups also should be included as an intervention, to help address children's perception. Groups are an effective treatment method for both adults and children because they can help participants discover similarities in circumstances. Groups also foster a greater sense of personal and family normalcy. For parents, group therapy is important because it offers them a means to deal with self-blame and inaccurate attributions.

Finally, because children and adults acculturate differently, particular efforts should be made to establish language and acculturation classes for parents. Any planned effort that facilitates these processes, however, should ensure that programs and social and mental health services match the needs and characteristics of the refugees, and the communities which they live in.

REFERENCES

Back, K. W. (19B0). Uprooting and self-image: Catastrophe and continuity. In G. V. Coelho and P. I. Ahmed (Ed.), *Uprooting and development: Dilemmas of coping with modernization*. New York: Plenum.

Berry, J. W. (1986). The acculturation process and refugee behavior. In C. L. Williams and J. Westermeyer (Eds.), *Refugee mental health in resettlement countries* (pp. 25-37). Washington: Hemisphere Publishing Corporation.

Canino, I. A., Earley, B. F., & Rogler, L. H. (1980). *The Puerto Rican child in New York City: Stress and mental health.* (Monograph No. 4). New York: Hispanic Research Center, Fordham University.

Cervantes, R. C., Salgado De Snyder, V.N., & Padilla, A. M. (1989). Posttraumatic stress in immigrants from Central America and Mexico. *Hospital and Community Psychiatry*, 40, 615-619.

Eisenbruch, M. (1988). The mental health of refugee children and their cultural development. *International Migration Review*, 22, 282-300.

Esquivel, G., & Keitel, M. (1990). Counseling immigrant children in the schools. *Psychology of Women Quarterly*, 11, 213-221.

Galan, F. J. (1992). Experiential focusing with Mexican-American males with bicultural identity problems. In K. Corcoran (Ed.), *Structuring change: Effective practice for common client problems*. Lyceum.

Goodstein, C. (1990). American societies: The new immigrants in the schools. Crisis, 98, 161-171.

Ho, D. (1995). Internalized culture, cultocentrism and transcendence. *The Counseling Psychologist*, 23, 4-24.

Hulewat, P. (1996). Resettlement: A cultural and psychological crisis. *Social Work*, 41, 129-135.

Hyuck, E. E., Fields, R. (1981). Impact of resettlement on refugee children. *International Migration Review*, 15, 246-254.

Karp, D. A., & Yoels, W. C. (1993). *Sociology in everyday life*. 2nd ed. Itasca, IL: Peacock.

McCall, G. J., & Simmons, J. L. (1982). *Social psychology: A sociological approach*. New York: Free Press.

Nikelly, A. (1997). Cultural babel: The challenge of immigrants to the helping professions. *Cultural Diversity and Mental Health*, 3, 281-285.

Okum, B. F., Fried, J., & Okum, M. L. (1999). *Understanding diversity: Learning-as-practice primer*. Brooks/Cole.

Pittman, F. S., III. (1987). *Turning points: Treating families in transition and crisis*. Toronto: Penguin.

Puig, M. E. (1997). Immigrant children: Mediating conflict between their parents and the host culture. Unpublished research study. Colorado State University.

Rinsley, D. B. (1971). The adolescent inpatient: Patterns of depersonification. *Psychoanalytic Quarterly*, 45, 3-22.

Roer-Strier, D. (1997). In the mind of the beholder: Evaluation of coping styles of immigrant parents. *International migration Review*, 35, 271-285.

Sluski, C. E. (1979). Migration and family conflict. *Family Process*, 18, 379-390.

Sue, D.W., & Sue, D. (1990). *Counseling the culturally different: Theory and practice*. New York: Wiley.

Szapocznik, J., Kurtines, W., Hervis, O., & Spencer, F. (1983). One person family therapy. In B. Lubin and W. A. O'Connor (Eds.), *Psychological dimensions of the acculturation process: Theories, models, and some new findings*. Boulder, CO: Westview.

Szapocznik, J., & Truss, C. (1978). Intergenerational sources of conflict in Cuban mothers. In M. Montiel (Ed.), Hispanic families. Washington, D.C.: COSSMHO.

Thomas, T. N. (1995). Acculturative stress in the adjustment of immigrant families. *Journal of Social Distress and the Homeless*, 4, 131-141.

Triandis, H. C. (1994). *Culture and social behavior*. New York: McGraw-Hill. U.S. Seventh Coast Guard District. (1995). Cuban Rescue Statistics Report. Wolcott, H. E. (1991). Propriospect and the acquisition of culture. *Anthropology and Educational Quarterly*, 22, 251-278.

Latinos Participating in Multiethnic Coalitions to Prevent Substance Abuse: A Case Study

Flavio Francisco Marsiglia
John Michael Daley

SUMMARY. This paper presents a case study of a neighborhood based coalition formed by two major participants, a neighborhood association formed by white and older neighbors and a school based parents association formed by younger Latino neighbors. Differences in their communication and organizational sales emerged after an external agency brought them together to form a substance abuse prevention coalition. This paper explores emerging themes as two different communities attempt to organize around shared community concerns.

Flavio Francisco Marsiglia, PhD, is Associate Professor at the School of Social Work, College of Public Programs, Arizona State University. He is the lead instructor for the Diversity and Oppression curriculum sequence and is the Principal Investigator of the Arizona component of the Drug Resistance Strategies Project (DRS-AZ). DRS-AZ is a culturally grounded drug use prevention project being implemented in 36 Phoenix middle schools, funded by a NIDA/NIH grant through Penn State University.

John Michael Daley, PhD, is Professor at the School of Social Work, College of Public Programs, Arizona State University. He teaches and researches on community development, organization and planning and intercultural social work practice.

[Haworth co-indexing entry note]: "Latinos Participating in Multiethnic Coalitions to Prevent Substance Abuse: A Case Study." Marsiglia, Flavio Francisco, and John Michael Daley. Co-published simultaneously in *Journal of Human Behavior in the Social Environment* (The Haworth Social Work Practice Press, an imprint of The Haworth Press, Inc.) Vol. 5, No. 3/4, 2002, pp. 97-121; and: *Latino/Hispanic Liaisons and Visions for Human Behavior in the Social Environment* (ed: José B. Torres, and Felix G. Rivera) The Haworth Social Work Practice Press, an imprint of The Haworth Press, Inc., 2002, pp. 97-121. Single or multiple copies of this article are available for a fee from The Haworth Document Delivery Service [1-800-HAWORTH, 9:00 a.m. - 5:00 p.m. (EST). E-mail address: getinfo@haworthpressinc.com].

97

Challenges and guidelines for developing multiethnic urban coalitions are also provided. *[Article copies available for a fee from The Haworth Document Delivery Service: 1-800-HAWORTH. E-mail address: <getinfo@haworthpressinc.com> Website: <http://www.HaworthPress.com> © 2002 by The Haworth Press, Inc. All rights reserved.]*

KEYWORDS. Coalitions, White/European Americans, Latinos, substance abuse

INTRODUCTION

The city government of a large southwestern community and the local state university were the initiators of a wide partnership to strengthen community based efforts towards substance use prevention among youth Local projects, Community Initiatives, organized at the neighborhood level were funded and evaluated by the partnership. This article documents the process of forming a Community Initiative (CI) that attempted to form a neighborhood based interethnic community coalition.

The proposal for the formation of the neighborhood base CI was developed by a social service agency (i.e., Behavioral Services) with many years of experience in the field of prevention. The agency staff adjusted their regular school based intervention model to the needs of the neighborhood, expanding the model to include a stronger community involvement. The CI design followed an empowerment approach (Wiel, 1996). The strengths of children, their families, and other community residents were seen as resources to be identified, supported and utilized (Saleebey, 1997). The participants' cultures were identified as sources of pride to be enhanced and to be utilized as a resource in the process of developing a community wide prevention program. The intervention aimed at narrowing the gaps between children, their parents, and other community members in order to enhance their communication and allow for an improved community spirit. The underlining hypothesis was that a more unified community based on mutual respect and an interest in the common good of all children would be able to delay, diminish, or eliminate the use of alcohol, tobacco, and other drugs (ATOD) among its youth. These efforts were envisioned to be lead by a multigenerational and multiethnic coalition of community members.

COMMUNITY COALITIONS

The community practice literature has attempted to understand the role coalitions play in community change. Weil (1996) discusses several key elements of contemporary models that have their basis in events over the past century such as the Settlement and Charity Organization Society movements at the turn of the century and the civil rights movement and social upheaval of the 1960s and 1970s. The complexities of social problems were recognized and scholars and practitioners acknowledged that broader strategies would be necessary to resolve such issues. Direct organizing for social justice issues, social action, and advocacy planning were seen as ways to empower people (Wiel, 1996). Weil goes onto identify coalitions as one of eight models for community practice that have been influenced by these antecedents.

The community practice literature often addresses coalitions' abilities to promote a cause or to improve or protect public sector organizations and programs. Caplow (1968, p. 165) defines a coalition as a combination of two or more actors who adopt a common strategy in contention with other actors in the same system. Mizrahi and Rosenthal identify coalitions as a group of diverse organizational representatives who join forces to influence external institutions on one or more issues affecting their constituencies while maintaining their own autonomy (1993, p. 14). Wiel (1996, p. 55) maintains that the purpose of coalitions is to build a multiorganizational power base large enough to influence social program direction and/or effectively demand resources for the purpose of responding to the common interests of the coalition.

Several authors describe coalitions as a way to improve or protect public sector organizations and programs. Weisner (1983) sees the formation of coalitions as a protective measure in response to fiscal uncertainty and waning public support. He contends that people join coalitions to advance their cause or maximize personal or organizational benefits and cites a variety of authors such as Riker (1962), Gamson (1961), Adrian and Press (1968) and Hill (1973) who have developed cost-benefit and exchange based theories of coalition behavior. Coalitions may increase the ability of different groups to access needed resources while avoiding a divide and conquer attitude generated by competition for scarce resources. Roberts-DeGennaro (1997, p. 92) believes that as resources become more difficult to obtain, coalitions can exert more power and influence and mobilize more resources than a single organization. Butterfoss, Goodman, and Wandersman (1993) describe seven ways in which coalitions are important: (1) enable organizations to become involved in new and broader issues without sole responsibility for managing the issues, (2) demonstrate and develop widespread public support, (3) maximize the power of individuals and groups through joint action, (4) minimize duplication of effort and services,

(5) mobilize talents, resources and approaches to influence an issue more than any single organization could, (6) provide an avenue for recruiting participants from diverse constituencies, and (7) exploit new resources in changing situations.

Boissevain (1974) identifies five characteristics of coalitions that distinguish them from more structured organizations: (l) they are temporary, (2) they have both core and peripheral members, (3) they are formed for a limited purpose, (4) they imply the joint use of resources, and (5) resources are attached to each member and may be withdrawn at any time. In addition, Feighery and Rogers (1989) categorize coalitions based on type of membership. *Grassroots coalitions* are composed of volunteers that are brought together in times of crisis. Professional coalitions are formed by employees of organizations at times of crisis or to address ongoing issues to increase their power and influence. *Community based coalitions* bring together grassroots leaders and professionals to influence long-term health and welfare concerns.

Forming Coalitions Within Diverse Ethnic Communities

In recent years a variety of factors are making the need for multiethnic coalitions particularly salient. Díaz-Veizades and Chang (1996) note the increase in interethnic conflict around the world. A large volume of work has focused on racial and ethnic issues related to the Los Angeles riots in 1992 (Yu and Chang, 1995). Calderon (1995) reviews a variety of topics such as Black-Latino political conflict, competition for scarce resources between ethnic groups, and conflict between immigrant and resident populations that are also garnering more attention. In the field of education, school populations are becoming more diverse and groups that were once considered minorities are becoming the majorities and demanding democratization in curriculum and course offerings (McCarthy, 1994). Nationalistic interests and the significance of ethnic group membership also appear to be contributing to inter and intra racial and ethnic group tensions (Brosio, 1997 Díaz-Veizades and Chang, 1996; Kamasaki and Yzaguirre, 1991; Soto-Ortega, 1970). Oliver and Grant (1995) discuss the lack of common interests and a rise in competition among groups on issues such as jobs, education, housing, health care, crime, and the role of government. They also note a decline in the role played by mediating institutions such as churches, unions, and political parties in addressing community issues.

Coalitions may make an important contribution in addressing and mediating these issues and conflicts. As Díaz-Veizades and Chang write, the creation of cross-cultural alliances and coalitions may very well be an important step in decreasing the level of cultural and ideological fragmentation which characterizes many urban centers around the globe (1996, p. 681). Brosio (1997, p. 2) argues that such fragmentation and culturalist focus hide the real issues such as power, privilege, access, and wealth and that coalitions are a way to organize across group lines to address these inequalities. While differences in multiethnic and racial communities are important, coalitions can provide a mechanism to build action around common interest on issues such as employment, income, housing, and medical care (Dymally, 1970; Shingles, 1991). Oliver and Grant (1995) recognize that at the macro level, these differences may be impossible to reconcile. They suggest that brief and issue oriented multiethnic coalitions developing at the neighborhood level may be able to surmount these differences around smaller, more specific issues. Such coalitions are necessary to enhance the chances of less influential groups becoming incorporated in a locality dominant coalition. One strategy available to less powerful ethnic groups is to seek partnership with other groups (Browning, Marshall, & Tabb 1995).

Functional Elements of Ethnically Diverse Coalitions

Coalitions addressing a variety of social and health problems are becoming more common (Mayer et al., 1998) and the literature has begun to identify variables associated with effective coalition functioning. Butterfoss, Goodman, and Wandersman (1996) found leadership roles, staff-committee relations, organizational climate, decision-making influence, and community linkages to be associated with coalition member participation and satisfaction. Interestingly, these independent variables did not relate to the quality of the coalition's plan or the primary outcome for coalition activities. Kumpfer, Turner, Hopkins, and Librett (1993) identified an empowering style of leadership as contributing to member satisfaction, perceptions of team efficacy, and ultimately, team effectiveness. A case study of two health promotion coalitions found coalition effectiveness to be related to a number of factors. Included among these factors are: a grassroots versus a bureaucratic source of vision for the coalition; higher levels of staff time devoted to coalition activities and a less prominent role for staff in carrying out coalition activities; frequent and productive communication among staff and members, high levels of cohesiveness; complexity of coalition structure during the intervention phase; and training and technical assistance (Kumpfer, Turner, Hopkins, and Librett, 1993).

While the theoretical and empirical literature on multiethnic coalition building is limited, many explanations for coalition formation rely on the self-interest of individuals and groups and on the realization that cooperation can maximize benefits (Regalado, 1995). Carmichael and Hamilton (1967) present four requirements for coalitions: (1) the coalition must recognize the self interest of its constituent parties, (2) there must be a belief that each party in the coalition stands to benefit, (3) there must be an acceptance that each party has its own base of power and decision making, and (4) there must be agreement that the coalition must deal with specific and identifiable goals and issues. Shared views and ideologies have also been advanced as a prerequisite for alliance: development (Himmelman, 1991; Sonenshein, 1993). Oliver and Grant (1995) hypothesize that in addition to common interests, there must also be parity in group size, economic status, and social resources. Several authors suggest that divisive issues, such as nationalism and identity politics must be addressed before functional coalitions can be developed (Brosio, 1997; Dymally, 1970; Kamasaki and Yzaguirre, 1991; Soto-Ortega, 1970). As Chechoway (1997, p. 25) writes, multicultural change is a process that recognizes the difference between groups while also increasing interaction and cooperation among them, recognizing differences and building bridges at the community level.

Additional studies have identified issues related to nationalist ideology and ethnic solidarity as potentially limiting a coalition's effectiveness (Calderon, 1995; Díaz-Veizades and Chang, 1996). Cultural and class differences within a multiethnic coalition were found to have the potential of creating barriers between its members (Calderon, 1995; Regalado, 1995; Díaz-Viezades and Chang, 1996). Organizational aspects of coalitions such as staffing patterns, resources to accomplish coalition objectives, and a clear statement of the coalition's purposes have been also identified as prerequisites for the formation of a successful coalition (Lichterman, 1995; Regalado, 1995).

This study researched the formation of a neighborhood based multiethnic coalition. The main research question guiding the study was: How did this neighborhood-based coalition deal with diversity in the process of organizing and mobilizing the community towards a common goal? Due to the unique geographic, political, and cultural characteristics of the Southwest, this study aimed at furthering our understanding of multiethnic coalitions in the Mexican U.S. border region. Issues of language, social class, marginality, discrimination, representation, and power sharing were at the core of our research.

THEORETICAL FRAMEWORK

We approached this study from a developmental perspective, focusing on the relationship between culture and human development. Vygotsky (1979) maintained that humans are active, vigorous participants in their own existence and at each stage of development they acquire the means by which they can competently affect their world and themselves. He spoke of *auxiliary stimuli* as components of a process experienced by humans for active adaptation. *Auxiliary stimuli* include the tools of the culture in which individuals were born or lived (practices, beliefs, and traditions), language, and other ingenious and indigenous means produced by the individuals as they communicate and organize.

The use of the developmental approach enhances our understanding of multiethnic group processes and the individuality of the group members. Guided by the principles of the developmental approach, this study explored how people of different cultures naturally organize and communicate and how different styles compete and perhaps complement each other. Paulo Freire (1994) calls these efforts "stepping back." Community members, through praxis, realize that they have some ownership over their lives and that they can together work towards creating a new reality for themselves. Community organizing is seen as a natural stage of development but not as a universal stage, each community may arrive to it from different experiences and through different means. Coalitions are necessary means to reconcile and integrate cultural differences towards achieving a common goal. From a developmental perspective we investigated how a particular inter-ethnic coalition was formed and how they integrated the *auxiliary stimuli* existing within each ethnic community.

METHODS

Intensive, semi-structured interviews were conducted by the first author, with a sample of twelve key members of the coalitions, at various locations, during the Spring of April 1997. The interviewees included the social service agency administrators (both Latinas) and the school principal (Latino); the project's two staff members (one African American/Latina and the other white/bilingual male); one school teacher (Latino); two members of the neighborhood association (both European American females), and four members of the parents' organization (three Latinas and one Latino). Interview guides developed by the university based research team were used in gathering information regarding the perceptions of the key participants. Purposive sampling was used to identify an initial set of expert informants representing the partner organizations and the Community Initiative staff. Informants were selected based on their higher levels of participation and corresponding knowledge about the coalition. These expert informants (Dexter, 1970) were interviewed with the purpose of assessing the progress made during the first year of the Community Initiative. Informal interviews and participant observations were conducted with students and other community members of the project sponsored activities.

The participants' responses were recorded verbatim, by hand, in the language used by each interviewee. Half of the interviewees responded in English, while the others responded in Spanish. All data were later transcribed electronically. In addition, the Spanish language responses were translated into English to allow for comparison and analysis. The translation process sought to preserve the essence of the respondents' messages avoiding literal translation in cases that such procedure would have resulted in a loss of meaning.

The data gathered through the interviews were analyzed by looking for patterns to compare, contrast, and sort pieces of information into categories until a discernible thematic attitude, opinion, or behavior became identifiable. Once patterns emerged, they constituted a coding scheme for the data to be compared to the guiding theoretical model. Triangulation of data from various sources was the main tool used for clarification and verification of contradictory information and testing for validity.

FINDINGS

The Neighborhood and the Partners

The *Los Fresnos* neighborhood has experienced demographic shifts from older established white middle class families to predominantly younger Mexican and Mexican American families of generally lower socioeconomic status. All census tracts within the Los Fresnos school attendance area show a poverty rate of at least 51% (U.S. Census Bureau, 1996). Based on family income level, eighty-five percent of the students in the district qualify for the national school lunch program (Arizona Department of Education, 1998). Since 1990, the school enrollment has grown by 42% and available anecdotal data predicts a continuation of this trend in the future. This growth mirrors an important ethnic and language shift. Forty percent of the district's students have been identified as limited English proficient. Eighty-one percent of the students are Latino, ten percent White, six percent are African American, two percent are American Indian, and one percent are Asian American. In addition, the families tend to have a high mobility rate. Older residents are predominantly white and English monolingual, whereas, the younger residents are primarily Latino and bilingual or Spanish monolingual.

The *Los Fresnos* neighborhood can be characterized as a community in transition. This condition provided an ideal opportunity for community development. As the CI began, there were multiple organizations and groups attempting to respond to various community needs in a fragmented and isolated fashion. Single need efforts were lead by particular ethnic and age groups. For example, the parents' organization was serving the needs of children and parents at school but only Latino parents participated. On the other hand, only older European American residents participated in the neighborhood association. Children and youth issues were not part of the neighborhood association agenda and neighborhood issues such as declining property values and safety were not addressed by the parents association. Interrelated issues between the two groups were treated as unrelated. An "us" vs. "them" mentality was blocking unified efforts to deal with local issues of violence, use of alcohol, tobacco, and other drugs (ATOD) and trafficking, gang activity, and poverty. Neighborhood activists described the difficulties they encountered in the past attempting to mobilize the different sectors of the community toward finding common strategies to meet these needs.

Los Fresnos Community Initiative (CI) as Proposed

The CI sought to mobilize the residents toward identifying local priorities and implementing interventions to strengthen the community and reduce the use of ATOD. In keeping with the mission of the city-wide partnership, the primary purpose of the CI was to assist the *Los Fresnos* residents build a safe and healthy neighborhood. There were three specific objectives established at the outset of the project: (1) To decrease ATOD consumption in the community (2) To strengthen partnerships between neighborhood organizations the city, the school, local businesses, families and youth in order to decrease risk factors while increasing protective factors in the community; (3) To revitalize and renovate the community by engaging the youth in community service learning projects and making intergenerational connections so that youth can work with elders on community projects.

The CI sought to strengthen families and communities as nurturing environments in which children and youth can live drug free lives. The project design was based on strength (Saleebey, 1997) and resiliency (Smith & Carlson, 1997) models. The strengths of the children and their families were seen as resources to supported and utilized in the community organization effort. The Latino culture of the youth and their families was identified as a source of pride to be enhanced and utilized as part of the ATOD prevention work. No evidence was found in any of the CI records about integrating the culture of the older residents involved in the neighborhood association.

Los Fresnos CI was a coalition of four stakeholders (i.e., interest groups). The first partner was Behavioral Services, a social service agency providing technical support (including hiring, training and supervising CI staff, project administration, resource development, fiscal and personnel management) and community capacity building. The second partner was Los Fresnos Neighborhood Association (LFNA), a five-year-old neighborhood based organization. The members of LFNA were European American, English monolingual, long term residents in the neighborhood, homeowners, mostly retired and elderly. Many had moved to Los Fresnos as young families and raised their own children in the neighborhood over a span of three decades. They had traditionally assisted the city in identifying neighborhood issues, recruiting new members, and participated in workshops on neighborhood issues organized by the city. The third partner was Parent, Students, and Teachers Together/Padres, Estudiantes, y Maestros Juntos (PEMJ), a newly created school based organization composed of Latino parents. Its main purpose was to mobilize parents to better serve the needs of their children. PEMJ sought to increase parent participation at school and make the school a more inviting place for these parents. The final partner was Los Frescos Intermediate School. The school was to be the site for many project activities. The parent organization and the CI staff (Community Mobilizer and a Prevention Specialist) were housed at the school.

As the project was being planned, Behavioral Services, the school districts' central staff and the neighborhood association played active roles. The school principal and the embryonic parents association were not involved. The host school principal supervised the parent Specialist who staffed the parents group and had a good working relationship with the neighborhood association leaders. The principal might have played an important role as mediator among partners as the project was implemented. However, staff of behavioral services and the school district central office excluded the principal because as the social service agency representative said "he would have not understood." Key staff of the school district and the social service agency had a good working relationship and as a staff member said, "spoke the same language." Both staffs had good intentions but by playing a broker role did not allow a stronger horizontal communication to emerge between the two key coalition partners: the neighborhood association and the parents association.

Project staff was to focus their efforts on community capacity building. The neighborhood association, through its participation in the project, was expected to become connected to other organizations (including the parents association) and enhance its community organizing and advocacy capacity. It was also expected that the coalition would provide opportunities for individuals, groups and institutions to come together and, often for the first time, communicate about shared concerns such as substance abuse, drug trafficking, domestic violence, and other safety issues. Once this communication structure was in place and people began to dialogue and work together on common needs, it was expected that community conditions would improve.

You Are Invited to Our Table....
The First Year of the Community Initiative

Two elderly sisters were the facto leaders of the neighborhood association. They were respectively the association's president and secretary since the association's inception in 1994. The president explains how the Community Initiative evolved.

> We (the neighborhood association) started the project. We went to Behavioral Services and asked them to write the proposal. They wrote it so it would be accepted. We put out what we wanted. No problems . . . went well and smooth, an easy process.

The leaders of the neighborhood association perceived their participation level as high in the planning process of the community initiative. They were active in neighborhood affairs in general with a particular interest in safety issues. The CI Community Mobilizer said: "The neighborhood association leaders are involved in everything." However, one year later they viewed their participation level in the CI as low. The president described the changes.

> We are not very involved in the CI any more. Illness has something to do with it. The president of the parents organization is the current leader of the CI. If I am still the president of the neighborhood association, next time we do something like this I will be more up front. If I do it alone, I'll take the credit.

The secretary of the neighborhood association spoke with some resentment about the credit she perceived the president of the parents' organization was getting for the Community Initiative work. She further explained.

> I wanted a survey to be done in order for us to get to know each other better. It never happened. We encouraged the project Community Mobilizer to get information from the principal regarding drug use by the students but he did not think it would work.

The neighborhood association leaders wanted data as a means to get to know the students and their parents. Students were administered a pre- and post-test survey, by the Prevention Specialist. The survey, focused on assessing the student's knowledge, attitudes, and behavior toward ATOD, was conducted on two occasions during the school year. The information was not shared with neighborhood association leaders because there was some fear that members of the neighborhood association would have used the information to feed stereotypical views of the youth and their substance use behavior. Ironically, an examination of the project outcome data shows low levels of self-reported ATOD use.

Neighborhood association leaders representing the neighborhood association, described themselves as founders of the coalition, and as having a messianic type of role in the community. Some of the narratives shared with the researchers spoke of a good neighborhood that started to change for the worst as "different people" started to move in. When asked who these different people were, the neighborhood association leaders responded: "Mexicans."

The neighborhood association members perceived themselves as instruments of acculturation. They invited the members of the parents association to attend their monthly meetings. The CI did not have a separate advisory board. The initial plan was for the parents to be integrated into the neighborhood association's structure. The neighborhood association meetings were conducted in English, following *Roberts' Rules of Order*, with agendas developed by the neighborhood association leaders, without consulting the members of the parent association. Spanish translation services were not provided. Parents attended two neighborhood association monthly meetings. Seventy-five members of the parents' organization attended the first meeting while the second meeting was attended by sixty-four. Approximately twelve (12) members of the neighborhood association participated in each of these meetings. The joint meetings were stopped after those two attempts. The project Community Mobilizer, who staffed these meetings, explained some of the reasons why the joint meetings were stopped.

> The cultural issues are too big to bring people together. Anglos felt lost among too many Mexicans. Traditional (meeting) facilitation methods [Roberts' rules] did not work. I needed to put on a show to bring people together. We needed to let it go. I felt I was juggling too many things. We got negative feedback from the two groups of participants. Language was an issue. Spanish speaking people wanted simultaneous translation services, English monolingual members said things like we are in America, they need to speak English here.

Cultural and language barriers, misunderstandings, and stereotyping became evident as soon as the parents group and the neighborhood association members started to interact. One of the social service agency representatives described how she perceived the first interactions between the partners:

> At the first meeting I was turned off by the lack of awareness about cultural diversity. Offensive terms and phrases were used such as: "Those people; they do drugs; illegals," and a lot of blaming came out. The second meeting was more positive. A more positive attitude evolved from the blaming to trying to do more. An additional problem was lack of experience.

These differences resulted in a strategic change in the way project staff would work with the two community partners. The social service agency administrators decided to have staff work separately with the neighborhood association and the parents association, rather than continue to bring them together.

The project Community Mobilizer and the social service agency administrators reported that, at the beginning of the implementation of the project with the parents' organization, the community's natural (culturally grounded) ways of organizing were not recognized. *Personalism* (Marsiglia & Zorita, 1996) was as an important cultural norm that recognizes and values the total person. In some ways this corresponds to the concept of primary group dynamics. Members of the parents association felt lost in the impersonal and rigidly structured meetings organized by the neighborhood association. Once this was recognized, more culturally appropriate, natural ways of organizing were integrated and an increase in effectiveness was noticed. For example, meetings for parents were held at family homes where food was shared and time for informal socializing was part of the meeting process. Topics identified for discussion by the parents included substance abuse, family violence, neighborhood safety, school absenteeism, homework, and English as a Second Language (ESL) classes for parents.

The Community Mobilizer was fluent in Spanish and had a strong affinity to the Latino culture. He and the administrators of behavioral Services naturally gravitated towards the parents association. Suddenly, the parents' organization became the focal point of the project. The leaders of the neighborhood association continued to play their traditional role of identifying community needs and effectively accessing city resources but they operated in isolation from the school-based activities. The neighborhood association's secretary explained.

> All the seniors involved say they want to remain involved, but there is not much action. They need to find a common denominator. When the chairperson tells them it involves working with children, the seniors become defensive, saying they have already raised their own children.

One of the Behavioral Services administrators added her perception of the neighborhood association members' relationship to the project Community Mobilizer.

> He is seen as the Messiah by the neighborhood association. They think that he should come in and fix things. They have unrealistic expectations and they are too dependent on him and the city. They have no concept of empowerment.

Behavioral Services representatives identified some of their own mistakes as the coalition was set up.

> Our strategies were not right. Trying to bring both groups together, forcing it too soon. Now they are going at their own pace. The project Community Mobilizer is working with them separately. Groups were resistant to joining together because of different ideas and points of view. LFNA was feeling outnumbered by the Spanish speaking community. A fear of being taken over, losing power. There is an inability to extending themselves. In the joint meetings there were 100 Hispanics and 10 Anglos.

The premature attempts to bring the community partners together were in part externally dictated by the funding proposal. The funding was to be specifically used for developing community coalitions. In an attempt to follow the guidelines of the funding source, the Community Mobilizer attempted to support the creation of a coalition between partners that were not ready and in some cases were unwilling to come together in a collaborative, democratic way. In the case of the parents' association, its members were going through the group formation phase of development, naturally looking inward. The neighborhood association was already formed and its members did not want to loose their hegemony over the neighborhood affairs. Issues of difference that were latent were brought to the surface by the attempted coalition without adequately preparing the participants before their (forced) encounters. The frustrations of both groups with quality of life issues boiled over during the joint activities. Issues of power, communication and trust joined with frustration about property values and change of ethnic composition and from the parents perspectives problems encountered as recent immigrants were not conducive to building a coalition.

Yet modest intergroup collaboration was possible and did occur. Three elderly male members of the neighborhood association participated in a bicycle rehabilitation project sponsored by the parents association. They met most Saturdays of one semester with many other Latino fathers and their children and fixed dozens of bicycles. Hands on activities appeared to have been more effective conduits for collaboration than formal meetings. The officers of the neighborhood association were informed about the progress made through the participating members and through the Community Initiative staff and had formed their own opinions about the project. The neighborhood association explained:

> We have seen an improvement in the children's attitudes and the
> way they dress and even the relations between the young and the
> old have made a change for the better.

Apart from the results of efforts to bring the parents association and
the neighborhood association together, there was some evaluation evidence to suggest that the Community Initiative was having a positive
impact in the children and their families. The CI strengthened the parents organization, which has planned and implemented activities of significance to the community such as recreational and sport activities for
children and youth, parent seminars about topics of interest, and cultural and arts activities. Many housewives were involved in the activities. Through the parent association parents became involved at the
school and became more familiar with their children's teachers. But the
CI has not brought together the different groups that it was set up to engage in the coalition.

"Thank you, but I prefer to stay en mi casa . . . " Lessons Learned.

After the first two joint meetings, the members of the parents' Association stayed away from the CI meeting called, by the neighborhood
association and used their time and resources to organize themselves.
They were in their initial stages of their own development and they were
not able to confront or negotiate the obstacles they encountered in the
coalition meetings. They needed more time as a group before attempting to form a coalition. The president of the parents association explained the reasons why their organization was needed.

> Por la necesidad de 1a escuela de envolver a la comunidad. Porque
> los padres no vienen a la escuela. Para apoyar a las familias. Unidos
> podemos evitar muchas de estas cosas que están pasando. (Due to
> the need the school has to involve the parents. Because the parents
> do not come to school. To support the families. United we can pre-
> vent many of these things that are happening [e.g., drug use])

Other parents referred to the president as their leader and reaffirmed
her definitions and comments. They constituted a very active group under her leadership. They made home visits as the main recruitment tool
and held most meetings at families' homes. When asked how they were
able to recruit over 150 members she answered:

A través del con facto humano. Conozco a todo el mundo. Los padres quieren participar cuando les decimos que es para los niños y que el proyecto es anti-drogas. (Through human contact. I know everybody. Parents want to join us when they learn that this is about children and it is a drug prevention project).

One of the most important outcomes of the CI has been the strengthening of the parent association. The CI through its Community Mobilizer has effectively supported the formation and development of the parents organization. The president praised the organizer by saying: *El nos ha abierto las puertas del conocimiento.* (He has opened the doors to knowledge.) Specifically the Community Mobilizer introduced the parents to available community resources, provided training on group facilitation, planning and organizing. He also assisted them in evaluating their activities and programs and deciding about their future course of action.

The parents have organized themselves while also planning and implementing important activities that benefited the whole community. They did not have a formal general monthly meeting. They met at families' homes and in smaller groups. Their influence was limited to the school and the neighborhood affairs such as "neighborhood watch" have been left to the neighborhood association. The president of the parents association commented:

> Los hemos invitado a muestras reuniones y les traducimos pero ellos no vienen. Nosotros vamos a las reuniones de ellos pero no tomamos parte en las decisiones. Nuestra prioridad es los niños. Nosotros conectamos la casa y la escuela. (We have invited them (the members of the neighborhood association) to our meeting and we offered translating for them, but they do not come. We go to their meetings but we do not take part in the decision making process. Our priority are the children. We connect home and school.)

Issues of cultural and language differences continued to block the formation of the coalition. The parent association offered English translation the neighborhood association members if they agreed to attend their meetings. The language used by both groups continued to describe and emphasize their own separate turfs, not a neutral overarching coalition.

The parents association's leadership evolved since the inception of the project and has gained confidence and effectiveness in its role. The external evaluation of this CI found that the program has had a noticeable impact on the participating children and the community. Specifically, both the children and their parents are taking the initiative in planning and implementing various activities. For example, the project Community Mobilizer shared the following vignette: "One girl said that once her mother became involved in the school, her grades went up because it made her see how much her mother cared about her." One of the teachers observed:

> The children identify with the activities organized by the parents' organization and they like to belong. The parents are very determined and committed to the success of the program. The program delivery staff are very effective. Members of the *parents' group have* shown leadership skills. There is trust between the participants, they are eager to help each other, and they get along well. Challenges, however, remain for the parents' organization. The Community Mobilizer noted:

> The active people are too involved. The president is trying to delegate authority because it is a new program and it is very labor intensive. Her leadership style makes it difficult to let go and delegate.

The president was exercising a traditional charismatic leadership style while a secondary leadership had not yet emerged. Parents were responding to her because she was a respected member of the community and because she had demonstrated commitment and care for their families. Personal and organizational efforts were directed inwards. The parents' organization needed its energy to build its own structure and deliver on its many projects rather than to open up and interact with a very different organization. The indigenous leadership structure was in need of support from the CI staff and it needed to be challenged toward a more democratic/participatory style and a broader leadership base. These challenges were typical of a new organization embedded in a traditional culture.

In summary, the CI had brought momentum and needed technical support primarily to the parent association and to a lesser degree to the neighborhood association. Students had benefited from its several programs and adults were gaining a renewed sense of pride and commitment toward their community. The school based parents organization was playing a key role in mobilizing the community. On the other hand, the neighborhood association was experiencing a sense of nostalgia for a neighborhood they remembered with pride. Suddenly, through their participation in the CI, they found themselves baring "their table" with the new neighbors. The CI provided some limited opportunities for the two main partners to come together and overcome some of the barriers they were facing. The attempts to bring these two groups together into a community coalition did not succeed. The project staff was working separately with the two main partners, addressing their own needs according to their different stages of group development and mission. The CI assisted the neighborhood association to become familiar with additional community resources and to extend their neighborhood based network.

DISCUSSION

Although the CI had been established primarily as a coalition between the neighborhood association and the parents' organization, neither community-based organization was ready to venture into the coalition. The parents' organization was numerically large and vibrant while the neighborhood association was numerically small and stagnant. Historically, the neighborhood association had represented *Los Fresnos* in city hall. But they did not represent the Latino neighbors, who were the majority of the current residents. There was a clash of cultures, each organization wanting to operate in a manner that felt right and comfortable. The leaders of both groups were unable and in some cases unwilling to work with each other. Because of these differences it is difficult to identify the CI as a coalition did its traditional sense (Caplow, 1968).

The partners were not able to exert more power and influence and mobilize more resources together than separately (DeGennaro, 1997). The CI's attempt to form a grassroots coalition (Feighery & Rogers, 1989) started before the potential coalition members were ready to share a common table. In part due to the different stages of development of the two organizations, the premature encounters between the groups, instead of decreasing cultural and ideological distance or fragmentation (Díaz-Veizades & Chang, 1996) gave each group ammunition to remain separate. The neighborhood association was not ready to share its power, privilege and access (Brosio, 1997) and the members of the parents organization were too busy building their group to go to places where they were not welcome. Neither organization had leaders who recognized the potential benefits of a coalition to their group. The neighborhood association could have benefited from the numbers and strength of the parents group and the parents could have benefited from the experience and connections to resources the neighborhood association had.

The organizational climate of each partner and the relations of each partner with the staff of the CI were positive but the groups linkages with each other were problematic (Butterfoss, Goodman & Wandersman, 1996). The two community based partners lacked a sense of common interests, were very different in size, had different economic status, differences in language use, different cultural backgrounds and organizational styles, and had different social and political resources. All these differences had been identified in the coalition literature as working against the development of effective coalitions (e.g., Oliver & Grant, 1995; Sonenshein, 1993; Himmelman, 1991).

This case study suggests ways in which community practice professionals might play a role in supporting ethnic minority communities in their participation in coalitions to prevent substance abuse. Minority organizations often need support as they attempt to catch up with years of discrimination, lack of representation, and exclusion from their communities. The Community Mobilizer in this case study had the complex task of bringing two very different main community groups together. He was hired after the grant proposal was written and after the externally based officials had initiated preliminary contacts between the partners. Probably the coalition meetings were started before the partners were ready to share a common table.

Mixed messages were given to the neighborhood association members about their role as gate keepers and leaders. They thought that the Community Initiative was exclusively their project and probably expected the parents to join their group. As the parents organization grew and increased its influence over the limited resources (such as the time of the Community Mobilizer), the neighborhood association felt marginalized.

We speculate that some of the prejudice and lack of communication across ethnic lines could have been lowered if the CI would have followed a different development plan, allowing each partner to develop its own internal strength before coming together with other partners (Vygotsky, 1974). As minority communities become the majority in many neighborhoods around the nation, they need to be represented as valued members in the new coalitions or alliances of minority groups. Should this not be realized, minority groups will be less and less willing to accept exclusionary organizations that do not represent nor serve their needs (Daley & Wong, 1994), or accept the expression of their own auxiliary stimuli (Vygotsky, 1979). Bringing partners together prematurely may only accentuate old stereotypes and intergroup animosity. The proposed coalition reflected the fact that the community had changed. The Latino families were not only numerically superior but through their parents organization demonstrated organizational strength. At the time we concluded our data gathering efforts the two organizations have discontinued their relationship. The parents' organization continues to be strong and has developed a coalition with the school teachers and principal. All the teachers involved in the coalition are white, demonstrating that when the conditions are right multiethnic coalitions are possible. The neighborhood association continues to hold its monthly meeting, often with only a hand full of its members in attendance. They continue to consider activities that may lead them to rebuild the neighborhood to its perceived former glory . . . those good old days when they and the neighborhood were perceived to have been young, active, and healthy. The idea of starting a new ethnically diverse coalition to improve community conditions continues to be in the minds of some neighbors.

Lessons Learned

As we reflect on the experiences of participants with this Community Initiative, several lessons might be drawn. First, as Daley (1998) has observed, antecedent conditions and contextual factors are significant factors in shaping the development of any community change episode. In the CI a number of antecedent conditions significantly influenced the development of the coalition. The two community partners lacked a history of collaborative work. Further, each had its own reasons for lacking trust in the other. The neighborhood association saw itself as losing ground in its efforts to return the community to its former glory and tended to blame the newcomers for the neighborhood's decline. The parents group understood their status as unwelcome newcomers and experienced the many indignities minority and recent immigrant groups experience as they settle in established neighborhoods.

Second, two key outside/external institutions (Behavioral Services and the school district's central staff), with the best of intentions for the CI excluded a key player, the local school principal, from the project planning and early implementation activities. The principal had trusting relationships with both partners and might have played a mediating role in bringing the groups together. At a minimum the principal might have alerted CI planners and staff of the need to move slowly in forming the coalition.

Third, CI planners and implementing staff seemed either unaware or unconcerned about the antecedent and contextual factors including the role of ethnicity, language and social class differentials between the two community partners. In retrospect, the influence of these factors was monumental, yet ignored in the planning and early intervention activities. Without specific efforts to ensure a smooth initiation of the coalition relationships of these groups, the clashes that occurred were predictable. In our opinion, these difficulties were largely avoidable. Bringing two such different groups into a coalition requires specific community practice and group facilitation skills and careful preparation. In the CI for example, preparations might have included working with the leaders of each group independently to ensure that they understood the benefits and costs of involvement. Then preparation might have brought the leaders of the two groups together in a small informal setting to develop relationships and explore the implications of involvement in the coalition. These activities might have raised the level of trust and intergroup competence. We understand that this is a long and challenging process to address intergroup dynamics, yet we find no evidence that these issues were addressed prior to introducing the unprepared partners at large public meetings. We cannot explain why the professionals who planned and staffed the CI did not anticipate the clashes that were noted when the community partners met in the public meetings.

Fourth, the need to produce a specific outcome, the community coalition, may have influenced CI planners and staff to move too rapidly. The CI was part of a larger, city-wide prevention program. This larger program created CIs in response to expressed dissatisfaction from funding sources, evaluators, and community members with the slow pace in which the program was being implemented. This institutional need to show results quickly might have shaped the work of CI planners and staff—forcing community partners into a coalition before they were ready. Does the experience of this CI suggest that intergroup coalitions are not feasible, or even desirable? We think not. However, this case study does highlight the challenges involved with forming effective interethnic coalitions. As with much of professional practice, the development of intergroup coalitions requires practitioner sensitivity to local conditions and dynamics, facilitative skills in intergroup work, commitment to nurturing leadership and persistence. Despite its success, the attempt to develop a coalition of diverse groups presented in this article, is remembered by some community members as one failed attempt that will hopefully pave the road for an inclusive and effective future coalition.

REFERENCES

Adrian, C. R. & Press, C. (1968). Decision costs in coalition formation. *American Political Science Review*, 62, 556-563.

Boissevain, J. (1974). *Friends of friends: Networks, Manipulators, and coalitions.* New York: St. Martin's.

Brosio, R. A. (1997). Diverse school populations and corresponding need for multiple identity coalitions. *(ERIC Document Reproduction Service No. ED* 410 349).

Butterfoss, F. D., Goodman, R. M., & Wandersman, A. (1993). Community coalitions for prevention and health promotion. *Health Education Research, 8,* 315-330.

Butterfoss, F. D., Goodman, R. M., & Wandersman, A. (1996). Community coalitions for prevention and health promotion: Factors predicting satisfaction, participation, and planning. *Health Education Quarterly*, *23*, 65-79.

Calderon, J. (1995). Multi-ethnic coalition building in a diverse school district. *Critical Sociology*, *21*, 101-111.

Caplow, T. (1968). *Two against one: Coalitions in Triads.* Engelwood Cliffs, NJ: Prentice-Hall.

Carmichael, S. & Hamilton, C. V. (1967). *Black Power*. New York: Vintage.

Checkoway, B. (1997). Core concepts for community change. *Journal of Community Practice*, *4*, 11-29.

Daley, J.M. (1997). The episode of purposive change: Field testing a practice model. *Journal of the Community Development Society*, *28*, 225-241.

Daley, J.M. & Wong, p. (1994). Community development with emerging ethnic communities. *Journal of Community Practice*, *1*, 19-24.

Dexter, L.A. (1970). *Elite and specialized interviewing*. Evanston, Illinois: Northwestern University Press.

Díaz-Veizades, J. & Chang, E. T. (1996). Building cross-cultural coalitions: A Case-study of the Black-Korean Alliance and the Latino-Black Roundtable. *Ethnic and Racial Studies*, 19, 680-700.

Dymally, M. M. (1970). Afro-Americans and Mexican-Americans: The politics of coalition. Inc. Wollenberg (Ed.), *Ethnic Conflict in California History* (pp. 155-171). Los Angeles, CA: Tinnon-Brown.

Feighery, E. & Rogers, T. (1989). Building and maintaining effective coalitions. Published as Guide No. 12 in the series *How-To Guides on Community Health Promotion*. Stanford Health Promotion Resource Center, Palo Alto, CA.

Gamson, W. (1961). *A theory of coalition formation*. *American Sociological Review*, 26, 373-382.

Hill, P. T. (1973). *A theory of political coalitions in simple and policymaking situations.* Beverly Hills, CA: Sage Publications.

Himmelman, A. T. (1991). *Communities working collaboratively for a change.* Washington, DC: Community Information Exchange.

Kamasaki C. & Yzaguirre, R. (1991). Black-Hispanic tensions: One perspective. Paper presented at the Annual Meeting of the American Political Science Association, Washington, DC.

Kegler, M. C., Steckler, A., Malek, S. H., & McLeroy, K. (1998). A multiple case study of implementation in 10 local Project ASSIST coalitions in North Carolina. *Health Education Research, 3,* 225-238.

Kumpfer, K. L., Turner, C., Hopkins, A., & Librett, J. (1993). Leadership and team effectiveness in community coalitions for the prevention of alcohol and other drug abuse. *Health Education Research, 8,* 359-374.

Lichterman, P. (1995). Piecing together multicultural community: Cultural differences in community building among grass-roots environmentalists. *Social Problems, 42,* 513-534.

Mayer, J. P., Soweid, R., Dabney, S., Brownson, C., Goodman, R. M., & Brownson, R. C. (1998). Practices of successful community coalitions: A multiple case study. *American Journal of Health Behavior, 22,* 368-377.

McCarthy, C. (1994). Multicultural discourses and curriculum reform: A critical perspective. *Educational Theory, 44,* 94-5.

Mizrahi, T. & Rosenthal, B. (1993). Managing dynamic tensions in social change coalitions. In Mizrahi, & Morrison, I.D. (Eds.), Community organization and social administration (pp. 11-40). New York: The Haworth Press, Inc.

Oliver, M. L. & Grant, D. M. (1995). Making space for multiethnic coalitions: The prospects for coalition politics in Los Angeles. In E. Yu & E. T. Chang (Eds.), *Multiethnic coalition building in Los Angeles* (pp. 1-34). Claremont, CA: Regina.

Regalado, J. A. (1995). Creating multicultural harmony? A critical perspective on Coalition-building efforts in Los Angeles. In E. Yu and E. T. Chang (Eds.), *Multiethnic Coalition Building in Los Angeles* (pp. 35-53). Claremont, CA: Regina Books.

Riker, W. (1962). *The theory of political coalitions.* New Haven, Conn.: Yale University Press.

Roberts-DeGennaro, M. (1997). Conceptual framework of coalitions in an organizational context. *Journal of Community Practice, 4,* 91-107.

Saleebey, D. (1997). *The strengths perspective in social work practice.* NY: Longman.

Shingles, R. D. (1991). Relations between Americans of Latino and African descent: A comparative framework for understanding differences and commonalities. Paper presented at the Fourth Annual Conference on Latino Issues, Wayne State University.

Smith, C. & Carlson, B.E. (1997). Stress, coping, and resilience in children and youth. *Social Service Review, 71,* 2, 231-56.

Sonenshein, R. J. (1993). *Politics in black and white: Race and power in Los Angeles.* Princeton, NJ: Princeton University Press.

Soto-Ortega, S. (1970). A Chicano response. In C. Wollenberg (Ed.), Ethnic Conflict in California History. Los Angeles. CA: Tinnon-Brown.

Vygotsky, L. (1979). *Mind in society the development of higher psychological processes.* Cambridge, MA: Harvard University Press.

Weil, M. (1996). Model development ill community practice: An historical perspective. *Journal of Community Practice, 3*, 5-67.

Weisner, S. (1983). Fighting back: A critical analysis of coalition building in the human services. *Social Service Review, 57*, 291-306.

Yu, E & Chang, E. T. (Eds.). (1995). *Multiethnic coalition building in Los Angeles.* Claremont, CA: Regina.

Culturally Competent Substance Abuse Treatment with Latinos

Juan Paz

SUMMARY. The Latino population in the United States is a complex and multifaceted population. Latinos are a very dynamic and mobile cultural group. The 2000 United States Census registered Latinos in practically every state. Clinicians involved in assessing and treating Latinos must consider a complex set of environmental and systemic cultural factors that have a direct impact on their problem and potential healing. Treatment must begin by systematically assessing the cultural fit between clinicians and clients. *[Article copies available for a fee from The Haworth Document Delivery Service: 1-800-HAWORTH. E-mail address: <getinfo@haworthpressinc.com> Website: <http://www.HaworthPress.com> © 2002 by The Haworth Press, Inc. All rights reserved.]*

KEYWORDS. Cultural competence, substance abuse, treatment, training, Latinos

LATINO DIVERSITY

The Latino population of the United States poses a special challenge to professionals in the substance abuse treatment field. Latinos can no

Juan Paz, PhD, is Associate Professor at Arizona State University School of Social Work where he has been on the faculty for the past 12 years. Currently he is Chair of the Advance Direct Practice Concentration. In addition, he has been a consultant to the Substance Abuse Mental Health Services Administration on issues of cultural competence.

[Haworth co-indexing entry note]: "Culturally Competent Substance Abuse Treatment with Latinos." Paz, Juan. Co-published simultaneously in *Journal of Human Behavior in the Social Environment* (The Haworth Social Work Practice Press, an imprint of The Haworth Press, Inc.) Vol. 5, No. 3/4, 2002, pp. 123-136; and: *Latino/Hispanic Liaisons and Visions for Human Behavior in the Social Environment* (ed: José B. Torres and Felix G. Rivera) The Haworth Social Work Practice Press, an imprint of The Haworth Press, Inc., 2002, pp. 123-136. Single or multiple copies of this article are available for a fee from The Haworth Document Delivery Service [1-800-HAWORTH, 9:00 a.m. - 5:00 p.m. (EST). E-mail address: getinfo@haworthpressinc.com].

longer be viewed from a simplistic framework that divides them into the Mexican American, Puerto Rican and Cuban subgroups. Latino demographics have changed dramatically in the past two decades. While Chicanos, Puerto Ricans and Cubans may be the predominant group in some cities, the influx of other groups has made it necessary to examine substance abuse treatment practices from a multi-ethnic and multi-racial perspective. For example, in New York, the new predominant group is now Dominicans and not Puerto Ricans. The city is also experiencing a growth in immigrants from Mexico. In Los Angeles and San Francisco, there has been a significant influx of Central Americans. While Chicago has a large Mexican origin population, the city is experiencing growth from other groups. The old paradigms that focused on the locality and region can no longer be applied. Instead, a thorough examination of Latino substance abuse issues requires professionals to study the dynamics of demographic growth, culture, cultural competence and current treatment methods being used in the field.

Latinos constitute a large social collective of approximately 30 million persons in American society whose survival is undergoing major challenges from within society's infrastructure. Defining Latinos poses a major task since Latinos are not a monolithic group. Latinos are a diverse group composed of persons of Mexican, Cuban, Puerto Rican, Caribbean, South and Central American descent. These social aggregates are made up of individuals of several ethnic and racial backgrounds as well as nationalities (African American groups, European groups and from the various indigenous tribes of the Caribbean, Central and South America). Historically, most Latinos were from the first three groups. However, recent mass migration from Central and South America has dramatically altered the Latino character. Latinos represent a wide spectrum of society, for example, they can include: Yaqui Indians from the Southwest, Blacks from Puerto Rico, Venezuela, or Colombia, Mizquitas from Nicaragua, Guaranis from Paraguay and Cholos from Peru.

During the 1980s and 1990s the influx of refugees and immigrants from Spanish speaking countries changed the fabric of many cities. For example, Washington, DC now has a substantial Latino population of over 200,000, which it did not have fifteen years ago. In Houston, the Spanish speaking population now outnumbers the African American population with over 600,000 individuals. During an interview with Leonel Castillo, (Personal Communication, 1992) former Commissioner of the Immigration and Naturalization Service, he indicated that the old practice of forcing Spanish speaking clients to learn English was no longer viable. The new trend is towards teaching human service professionals to speak Spanish as well as cultural factors that influence their client's behavior. This signals a large shift in the traditional social service delivery paradigm because the goal is no longer to assimilate Latinos into society. Instead, it is necessary to evaluate their level of acculturation and adaptation into the larger society. The new focus is on making health and human service systems culturally competent.

During the 1970s and 1980s the human service literature called for developing bilingual-bicultural services for some Spanish speaking groups. Specifically, Mexican Americans, Puerto Ricans and Cubans. Today the treatment field has evolved to recognize the development of multi-ethnic, multi-racial services in major urban cities throughout the United States. In order to arrive at an understanding of the complex Latino reality in this country it is necessary to develop a broader perspective such as the concept of the *Raza Cosmica* or *Cosmic Race* elaborated by Dr. Jose Vasconcelos the well-known Mexican philosopher.

LA RAZA COSMICA/THE COSMIC RACE

In *La Raza Cosmica/The Cosmic Race*, (1979) Vasconcelos was an early visionary this past century and saw the blending of the Mexican mestizaje as an example of how ultimately there would be a fusion of various ethnic and racial groups. (In Mexico, this consisted of the Spanish and Indian.) His theory was that through a process of interracial mixing a new race, a race of the future, a universal race would evolve. This would be a race in which all other races would disappear. With the development of *La Raza Cosmica*, a new age in the evolution of a new Humanity with a strong creative power was to take place, this was called the Spiritual or Aesthetic Era. The Cosmic Race concept is one that is often used by Latino leaders to signify a unique dynamic population composed of multiple races and ethnic groups.

CULTURAL COMPETENCE

The need to develop culturally competent substance abuse treatment programs has arisen from two directions. First, there is a significant need to develop effective and efficient treatment programs for a rapidly growing Latino population. States with significantly large Latino populations such as Arizona are faced with having to provide services based on traditional paradigms such as the medical model, which is limited in scope. The medical model does not take into account the influence of cultural systems on an individual's behavior. In some cases, the traditional market is ill equipped to provide culturally competent treatment services. During the past year this writer has been called upon several times to refer clients from for-profit in-patient treatment facilities to culturally competent facilities. In addition, some recent cases in which two Latino adolescents died while in treatment at in-patient facilities has raised concerns over the lack of appropriate culturally competent treatment. In one case the parents of a Latino male adolescent spoke no English and were not clearly informed regarding their sons' treatment and the circumstances surrounding his death.

The Second major factor is the fact that Latinos have become the fifth largest Spanish speaking market globally. It is also among the strongest of the markets because it is based on the U.S. dollar and American economics. Evidence of this are the two Spanish language networks (Telemundo and Univision) broadcasting programs nationally and internationally. Every major metropolitan area with a significant Latino population has either Spanish language radio and/or newspapers. In other words, Latino consumerism is growing and with it come market demands.

The concept of cultural competence has its roots in the field of competency based education (Pottenger, Goldsmith, & Klemp, 1979). The focus in competency based education is to identify clearly elaborated skills and competencies that are observable and measurable. Skills are defined as "the ability to demonstrate a set of related behaviors and/or processes (such as logical thinking)." Competency refers to the quality of performance: the focus is on what the clinician can do. The American Heritage Dictionary of the English Language defines competence as "(1) Properly or well qualified: capable, (2) Adequate for the purpose: suitable, sufficient, (3) Legally qualified or fit: admissible."

Culturally competent substance abuse treatment service delivery refers to clinicians and agencies that demonstrate knowledge, values and skills for working with individuals from a different cultural background. Romero (1996) defines cultural competence as "personal qualities of the care provider that are a function of personal growth and ongoing examination of one's own cultural influences, i.e., beliefs, values and attitudes and how these impact the therapeutic encounter."

The "cultural" component in cultural competency has its roots in the social sciences, specifically, anthropology, philosophy, sociology, psychology and social work. Anthropology and philosophy, have demonstrated that in order to survive, a culture must evolve. Historically, it has been noted that the Roman Empire grew and flourished when it acquired the cultural practices of those it conquered. The fall of the Roman Empire came about when the culture stagnated. In much the same way the Latino culture in the United States is in a state of flux while it is changing the fabric of our society. As several Latino groups have settled in this country they have engaged in a process of "selective cultural adaptation." Selective cultural adaptation is defined by this writer as the process of examining one's own cultural value base and deciding which values are significant enough to retain and which values can be changed or adapted.

WHY CULTURAL COMPETENCE?

Cultural competence has gained prominence in the past few years because it enhances efforts at evaluating effective and efficient programs with Latinos. Evaluation of culturally competent substance abuse treatment programs require methodological clarity and precision in the delivery of treatment services in order to strengthen the reliability and validity of the protocols being used. Another critical dimension of service delivery is to examine the theoretical approach guiding the treatment and to inquire from a group of key informants whether or not the major concepts being utilized are conceptually equivalent cross culturally. Determination of conceptual equivalence involves asking whether a specific concept in one culture exists and manifests itself in the same fashion in another culture. For example, among some groups alcohol and tobacco are not considered drugs. In these cases clinicians are required to clarify with the client the fact that alcohol and tobacco are indeed drugs.

Using a building block approach we can begin to lay a foundation regarding Latino cultural competence by identifying the knowledge values and skills that are required in order for a clinician to be culturally competent. Knowledge, values and skills are the critical elements required for human service professionals to learn methodologically sound interpersonal treatment skills. Instead of using lists that identify specific cultural characteristics or typologies that often reinforce stereotypes, the fonts of knowledge regarding the specific concepts are presented here. Practitioners have the task to research each of these fonts of knowledge further.

KNOWLEDGE/CONOCIMIENTO

An initial task in elaborating a culturally competent framework is the establishment of a theoretical knowledge base for practice. Research and evaluation of Latino specific programs drive the substance abuse treatment knowledge base. Latino researchers have made significant contributions. Szapocznik (1988), Amaro (1988), and Delgado (1998) have studied the impact of various cultural variables that must be considered when engaging Latinos in treatment. Szapocznik (1989) at the Family Guidance Center in Miami, Florida has demonstrated how the use of brief strategic therapy can be very effective when working with Hispanic youth with drug abuse problems. They have further studied the use of brief strategic family therapy with one person. The theory of this approach is that brief strategic therapy with one member of the family will result in change in the family system. In this approach, the therapist uses cultural conflicts between different family members as a mechanism to address the symptoms of drug abuse. Amaro (1988) has extensively studied the traditional value base of the Latino culture and its negative impact on Latinas. In the Entre Familia Program, Amaro has elaborated a framework that views Latinas using drugs from an ecological perspective. Latinas need to be viewed from within their cultural milieu; they celebrate birthdays and special holidays. Other services include social support and support for their families. Treatment of these women addresses their socio/cultural experience using *platicas/informal chats* as well as comprehensive services to provide their children a stable environment Delgado, (1998) in his most recent research among Puerto Ricans has demonstrated the importance of viewing clients with regards to their assets as opposed to the traditional deficit based perspective.

The characteristics of the drug user as well as the type of drug being used are also changing. For example, ten years ago Latina adolescents were using drugs at a level lower than males (Human and Delgado, 1983). However, recent research has found that adolescent Latinas now use drugs at the same levels as males (ONDCP Report, 1997, Nuestra Juventud Project, 1998). Estrada, (1982) also has documented that fact that alcohol is a gateway drug to marijuana and other more lethal substances. Several practitioners also report that alcohol is the predominate drug of choice for the majority of adults. While the same is true for adolescents, an alarming new trend is the increasing use of inhalants.

Substance abuse is not an isolated problem. Drug abuse often converges with problems in other fields of practices; these include child welfare, family preservation, HIV/AIDS and mental health. Substance abuse has become a regular element of child welfare training.

Child Welfare

In the child welfare field alcohol and other drug use are factors in cases of child abuse and foster care (Day, Robison, & Sheikh, 1998).

The goal in the child welfare field is to provide a safe and stable environment for children and adolescents. A notable number of child abuse cases involve parents whose patterns of alcohol and drug abuse interfere with their ability to provide adequate care for a child. In these cases a judge often mandates the removal of that child from the parents' custody and orders the child into foster care. The parents are then mandated into treatment with the understanding that once they provide sustained evidence of improvement their child is returned to them. In cases where a parent does not undergo successful treatment, termination of parental rights occurs and the child can subsequently be adopted.

A different type of case often arises. In these cases a child or adolescent is using drugs at a level that negatively impacts a family's functioning. In these cases the youth is often placed in a foster home where he undergoes various types of treatment. In these cases the parent is educated about drug use and provided services to strengthen their parenting skills.

In their efforts to train child welfare workers more adequately the Child Welfare League recently published, "Ours to Keep: A Guide for Building a Community Assessment Strategy for Child Protection." It includes several substance abuse assessment tools. The Substance Abuse Subtle Screening Inventory (SASS, 1994), is a 52-item true or false instrument that screens for chemical dependence in a subtle matter. This is a very helpful instrument especially in cases where it is difficult to openly gather information about chemical dependence with some resistant clients. The inventory of Strengths in Substance Abuse Affected Families (Levenson, 1995) is an assessment tool measuring the parents functioning, parenting, and support systems. It assesses a parent's ability and willingness to seek treatment. The CAGE four item instrument (Brooks & Rice, 1997) is simple and quick for assessing whether or not an individual has problems drinking or using other drugs. It is this writer's perspective that these tools are suitable for use with Latino families and children if ample attention is given to their translation and use.

The guide also provides four culturally competent assessment questions for working with people of color. The questions are for people of color; they are not Latino specific. This writer added the descriptor Latino and Spanish language. These include (1) What are the Latino family's cultural beliefs, customs and practices? (2) What are the Latino family's language skills, both in English and Spanish? (3) What strengths and protective factors do the Latino family's cultural beliefs, customs and practices contribute? And (4) How can the assessment and child protection services be tailored to fit the Latino family's language and culture?

FAMILY PRESERVATION

The family preservation field is another arena that is involved working with persons who have substance abuse problems. In the delivery of family preservation services, the goal is to maintain and promote the integrity of the family. In "The Power of La Familia: A Family Preservation Approach in the Latino Community," Navarro (1996) elaborates a family centered collaborative model. She identifies eight core service programs provided through family preservation in Los Angeles County. These include: in-home counseling, in-home emergency caretaker (respite care), mental health services, parent education, homemaker services, support groups, substitute adult sponsor, and transportation. Its primary component is a bilingual home-based counseling program staffed by clinicians. Maintaining family contact is very important with up to four home visits per week. The goal of La Familia model is to reach parents who lack self-confidence and who have little trust in the existing formal social service agencies. Some unique features of this model include counselors that are available 24 hours a day for crisis help. Parents and children have access to family life education groups plus support groups for parents and children. Other resources include nutrition, English and citizen classes, an outreach worker links families to health, housing and child care services.

HIV/AIDS

HIV/AIDS is another field of practice where substance abuse issues impacts Latinos in larger proportions than for the population overall. A recent report issued by the National Coalition of Hispanic Health and Human Services Organizations (1998) reveals that for Latinos, injection drug use is the main form of infection in the Eastern part of the United States and Puerto Rico. However, it is important to note that intravenous drug use is a historical issue for some communities along the U.S. Mexico border. In fact, in some families there may be patterns of intergenerational intravenous drug use.

Latino researchers have found that Latinas who use drugs intravenously are often initiated into it by their male partner who himself is an intravenous drug user. This is born out by the fact that the number of Latinas with AIDS has grown disproportionately to their number in the general U.S. population. The Center for Disease Control (1998) reports that 33% of AIDS cases report injection drug use as their main model of transmission. Latinas currently comprise 20% of all reported AIDS cases and 19% of new cases among reported cases of women. Yet, they only represent 10% of the total population. The number of AIDS cases per 100,000 accounts for 23 Hispanics and 3.8 non-Hispanic white women. Among new cases, 47% of Hispanic women report heterosexual transmission as their main mode of infection.

Despite these statistics, the Kaiser Foundation in a national study of 802 adults found that 57% of Hispanic women had not been tested for HIV. From these, 24% reported they were not tested because they were sexually inactive and 43% reported they were married in a monogamous relationship. This data strengthens the belief that efforts at the prevention of HIV as well as HIV treatment must examine the quality of their relationship with their male partners. The results of this research point to the need to reach a broader portion of the Latino population. More AIDS/HIV education courses, which provide information about the virus, condom use and skills building, are called for. Outreach and prevention efforts that are grounded in the Latino culture are seen as necessary for curbing the rise in Latino HIV/AIDS cases.

Mental Health

Cultural competence also made has some advances in the mental health field. The fourth edition of the American Psychiatric Association's *Diagnostic and Statistical Manual of Mental Disorders (DSM IV 1994)* describes three types of information that is influenced by an individual's culture. The manual is very clear in recognizing the importance of ethnic and cultural considerations in situations where a clinician uses the DSM IV to evaluate an individual from different ethnic or cultural groups. It further stipulates that "A clinician who is unfamiliar with the nuances of an individual's cultural frame of reference may incorrectly judge as psychopathology those normal variations in behavior, belief, or experience that are particular to the individual's culture" (DSM IV, 1994, PP xxiv).

The DSM IV provides clinicians with an outline of the types of information that is needed in order to attain an accurate assessment of the client from within the client's cultural context. The focus is on how an individual's behavior is influenced by his/her cultural context. This information includes: "(1) a discussion in the text of cultural variations in the clinical presentations of those disorders that have been included in the DSM-IV Classification; (2) a description of culture-bound syndromes that have not been included in the DSM-IV

Classification, (3) an outline for cultural formulations designed to assist the clinician in systematically evaluating and reporting the impact of the individual's cultural context." These three types of cultural information serve as a guide for clinicians to improve the methodological soundness of their diagnosis and ensuing treatment plan.

Some of the culturally bound syndromes in the DSM IV include syndromes from numerous cultures all over the world (i.e., Malaysia, Ethiopia, Portugal, Latin America and Europe). The Latino culturally bound syndromes are (1) ataque de nervios/a nervous breakdown (2) bilis/bile and colera/anger, (3) locura/madness, (4) mal de ojo/evil eye, (5) nervios/nerves and (6) susto/scared to death or nervous breakdown. These culturally bound syndromes often co-exist with substance abuse diagnoses, as was the case in a tragic accident in south Texas in 1989.

South Texas Case Study

On Sept. 21, 1989 a Coca-Cola truck (Mission Schools Special Supplement, 1989) hit a Mission High School bus carrying 81 youths. The bus careened into the deep waters of Caliche Quarry. This tragedy resulted in the death of 21 youths. The scene of the accident was a very sad scene with some persons at the site jumping into the waters in their efforts to save some of the youths' lives. This accident made a deep impact in the entire community but more specifically to the families of the youth who were mostly from traditional Hispanic families of Mexican origin from rural south Texas.

Shortly after the accident several families experienced problems related to the accident. Some youth experienced susto and nervios together with visons of their deceased sibling(s). Some parents experienced ataques de nervios and susto along with post-traumatic stress syndrome and co-existing alcohol problems. Myrta Cardona, MSW, a social worker with the Mission School District assigned to work with the families initiated strategies to provide traditional therapeutic services along with the help of a curandero(a)/indigenous healers. They utilized indigenous healing practices such as limpias/spiritual cleansings using prayers, building altars for the deceased, Masses and prayer vigils. As a result of these efforts the families began to heal. This is one example of how traditional therapeutic interventions and traditional indigenous practices can be merged to benefit the client (Mission School District Special Supplement, 1990).

VALUES

Values are the driving forces that guide the way in which our society is organized. An individual's behavior is influenced during childhood by fundamental values imparted by their families. Values directly impact our attitudes or beliefs towards our families and society. In the helping professions, values are transmitted to students through their education and socialization into their chosen fields. In social work, for example, the profession is concerned with meeting the needs of disenfranchised individuals using objective interventions. Often when individuals in need of help meet a professional who shares similar cultural values a cultural fit takes place between the client and helper. In cases, where the cultural values of an individual are different from those of a professional the result is a lack of fit.

In these cases cultural competence training for the clinician needs to be implemented by the agency. At the organizational level, an agency's administration needs to determine whether or not it is culturally competent. Benchmarks of institutional cultural competence include (1) evidence that the agency recognizes and values cultural diversity (2) adherence to a mission statement embracing diversity, (3) hiring of culturally competent staff, (4) the delivery of well articulated culturally competent services, and (5) management and the board of directors that represents the ethnic/racial composition of the community? Furthermore, Cross et al. have elaborated a continuum that appraises the organizational cultural competence. These encompass (1) cultural destructiveness, (2) cultural incapacity, (3) cultural blindness, (4) cultural pre- competence, (5) cultural competence and (6) cultural proficiency. In sum cultural competence is important not only at the interpersonal level but also at the agency/organizational level.

SKILLS

A culturally competent substance abuse treatment knowledge base ideally consists of skills that are identified as benchmarks for practice. They must be guided by a theoretical framework that that is founded on research, policy and practice wisdom from both practitioners and researchers in the field. The previous discussion of past and present substance abuse treatment research has yielded the following skills.

Skills at Initiating a Helping Relationship

In order to work effectively with Latinos, clinicians need to demonstrate their skills at assessing whether or not there is a fit between themselves and the client. First it is important to establish the type of clinician/client relationship. The literature points to a clinician/client dyad where both see themselves as peers sharing power. Other basic skills are necessary to determine whether or not the clinician would be able to engage the client. These include: (1) Assessing their own cultural base and whether or not it fits with the Latino client's; (2) Assessing whether or not they are able to communicate with their client, either in the client's language or through the use of a translator; (3) Assessing to what extent clients identify with their own culture as well as whether or not the client has a positive world view; (4) Assessing the client's level of acculturation to the larger American society; and (5) What barriers has the Latino client encountered in the problem solving process? Once a clinician has performed these assessments it is necessary to verbally validate and affirm the responses to these questions. Outward affirmation of both cultures is necessary to achieve a level of understanding and begin a relationship.

Skills at Building a Helping Relationship

Once the relationship has been established, a clinician needs to demonstrate more advanced skills at nurturing the helping relationship. This calls for developing a level of interpersonal competence that is culturally syntonic with Latinos. The following concepts/skills are found in the mental health field. *Respeto* is the ability/skill of the clinician to demonstrate respect to his clients. *Simpatia* is the ability/skill to connect with the client by demonstrating empathy, sincerity, and warmth. *Confianza* is the ability/skill to establish and maintaining trust with the client. *Personalismo* is the ability to be person centered and establish individual rapport with the client. *Dignidad* is the ability to support the dignity and worth of an individual. *Platicas* are the ability/skill of the clinician to engage the client in therapeutic conversations that are more relaxed. *Dar Anitmo* is the ability/skill at helping the client work through his/her issues through affirmation, validation and motivation.

Skill in Measuring Acculturation

The assessment of acculturation is a very important factor because it provides insight about the client's ability to adapt and respond to the demands of his family and the larger society. This writer is familiar with two approaches. The first, the Acculturation Rating Scale for Mexican Americans-II: A Revision of the Original ARSMA Scale, analyzes values, socialization, language preference and food preferences (Cuellar, Arnold, & Maldonado, 1995). The second approach was used to study the cultural context of an individual in his/her attempts at acculturation (Szapocznik, Scopetta, Kurtines, & Aranalde, 1978). This approach was used in research conducted by Szapocznik et al. to study the effectiveness of strategic family therapy in families with drug abuse problems.

CONCLUSION

The preceding discussion of cultural competence with Latino populations has reviewed some of the key elements that are necessary to training culturally competent clinicians. The task of organizing cultural competence training specific to each community is one that has to follow the demographic growth of each community, migration patterns, manifestations of substance abuse patterns in the region, acculturation and adaptation of the various latino groups that exist in the community.

Finally, it is important to note the relationship of research to the increased development of knowledge, values and skills for working with Latino populations. The theory, concepts and approaches reviewed are only the beginning efforts at documenting the unique needs of Latinos. More policy initiatives that recognize the impact of culture on drug, tobacco and alcohol problems are required to stimulate the growth of this knowledge base.

REFERENCES

Amaro, H. (1988). Women in the Mexican American Community: Religion. Culture and Reproductive Attitudes and Experiences. *Journal of Community Psychology, 16,* 6-19.

American Psychiatric Association. (1994). *The Diagnostic and Statistical Manual of Mental Disorders Fourth Edition.* Washington, D.C. American Psychiatric Association Press.

Brooks, C. & Rice, K. (1997). *Families in Recovery Coming Full Circle.* Baltimore, MD. Paul H. Brookes Publishing Co.

Centers for Disease Control, (1995). HIV/AIDS Surveillance Report. Atlanta. Georgia. U.S. Dept. of Health and Human Services Public Health Service.

Cross, T.L., Bazron, B.J., Dennis. K.W., and Isaacs, M. (1989). *Towards a Culturally Competent System of Care Volume 1.* Washington. D.C. CASSP Technical Assistance Center Georgetown University Child Development Center.

Cuellar, 1., Arnold, B., and Maldonado. R. (1995). Acculturation Rating Scale for Mexican Americans-Il: A Revision of the Original ARSMA Scale. *Hispanic Journal of Behavioral Sciences Vol. 17, No. 3.* Pp. 275-301.

Day, P., Robison, S. and Sheikh, L., (1998). *Ours to Keep: A Guide for Building a Community Assessment Strategy for Child Protection.* Washington, D.C. Child Welfare League of America Press.

Delgado, M. (1998) Community Asset Assessment and Substance Abuse Prevention: A Case Study Involving the Puerto Rican Community. In M. Delgado. (Ed.) *Social Services in Latino Communities.* New York. The Haworth Press, Inc.

Delgado. M. and Humm-Delgado. D. (1983). *Hispanic Adolescents and Substance Abuse.* In *Adolescent Substance Abuse.* New York. The Haworth Press, Inc.

Estrada, A., Rabow. J. and Matts. R.K. (1982). Alcohol Use Among Hispanic Adolescents: A Preliminary Report. *Journal of Behavioral Sciences.*

Levenson, J. (1995). *Inventory of Strengths in Substance Abuse Affected Families.* Unpublished Manuscript.

Navarro, C. (1995). The Power of "La Familia:" A Family Preservation Approach in the Latino Community. In H. Curiel, (Ed.). *Selected Papers in Substance Abuse Prevention & Family Focused Approaches in Social cork Practice with Minority Populations.* Norman. Oklahoma. Southwest Regional Center for Drug Free Schools & Communities.

Paz, J. (1998). The Nuestra Juventud Substance Abuse Prevention Project. Annual Report. Eloy, AZ. Pinal Hispanic Council.

Pottenger, P.S., Goldsmith, J.R., and Klemp, G.O. (1979). *Defining and Measuring Competence.* San Francisco. Jossey-Bass, Inc.

Romero, J.T. (1996). Culturally Competent Treatment Services for Hispanics. In H. Curiel, (Ed.) *Selected Papers in Substance Abuse Prevention & Family Focused Approaches in Social Work Practice with Minority Populations.* Norman, Oklahoma, Southwest Regional Center for Drug Free Schools & Communities.

SASSI Institute. (1994). *Substance Abuse Subtle Screening Inventory.* Bloomington, IN. Author.

Szapocznik, J., Kurtines, W. (1989). Brief Strategic Family Therapy for Hispanic Youth. In L. Beutler, (Ed.) *Programs in Psychotherapy Research.* Washington, D.C. American Psychological Association.

Szapocznik, J., Scopetta, M.A., Kurtines, W., & Aranalde, M.A. (1978). Theory and Measurement of Acculturation. *Interamerican Journal of Psychology, 12,* Pp. 113-130.

Vasconcelos, J. (1979) La Raza Cosmica. In D.T. Jaen. (Ed.) *Jose Vasconcelos: The Cosmic Race/La Raza Cosmica. Bilingual Edition with Introduction and Notes.* Los Angeles, Centro de Publicaciones Bilingual Edition.

Latino Immigrants:
Patterns of Survival

Maria E. Zuniga

SUMMARY. The Latino population continues to increase dramatically with some of the increase due to continuous immigration, both documented and undocumented. This article examines some of the demographic within group diversity that exists. The immigration experience is highlighted for the particular stresses that occur. The unique issues related to living in the United States without legal papers are noted. For those immigrants who are refugees, the impact of civil war and violence on their ability to adapt to this new culture is underscored. The consequences of immigration are noted in how children are affected. An Ecological Perspective illustrates how their adaptations can be classified into such specific areas as identity, relatedness, competence and autonomy. Some of the resources to support viable adaptation are delineated. *[Article copies available for a fee from The Haworth Document Delivery Service: 1-800-HAWORTH. E-mail address: <getinfo@haworthpressinc.com> Website: <http://www.HaworthPress.com> © 2002 by The Haworth Press, Inc. All rights reserved.]*

KEYWORDS. Immigration, adaptation, ecological perspective, acculturation, undocumented vs. documented refugee

---

Maria E. Zuniga, PhD, LCSW, is Professor at the School of Social Work, San Diego State University.

[Haworth co-indexing entry note]: "Latino Immigrants: Patterns of Survival." Zuniga, Maria E. Co-published simultaneously in *Journal of Human Behavior in the Social Environment* (The Haworth Social Work Practice Press, an imprint of The Haworth Press, Inc.) Vol. 5, No. 3/4, 2002, pp. 137-155; and: *Latino/Hispanic Liaisons and Visions for Human Behavior in the Social Environment* (ed: José B. Torres, and Felix G. Rivera) The Haworth Social Work Practice Press, an imprint of The Haworth Press, Inc., 2002, pp. 137-155. Single or multiple copies of this article are available for a fee from The Haworth Document Delivery Service [1-800-HAWORTH, 9:00 a.m. - 5:00 p.m. (EST). E-mail address: getinfo@haworthpressinc.com].

137

INTRODUCTION

The United States as a nation of immigrants displays major ambivalence towards present day immigration. The United States, Germany and Canada have the largest number of immigrants amongst advanced industrial countries: 6.8 million foreign residents in Germany in 1994 and 8.6 percent of its population. For the U.S. in 1993 there were 23 million foreign-born residents or 8.9 percent of the population (Bade & Weiner, 1997); for Canada, 16 percent were immigrants in the late 1980s, (Edmonston & Passel, 1994). In the U.S., legal immigration from Asia, Latin America, the Caribbean, and Africa composed 82 percent of all immigration to the United States in 1990 (U.S. Immigration and Naturalization Service, 1991). Latin American immigrants rank second to Asians as groups who immigrate legally and composed 20 percent of all immigrants in 1990, (Edmonston & Passel, 1994). The 1990 census indicated that a total of about 7,150,000 persons living in the U.S. were either born in Mexico, the Caribbean and Central America. Sixty percent of the Latino group was Mexican origin. In descending order of population were Cubans, Salvadorans, Dominicans, Jamaicans, Haitians, and Guatemalans (Munz & Weiner, 1997).

Presently, countries with increases in immigration are experiencing major political concerns due to assertions that migrants impose fiscal costs on governments, that they have a negative impact on the local labor market, and cause social conflicts due to their diversity of ethnicity, race or religious affiliation, (Edmonston & Passel, 1994).

The diverse and massive immigration that occurred in the United States during the last part of the 20th century evoked a range of responses similar to those above. Many people voiced concern that immigrants were overwhelming social resources. Demographer David Hayes Bautista in California reported that many people held a pervasive sentiment that the state's problems, economic issues and even pollution, were caused by Latino immigrants (1992). The millions of dollars spent by the federal government to "secure" the border with Mexico, underscored extraordinary attempts to curtail the immigration of "illegal aliens." Despite the variety of sentiments, most of which were very negative, and the variety of social policy initiatives to curb these phenomena, the immigration continues both for documented and undocumented persons. Immigrants from these countries are here and often are confronting major psychological trauma and situational stress. Human service workers must have more informed and incisive insights about their person-environment issues and service needs so as to offer competent interventions.

For this paper the focus will be on the immigration of those from Mexico and Central America, a large percentage of which has been outside legal avenues. The term "illegal alien" is identified as a term that the writer urges workers not to use but replace by the term undocumented immigrant or other less negative terms. The hostile reaction to those who have and continue to cross the U.S.-Mexico international border outside the legal pathway does not need to be strengthened by concepts that dehumanize these individuals. In addition, many immigrants in those groups from war-torn countries in Central America, are actually refugees. The definition of refugee according to the 1967 United Nations definition are people fleeing political oppression (Potocky-Tripodi, 1999). However Nicaraguans who came here during the Somoza and Sandinista regimes in the late 1970s and early 1980s, although fleeing political oppression, were not considered refugees according to U.S. policy. Since they were here without documentation the government classified them as undocumented immigrants. The distinction between an immigrant and an actual refugee is critical to assessment purposes. The history and resultant trauma that occurs with refugee status may be quite different than the experience of those who chose immigration in a free manner.

The goal of this paper is to elucidate what happens to immigrants, especially those who are undocumented when they come to the United States. How do they adapt and cope with this new experience, situation, and culture? What are the stresses that often characterize their experience? Importantly, what may be resources or domains of strength that soften this hard experience, and enable them to succeed. In particular, what might be areas human service workers may need to assess, especially for immigrants who have come from the political strife and civil wars that occurred for so many years in places like El Salvador, Guatemala, and Nicaragua? What should we be sensitive to in how these experiences have affected children, adolescents, and entire family systems?

A ecological perspective (Germain & Gitterman, 1980) will be used to assess the interplay between the person and this new environment in which immigrants have been thrust. How do cultural, economic, health and educational systems impact these new immigrants? The ecological theme of adaptation is the centerpiece for examining the experiences of these immigrants. This includes the focus on identifying the strengths those individuals present that can be easily overlooked. How did these immigrants cope before and how can they learn to cope anew in this stressful situation. This perspective provides a focus for comprehending how individuals view themselves or their identities in light of this new cultural context. How do they evaluate their skills or competencies; what networks or supports are called upon as resources to curb their isolation? How do they carve out a mode of functioning independently, despite all the barriers that impede this goal. Importantly, utilizing the four domains of an ecological view, the focus on a person's identity, autonomy, relatedness and competence will be themes that will guide this examination (ibid).

HISTORICAL OVERVIEW OF IMMIGRATION

A brief overview of the immigration trends in the latter part of the 20th century based on the work of Bean, Cushing and Haynes (1997) depicts who these immigrants are. They note that after World War II immigration in the U.S. dropped tenfold, decreasing from over seven hundred thousand per year during the first 20 years of the century to less than seventy thousand from 1925 to 1945. Then, for nearly fifty years legal immigration moved upward reaching all-time highs set in the first 20 years of the century, during the 80s and 90s; in this latter time it was composed of legal, undocumented, and refugee immigrants. The 1986 Immigration Reform Act which provided amnesty to those who were living here undocumented, the large majority of which were Latinos, contributed to this immigration surge. The result was the largest increase of immigrants in U.S. history, (Bean et al., 1997). Presently, it is estimated that illegal immigration from all countries results in about 200,000 undocumented persons per year, (Edmonston & Passell, 1994).

The change in national origins is also important. Prior to 1960 the majority of immigrants were from European countries or Canada. In the 60s this pattern changed when family reunification criteria rather than national origins quotas became the policy for providing entry visas (Bean et al., 1989). In the 1980s 12.5 percent of legal immigrants were from Europe or Canada while 84.4 percent were from Asian or Latin American countries, especially Mexico. The 90s witnessed an increase of European immigration, especially from Russian changing the percentage to 20.6 from Europe and Canada and 75.9 from Asian and Latin American (U.S. Immigration and Naturalization Service, 1995, as cited by Bean et al., 1997). These authors highlight that the Euro-American and African-American biracial society changed to a multiracial and multiethnic society. The year 1990 could designate almost one fourth of the U.S. population as Afro-American, Latino, Asian or Native American. By 1990 African Americans no longer composed a majority of the minority population (Passel and Edmonston, 1994).

An important aspect of the changed immigration demographics is the changes in educational levels. Bean et al. (1994) point to the change in educational levels of recent Mexican immigrants compared to those who immigrated in the 1960s. Between 1960 and 1964 Mexican immigrants were on average 19 years old and had completed more than eight years of school. Since that time Mexican males have completed less than six years of school and average an age of over 30 with the same pattern for female Mexican immigrants. For male and female Central and South Americans immigrants a similar pattern of decreasing education and increasing age holds true. Consequently, these immigrants will all encounter a more difficult time becoming integrated into the United States than earlier immigrants do. They typically work in low-skill, low-paying jobs that restrict them to old urban areas, with overcrowding and poor social conditions (Bean, 1994).

CENTRAL AMERICAN IMMIGRANTS/REFUGEES

Melville and Lykes (1992) estimate that there are more than a million Salvadoran and 200,000 Guatemalan refugees in the United States. The geographic distribution of these groups is different than that of Mexicans who tend to cluster in California, Texas, and Illinois. For Cubans the clustering is in Florida, New Jersey and New York. Those from El Salvador move to California, Texas and New York. Those from Nicaragua and Honduras have also settled in Florida, California and New York while Guatemalans settle in California, New York and Illinois (Munz & Weiner, 1997).

An important feature of the Central American immigration is that the vast majority of the immigration during the 50s was a consequence of civil war and human rights abuses and was heavily composed of children and youth (Benjamin & Morgan, 1989). These youth migrated in order to survive. As Zea et al., (1997) highlight, massive exposure to violence characterizes this population. These children and teens witnessed mutilations, torture, and disappearance of kin, killings, massacres of entire communities, bombings and relocation.

The war or civil strife forced fathers to leave their families sometimes to avoid being killed or drafted. Mothers would later join fathers in the states, leaving young children behind. While these youth waited to be brought to the U.S. once their parents had enough money, they continued to be exposed to the atrocities of civil strife, now without the buffering roles of their parents (Zea et al., 1997). The psychological themes that are critical to understand in working with this population will be elucidated later.

HOSTILE REACTIONS

As noted earlier, mass immigration provokes many different reactions from governments and its citizenry. The dynamic increase of Latinos immigrant, especially those here without papers, has often resulted in very hostile and discriminatory attitudes. In San Diego, during the 1990s these negative attitudes fostered such a high degree of xenophobia that two young men, decided to "hunt down" Mexicans. They were later brought to trial for shooting and killing someone who they assumed was an undocumented Latino. This person was a legal resident of Mexican origin. The point of this vignette is to underscore the hostile and even dangerous ambience that Latino immigrants often encounter when they cross to the United States. Comprehension of the immigrant experience must consider if and to what extent the immigrant has to also address racism and prejudice as they strive to adjust to this new cultural order. Since there tends to be an overrepresentation of immigrants from low socioeconomic levels, it is probable that they have encountered discrimination in their countries of origin that is class based. However, experiencing discrimination due to their phenotype may be a very new experience which could easily attack their identity and which they will need to counter with new coping devices.

STRESSORS OF THE IMMIGRATION EXPERIENCE

The context in which the migration experience takes place is important for assessing what the immigrant brings with him/her in terms of preparedness and motivation for the this change. For some it is a well-planned and thoughtful process that is viewed with optimism for a better life. For others it is being forced out of their country due to political realities that is even life threatening. As Sluzki, a family therapist indicated "They look forward with hope or backward with fear," (1979, p. 379). Sluzki (1979) outlined five stages of migration so that workers would have a framework for identifying sources of family conflict. Workers can use this framework for assessing where the immigrant family or individual is positioned along the immigration trajectory and if presenting problems are related to specific stage processes.

For example, in the *Preparatory Stage* the person or family makes the decision to leave. Is this decision made in an orderly and thoughtful manner with everyone agreeing to this major change or is it made at the last moment without the opportunity to ritualize goodbyes to family and friends? This latter kind of departure aggravates the grief and loss themes that naturally correspond to such a major life move. When some members have not been in agreement with the move they may later blame the person who made this decision. Issues of loss and mourning are intricately woven in the immigration process and can heavily mire the family in dysfunctional dynamics if mourning is disallowed, is incomplete, or extended.

In the second stage, *The Act of Migration*, there may be a variety of circumstances that make the experience unique for each person or family. For some they may be in the U.S. in a matter of hours with a swift and readily peaceful plane trip. For others, it may be a treacherous journey to escape detection, or protracted time spent in refugee camps as they awaited entry to the U.S. For some Central Americans, immigration meant traveling laboriously through other countries like Mexico before entering the U.S., as the film "El Norte" vividly depicts; The fear of authorities and the military caused by their horrible experiences during civil wars exacerbated fear and trauma themes in their journeys. For those who enter without documents the horrors of exploitation, assault and rape can be realities that will impress traumatic memories that will impact their future ability to adapt and to cope. In San Diego County, tightened border surveillance has pushed those crossing without documents to the eastern part of the county. In winter, there are dozens who freeze to death as they cross mountainous terrain; in the summer this same trek takes them through desert-like conditions during which each year many die of dehydration and exposure. For those who are able to complete the journey, memories of relatives or friends who died in the process result in grief and guilt issues which are tremendous. Assessment must consider what was this crossing experience like; if and how was trauma experienced as part of this process. These kinds of trauma will lurk in the immigrants' psyche, contributing to depression and anxiety that will not be easily eradicated from their new lives without intervention.

In Stage Three or the *Period of Overcompensation,* Sluzki (1979) highlights that often there is a honeymoon period after entry to their new country, that negates the losses that have actually occurred. It is a time when the person or family is in a heightened task oriented stage, not recognizing the incongruency of their cultural situation. However, the lack of fit from their accustomed values, roles and expectations, and those of the new society eventually begin to be felt as the family finds itself confronting many conflicts and pressures that are fatiguing. Many families react by rigidly hanging on to old cultural patterns and rituals. However, the problems begin to raise their ugly heads.

In the Fourth Stage or *Period of Crisis or Decompensation*, symptoms begin to be noticeable; conflicts become more overt and heightened. Often the family is drawn into interaction with societal institutions, due to child abuse, family violence or some other issue and need that highlights their crisis. Resources they could call on in the old country to address issues are typically not available. It is not unusual that conflicts between children and parents come to a head as the younger generation integrates new values and roles that threaten the family's cultural framework. The family system is dramatically challenged to undergo a new configuration of values and styles that will allow them to keep some of the old but hopefully integrate new ways of thinking and behaving that will enable them to cope more effectively in this new society. That is a major charge for families to address. Often, if one spouse has more readily entered into societal roles due to employment, the other spouse who is not acculturating at the same rate will be left behind; creating a spousal cultural chasm that exacerbates couple and family problems. If women have employment opportunities rather than the male, then role and gender conflicts will challenge these traditional families.

After a few years the family system may find itself embroiled in conflicts they have not developed new skills to address. They are not coping well. Or, through struggles they have developed a new system of adaptation that integrates both new and old for a reconfiguration of the family's coping abilities.

In the Fifth Stage or *Transgenerational Impact*, the effects of the family's ability to work through an integration process of new and old values, behaviors, and coping mechanisms will enable the younger generation to function in society in a viable manner. If a value and behavior revision has not occurred, the younger generation will display Culture clashes within their family or with the larger social culture, sometimes resulting in delinquent behaviors.

Sluzki's framework (1979) helps the interventionist to consider what these immigrants experience and the price they pay for their journey, whether freely chosen or imposed on them by political strife. This consideration enables the human services worker to assess the themes outlined above, to detect intervention points that can offer problem-solving processes for addressing the issue, conflict, or grief reaction that is causing maladaptation. For therapists, this framework enables them to trace back to those experiences the immigrant may be resistant to processing since these painful memories have imposed major psychological trauma.

An important reality to consider for both immigrants who are undocumented as well as for refugees, is to what extent they are suffering from Post Traumatic Stress Syndrome (Cervantes et al., 1989). For Central American refugees, the trauma of civil war, experiencing torture and death, and the lack of power in being able to change these adversities truly stresses the human psyche. Effects of these kinds of trauma on children and youth are especially critical to assess since their developmental stages insure fewer skills for use in addressing this adversity. Importantly, the experiences of undocumented immigrants also produce trauma. The incidence of Trans-border assaults, rapes, robberies and then the terrifying experience of being hunted down by the Border Patrol, will result in similar emotional trauma (Cervantes et al. (1989).

Effects on Families

A community survey undertaken by Espino, Berry-Caban and Gimenez (1986) cited by Espino (1991) in Washington D.C. showed a very high incidence of neglect amongst Central American immigrants. For example, the conditions of poverty that often characterize their lives have resulted in inadequate supervision of children, environments that are physically dangerous, inadequate health care and the parentification of older siblings that interferes with their educational and developmental needs. Such environmental conditions as overcrowding have exposed children to sex and violence that challenges emotional well being. Furthermore, the changed family constellations, with blended families resulting from new unions in the United States and the children of unions from their country of origin have created both step and half-sibling combinations. For some these combinations create rivalries between siblings and parents, often times resulting in heightened family conflict. This range of adverse familial conditions does not foster the kind of climate needed for healthy development, emotional or cognitive (Espino, 1991).

Isolation Issues and Their Relevance to Relatedness

The immigration experience typically implies that some family and friends will be left behind in the country of origin. For some from war torn countries, relatives, friends, boyfriends have been killed, often before their own eyes. The separation of families ruptures the support the immigrant had been accustomed to. Due to language, cultural and economic issues, immigrants will often find themselves without the moral support and networks that had enabled them to function. In Jacob's (1994) Investigation of the social integration of Salvadoran Refugees in Canada he found that social relationships were critical to satisfying the refugees' need for communication and to mitigate isolation. These Salvadoran refugees found the workplace as the most significant non-family support network. Despite some negative aspects of their employment, they still attached great meaning to the quality of their interactions. Another feature that Vasquez (1983) as cited by Jacob (1994) encountered was that Salvadoran refugees went through a process of introspection as they mourned for their country. They tended to reject what surrounded them while feeling they were being rejected, adding further to their sense of aloneness. The theme of isolation will be present for most refugees and immigrants; the degree will depend on the meaning ascribed to their situation. Some with family and linkages to an actual Salvadoran community will feel more or less isolated, depending on their subjective interpretation. While isolation is an issue of concern with any client, it imposes a heavier impact for an immigrant who has already suffered familial, cultural, resource and network losses.

Competency and Identity Themes

From the sample of Washington D.C. immigrants (Espino et al., 1987) discovered issues in Education for children/youth that place them at high risk for delinquency behaviors, and retardation of social and developmental skills. In illustration, this study of the academic and cognitive functions of children indicated that 35 percent were functioning two or more years below expected grade level. Although some might interpret the delay as related to lack of English proficiency, when these children were given school achievement tests in Spanish, 72 percent scored a two or more year delay in reading and 73 percent a similar delay in mathematics. Some teens were reading at first and second-grade levels. As Espino (1991) noted, once a child or teen reaches this grave level of academic delay, achievement motivation becomes very poor and they are at risk of severe self-esteem and shame issues associated with their efforts at school skills. Their self-identity suffers and they perceive themselves as inadequate and incompetent. Consequently these youth are attractive to the kinds of activities that mask these deficits, some of which are delinquent. This fits into Sluzki's last stage of transgenerational impact. When immigrants are ghettoized and unable to develop coping skills in the broader society, their children will similarly miss out on these skills and can easily resort to behaviors that are antisocial. Thus the reading and learning impairments hamper the youth's ability to interpret cues, or to learn the kinds of information for making developmentally sound judgments, further hampering their ability to adapt well to urban life. These youth will not master the verbal skills that will allow them to interact with adults from a broader range of socioeconomic groups. As a reaction they are restricted to many areas of the city and activities they could benefit from, and withdraw and function in a limited but familiar territory. Their identity and sense of competence suffer further setbacks. This is the time when gangs become attractive, especially for teens that are cognizant of their sense of inadequacy, feeding into a negative reaction of rebelliousness and delinquency. Certainly, drug abuse risk factors are prevalent as well as teen pregnancy.

Autonomy Issues

Despite their levels of poverty, inadequate wages and employment conditions, studies of Latino immigrants have shown that they tend not to depend on government subsidies to the extent that is often ascribed to them. For instance, in Espino's work in Washington D.C. it was discovered that these immigrant women did not participate in the WIC (Women, Infant, and Children) program for infants and pregnant women, despite the fact they were eligible (1991). These undocumented immigrants lived off their limited incomes and did not obtain any federal income supplements. Earlier work in San Diego County revealed that out of 5,000 amnesty applicants only 2.8% reported receiving AFDC payments in the previous five years, 2.5% had received "General Assistance" and 6.6% had received food stamps (Comprehensive Adult Student Assessment System, 1989). Hayes-Bautista et al., (1992) reported although Latinos in California had the highest rate of poverty they were the least likely to utilize welfare programs. When controlling for income, Latinos were half as likely as Anglos or Asians to receive AFDC payments and about one fifth as likely as African Americans were. Part of this lack of dependency may be explained by the high labor participation rate Latinos tend to have.

The California Identity Project data confirm Latinos' strong dedication to the work ethic; a disinclination to use government programs and the highest rate of participation in the work force for the past 50 years as compared to any other group (Hurtado et al., 1992). The paradox is that despite this work participation they are the group that is the poorest in California due to low level employment. Third-generation Latinos are as likely as immigrants to be blue-collar workers. This implies they will also have less employment benefits like health insurance, vacation days or retirement plans. Yet, they do not want to depend on others (Hayes-Bautista et al., 1992). For those who are undocumented this reluctance to utilize government resources may be heightened by their fear of apprehension (Zea et al., 1997).

THE CENTRAL AMERICAN EXPERIENCE

The massive influx of children and youth to the U.S. as a result of the civil strife in such countries as El Salvador and Nicaragua compelled researchers to examine the effects of this entire trauma. Arroyo and Eth's (1985) study of 28 Salvadoran and Nicaraguan youth and their parents identified some alarming outcomes. Their exposure to violence had resulted in suicidal behaviors, serious antisocial acts, insomnia, separation anxiety, defiance, somatic complaints without organic etiology and school related problems. Aside from these more serious effects, Mancilla (1987) as quoted by Zea et al. (1997) found in a sample of 30 Salvadoran youth that they severely missed their hometown and country, adding to the burden they already carried.

Moreover, Melville and Lykes' (1992) study of Guatemalan children indicated that one of the more difficult aspects they identified was the severe hunger they endured when they fled their hometowns and until they reached refugee camps. In addition, once in the U.S. they also experienced hunger because of their parents' inability to secure steady employment due to language barriers and especially their undocumented status.

In the research of Central America and Mexican immigrants by Cervantes, Salgado de Snyder and Padilla (1989) Post Traumatic Stress Disorder (PTSD) was found to derive not just from the violence of war but also from the immigration experience as well. When they used the Center for Epidemiology Depression Scale they found a significant difference in generalized psychological stress between the sample of Latinos who were immigrants versus those who were not. This research needs to be examined with caution due to the confounding that occurred when they included both Mexican immigrants and refugees in the sample. However the significant stress differences between Mexican immigrants and Mexican non-immigrant participants of the sample, underline the impact of the immigration experience itself (Zea et al., 1997).

Aside from the effects of war trauma coupled with the stress of the immigration trek, those refugees and their children who were not granted asylum have to address the daily anxiety of being discovered and deported. In addition, when there is a threat of INS authorities being called in, families will pick up and move to insure their safety. All of these features wear on the emotional reservoir of both adults and children (Zea et al., 1997).

RESOURCES

Zea et al. (1997) identified three protective factors that were salient for refugee children. These factors were gleaned from the literature and from their research. Social support, psychosocial competence and cognitive factors helped refugees cope.

The literature on social support shows how those who believe or experience tangible or intangible forms of help enable individuals to feel cared for (Barrera, Sandler & Ramsey, 1981). This results in increased resilience and serves as protective factors during such periods as war times.

If a parent offers social support, research from World War II has shown that children experience more positive psychological outcomes. As Zea et al. (1997) note, the research of Melville and Lykes (1992) showed that Guatemalan children felt they recovered from trauma because of the support of their parents. The work of Diehl et al. (1994) with children mainly from El Salvador showed that those children who had endured extreme exposure to war violence and were separated from their fathers exhibited more PTSD symptoms. One interpretation was that in Central America the role of father as protector might be of more importance than that of the mother due to their strong patriarchal culture, thus this interesting finding. Using the ecological model, the importance of relationship, in this instance with parents is a critical protective or coping factor.

Psychosocial competence has been defined by Tyler, Brome, and Williams (1991) as those who believe they have control over the outcomes of their lives, those who have moderate self-efficacy, those who have an active coping style, and those who have some trust in the world around them. Masten et al. (1990) indicate that persons who demonstrate resilience or the capacity for successful adaptation regardless of the threat they face, are psychosocially competent persons. Mancilla's (1987) research of Central American youth found that those who had lower psychosocial competence scores and had obtained less social support in El Salvador were faced with more difficulties in coping after migration to the United States. Thus youth who have some of the attributes of psychosocial competencies may be better equipped for learning how to adapt in the aftermath of immigration.

The third factor that Zea et al. (1997) identify as a buffering factor is cognitive. Intelligence and problem-solving skills help the individual compensate for trauma. Zea et al., found that children who had been more exposed to the violence of war were more easily distractible. Arroyo and Eth's (1985) research found that Central American children who had experienced the violence of war had frequent thought intrusions. It is no wonder that Espino et al.'s (1987) research on the educational levels of Central American children showed delayed and poor academic performance. This is similar to Sattler's (1982) idea that exposure to war violence contaminates intellectual development for some children similar to how anxiety or depression interferes with IQ. Zea's et al. (1997) work also showed that intelligence serves as a mediator of the impact of violence. For example, under high levels of experiences with violence children with lower Verbal IQ scores had more PTSD symptoms. Under moderate levels of exposure to violence IQ did not have an effect. Thus it may be that having a high IQ can offer the resources that will enable children to cope with high degrees of stress. Although research in this area is still sparse, it does indicate how social support; psychosocial competence and intelligence may mitigate the adverse experiences of war trauma. The Ecological Model highlights that social support or relatedness is crucial for understanding this population as well as the more personal indices of competence. Other kinds of environmental factors are also instrumental in helping immigrants adapt.

CONTEXTUAL SUPPORTS

Although the concentration of immigrants in poor neighborhoods contribute to problems, having them living in close proximity to others from their country so they can speak their language and pursue native rituals provides the kind of support that may enable them to begin forays into their new cultural environment. De Anda's (1984) model of bicultural development highlighted that identified support structures that benefit immigrants should always be considered in work with this population. Do they have family already in the area that can act as the cultural brokers, sharing their experiences and providing the do's and don't that will enable them to learn from others' mistakes? Often these brokers may not be kin but a member from the same town the immigrant comes from and with whom they feel the cultural connection that mitigates their isolation. These brokers teach new immigrants where rent is affordable, what stores have their cultural foods, where English classes are the most accessible. Many recent arrivals rely on brokers to find employment. These brokers may also provide linkages to recreational and social activities. This kind of networking provides ties to the old culture as a way to stabilize the immigrants' situation. The important principle is that the cultural supports should help the immigrant to begin to reach out to their new cultural scenario rather than stay immersed in their old culture, which does not facilitate the acculturation processes needed. Not reaching out will only insure that the second generation will be constrained in the acculturation process as well.

Other important resources to assess for are religious institutions that immigrants may connect to. Some churches will provide resource information that will enable the immigrant to cope more effectively. Certainly, the support derived from spiritual or more formal connections to belief systems is a valuable resource for helping them cope emotionally and for providing a context that will enable them to feel connected to others.

Some communities may have such agencies like Catholic Social Services that provides specialized immigration services for all immigrants and refugees, including Latinos, offering help with documentation as well as services for employment training, job securement and English classes.

An important feature to services that are formal is to educate immigrants about what kind of resources, if used, could make them ineligible for future legal documentation versus those that have no impact, (Zuniga, in press). This is why knowledge of recent immigration policy is necessary in working with this population. Such institutions as the National Council of La Raza have specialists who offer updated interpretations of national policy (NCLR, 1998 or organizations as the California Immigrant Welfare Collaborative, (1-13-00).

Given the cultural traditions of individuals from Central America and Mexico, Zea et al. (1997) explain that social support at the community level may be more important to these immigrants than at the individual level due to the value they place on relationships. The Ecological Model (Germain & Gitterman, 1980) highlights the role of relatedness as crucial in everyone's life. For these immigrants this connection and support appears to have even heightened value.

CONCLUSION

This overview on Latino immigrants and refugees has delineated the variety of ways in which they are challenged when they come to the United States. In answer to the questions posed at the beginning of this chapter the literature details that immigrants and refugees from these countries adapt and cope with their immigration in a variety of ways, depending on prior experiences with trauma and with mitigating factors such as social support. Some of the stresses that characterize the experiences of these immigrants includes the exposure to war related trauma, especially for children and youth. Both refugees and immigrants suffer the loss of their homeland, friends, and relatives. They are faced with proceeding through the stages that Sluzki (1979) identified as very characteristic of an immigrant's experience. Certainly, this immigration process impresses their sense of identity, perhaps compromising their sense of self as they sort through cultural confusion, and more importantly, changed roles, statuses and for many the experiences of discrimination.

Many refugees have witnessed the death of family members, neighbors, and friends. The losses they have incurred and the new environment in which they find themselves challenges them to develop human contacts that are meaningful and supportive. If they are not able to find and use community and cultural supports, their emotional, psychological, and situational needs will not be met and they will become more vulnerable and more isolated. Relationships for them are critical. The importance of relatedness is also enhanced by their cultural relational tradition. The barriers of language and lack of documentation may cause them to be intermittently or underemployed, incurring continued poverty and related risk factors. Although refugees as compared to immigrants may have more severe trauma to address given the impact of war and torture, both groups appear to suffer from the stressful process of entering the United States without documents. In addition, the daily torment of fear of apprehension by immigration authorities is a constant threat to their emotional health. For refugees the impact of war trauma must be considered by workers to assess if they are suffering from PTSD. For-all immigrants the worker must assess if the immigration process itself, especially for the undocumented was traumatic in its own right, also contributing to PTSD. It is amazing that these immigrants do not seek more government resources in light of their desperate circumstances that daily challenge their autonomy. Like autonomy, their sense of competence will also be difficult to achieve. Cultural and situational change will be confusing and may at times restrict their sense that they have skills and capabilities.

However, there are avenues that can be pursued to attempt to adapt despite the adversity they encounter. They may have access to resources that have been identified as important for immigrants. The use of cultural brokers, kin, and community informal and formal resources enable them to survive. Church related resources enable them to receive help without jeopardizing future legalization aspirations.

Zea et al.'s (1997) specification of three salient coping resources, psychosocial competence, cognitive factors, and social support enable workers to look for these coping variables that they could call upon to facilitate adaptation for immigrants. The research on the effects of trauma on children and youth is particularly helpful for workers who may not be accustomed to considering how war trauma and civil strife affect personal coping. Recognizing the particular vulnerability of children and youth in relation to adapting and succeeding in school and social environments may enable workers to focus their intervention as well as prevention efforts in these need areas. Germain and Gitterman's Ecological model, (1980) and Sluzki's stage theory (1979) enables the worker to consider the special historical, stage and situational experiences that impact the immigrant's interaction with societal systems and their ability to function in and adapt to these new systems. Workers and social agencies must help with the integration of these immigrants into societal systems. More systematic and organized forms of specialized services focused on their individual and group needs must be developed (Jacob, 1994). Most importantly, human service workers must examine their own politics and attitudes toward immigrants, refugees, and in particular those who are undocumented. Residues of prejudice or racism must be identified and eradicated so as not to raise further barriers that these human beings must overcome.

REFERENCES

Arroyo, F., & Eth, S. (1985). Children traumatized by Central American warfare. In S. Eth & R.S. Pynoos (Eds.), *Post-traumatic stress disorders in children.* (pp. 101-120). Washington, DC: American Psychiatric Press.

Bade, K.J. & Weiner, M. (1997). *Migration Past. Migration Future: Germany and the United States.* Providence, RI: Berghahn Books.

Barrera, M., Jr., Sandler, I.M., & Ramsay, T.B. (1981). Preliminary development of a scale of social support: Studies on college students. *American Journal of Community Psychology, 9*, 435-447.

Bean, Frank, J. Chapa, R. Berg, K. Sowards, (1994). Educational and Sociodemographic Incorporation among Hispanic Immigrants to the United States. In Barry Edmonston and J. S. Passel, (Eds) *Immigration and Ethnicity: The Integration of America's Newest Arrivals.* Washington, DC: Urban Institute Press.

Bean, Frank, R. Cushing, and C. Haynes (1997). The Changing Demography of U.S. Immigration Flows: Patterns, Projections, and Contexts, in Klaus Bade & Myron Weiner, (Eds.) *Migration Past. Migration Future: Germany and the United States,* pp. 121-152.

Bean, Frank, George Vernez, and Charles B. Keely, (1989). *Opening and Closing the Doors: Evaluating Immigration Reform and Control.* Washington, DC: Urban Institute Press.

Benjamin, M.P., & Morgan, P.C. (1989). *Refugee children traumatized by war and violence: The challenge offered to the service delivery system.* Washington, DC: CASSP Technical Assistance Center, Georgetown University Child Development Center.

California Immigrant Welfare Collaborative, 926 J St., Suite 408, Sacramento, CA. 95914

Cervantes, R.C., Salgado de Snyder, V.N., & Padilla, A.M. (1989). Posttraumatic stress in immigrants from Central American and Mexico. *Hospital and Community Psychiatry,* 40, 615-619.

Comprehensive Adult Student Assessment System. (1989). *A Survey of Newly Legalized Persons in California.* San Diego: San Diego Community College Foundation for Educational Achievement.

De Anda, Diane. (1984). Bicultural Socialization. *Social Work.*

Diehl, V.A., Sea, M.C., & Espino, C.M. (1994). Exposure to war violence, separation from parents, post-traumatic stress, and cognitive functioning in Hispanic children. *Interamerican Journal of Psychology,* 28, 25-41.

Edmonston, B. & Passel, J.S., (Eds.) 1994. *Immigration and Ethnicity: The Integration of America's Newest Arrivals.* Washington, DC: Urban Institute Press.

Espino, Conchita M. (1991). Trauma and Adaptation: The Case of Central American Children. In Frederick Aherarn and Jean Athey, (Eds.) *Refugee Children: Theory, Research. and Services.* Baltimore: Johns Hopkins University Press.

Espino, C, Sanguinetti, P., Moreno, F., Diehl, V. and Sea, M.D. (1987). Psychological testing of Hispanic children: The role of war violence. Paper presented at the meeting of the American Psychological Association Meeting, New York, NY.

Espino, C., Berry-Caban, C., and Giminez, S. (1986). Characteristics of Hispanic families experiencing child abuse and neglect. Unpublished manuscript.

Germain, C., & Gitterman, A. (1980). *The life model of social work practice.* New York: Columbia University Press.

Hayes-Bautista, David, A. Hurtado, R.B. Valdez, A.C. Hernandez. (1992). *No Longer a Minority: Latinos and Social Policy in California.* Los Angeles: UCLA Chicano Studies Research Center.

Hulewat, Phyllis, (1999). Resettlement: A Cultural and Psychological Crisis. In P. Ewalt, E. Freeman, A. Fortune, D. Poole, S. Witkin (Eds.). *Multicultural Issues in Social Work: Practice and Research.* Washington, DC: NASW, pp. 669-678.

Hurtado, Aida, Hayes-Bautista, D. Valez, R. Hernandez, A. (1992). *Redefining California: Latino Social Engagement in a Multicultural Society.* Los Angeles: UCLA Chicano Studies Research Center Publications.

Jacob, Andre. (1994). Social Integration of Salvadoran Refugees. *Social Work* January, Vol. 39, No. 1, 307-312.

Mancilla, Y.E. (19887). Exposure to war-related violence and psychosocial competence of adolescent males from El Salvador. Unpublished manuscript.

Masten, A., Best, K. M., & Garmezy, N. (1990) Resilience and development: Contributions from the study of children who overcome adversity. *Development and Psychopathology,* 2, 425-444.

Melville, M.B., & Lykes, M.B. (1992) Guatemalan Indian children and the sociocultural effects of government-sponsored terrorism. *Social Science and Medicine* 34, 533-548.

Munz, R. & Weiner, M.(1997). *Migrants Refugees and Foreign Policy.* Providence, R.I.: Berghahn Books.

National Council of La Raza, (1998). *U.S. Hispanic Demographic Profile.* Washington, DC: Policy Analysis Center. 1111 19th St. N.W., Suite 1000, Washington, DC 20036.

Potocky-Tripodi, M. (1999). Refugee Children: How are They Faring Economically as Adults? In, P. Ewalt, E. Freeman, A. Fortune, D. Poole, S. Witkin (Eds.). *Multicultural Issues in Social Work: Practice and Research.* Washington, DC: NASW, pp. 622-633.

Sattler, J.M. (1982) *Assessment of children's intelligence and special abilities.* Boston: Allyn and Bacon.

Sluzki, Carlos. (1979). Migration and Family *Conflict. Family Process* 18, 379-390.

Tyler, F.B., Brome, D.R., & Wiliams, J. (1991). *Ecology ethnic validity and psychotherapy: A psychosocial competence approach.* New York: Plenum Press.

U.S. Immigration and Naturalization Service. (1991). *Statistical Yearbook of the Immigration and Naturalization Service.* 1990 Washington, DC: U.S. Government Printing Office.

U.S. Immigration and Naturalization Service, (1995). *Statistical Yearbook of the U.S. Immigration and Naturalization Service* 1994. Washington, DC: U.S. Government Printing Office.

Vasquez, A. (1983). L'exil, une analyse psychosociologique (Exile, a psychosociological analysis). *L'Information psychiatrique,* 59(1), 12-18.

Zea, Maria C. Diehl, V., Porterrield, K.S. (1997). Central American Youth Exposed to War Violence. In Maria C. Zea, V. Diehl, and K.S. Porterfield, (Eds.) *Psychological Interventions and Research with Latino Populations.* Boston, MA: Allyn & Bacon.

Zuniga, Maria. (in press). Working with Latino Families: Ethical Considerations, in R. Fong and S. Furuto, (Eds.) *Interventions with Diverse Families.*

Voices of Hispanic Caribbean Women: Migration, Family and Work

Nilsa M. Burgos

SUMMARY. Few studies on Caribbean women in the United States are based on women's realities or view these issues from their perspective and even fewer compare Caribbean women living in the United States to each other. Gender as an important factor of emigration experience has been neglected. This article presents (1) the results of a qualitative study describing changes in Caribbean women's lives after living in the United States for a period of ten or more years, and (2) a discussion of problems confronted by Latinas in a society different from their native countries of origin. The voices of Caribbean women on the process of migration, family values, and work experiences, are analyzed from a gender perspective. Implications for human services professions practice and recommendation for future research are also presented. *[Article copies available for a fee from The Haworth Document Delivery Service: 1-800-HAWORTH. E-mail address: <getinfo@haworthpressinc.com> Website: <http://www.HaworthPress.com> © 2002 by The Haworth Press, Inc. All rights reserved.]*

KEYWORDS. Caribbean, Hispanic women, migration, family, work

Nilsa M. Burgos, PhD, is Professor and Researcher at the University of Puerto Rico graduate School of Social Work. Her research focus has been on gender issues, family, and employment. She has published two books and numerous articles for journals in Puerto Rico, Latin America, and the United States.

[Haworth co-indexing entry note]: "Voices of Hispanic Caribbean Women: Migration, Family and Work." Burgos, Nilsa M. Co-published simultaneously in *Journal of Human Behavior in the Social Environment* (The Haworth Social Work Practice Press, an imprint of The Haworth Press, Inc.) Vol. 5, No. 3/4, 2002, pp. 157-174; and: *Latino/Hispanic Liaisons and Visions for Human Behavior in the Social Environment* (ed: José B. Torres, and Felix G. Rivera) The Haworth Social Work Practice Press, an imprint of The Haworth Press, Inc., 2002, pp. 157-174. Single or multiple copies of this article are available for a fee from The Haworth Document Delivery Service [1-800-HAWORTH, 9:00 a.m. - 5:00 p.m. (EST). E-mail address: getinfo@haworthpressinc.com].

INTRODUCTION

Few studies on Caribbean women in the United States (U.S.) are based on women's realities or view these issues from their perspective and even fewer compare Caribbean women living in the U.S., to each other. Gender as an important factor of emigration experience has been neglected in the social science literature. There are important exceptions of research about Dominican, Cuban and Puerto Rican women on topics such as: work, education, family, sexuality, welfare and family roles (Candelario & López, 1995; Fernández-Kelly, 1985; Grasmuck & Pessar, 1991; Hernández & Rivera-Batiz, 1997; Ortíz, 1996 and 1995; Pessar, 1995; 1986; Prieto 1992; Torruellas, Benmayor & Juarbe 1996). This article presents the results of a qualitative study conducted in 1997, focused on three main variables: migration, family and work.

The purpose of the study was to describe changes in Caribbean women's lives after living in the U.S. for ten years or more; and to contribute toward the understanding of their problems confronted in a society different from the one in their country of origin. The information offered by the participants is analyzed and compared with the review of the literature. I also used my perspective as a Puerto Rican that has lived in the U.S. for different periods of time and for six months in the Dominican Republic. Implications for human services professions practice and recommendation for future research are offered at the end of the article.

Migratory periods vary among the Dominican Republic, Cuba, and Puerto Rico. In Puerto Rico, the largest movement of migrants to the U.S. occurred in the 1950s, while for the Dominican Republic it occurred during the 1960s. This took place when the restrictive policy of migration held by the Trujillo dictatorship was eliminated. The Cuban emigration had two great periods: during the sixties, as a result of the triumph of the Revolution and in the eighties with the opening of Mariel's harbor. Pedraza (1998) adds another period during the first years of the present decade when people escaped from the economic crisis (período especial).

Migratory statistics demonstrate that in different periods of time, a greater number of women from Puerto Rico and the Dominican Republic left their native countries. That was the case in the forties when female workers in the Puerto Rican manufacturing sector were recruited to work in New York. Recent statistics show more Dominican women than men living in the U.S.: 302,000 (59%) of a total 515,000 among female immigrants born in Dominican Republic; and 398,000 (52% of

772,000) for female immigrants born in Cuba (U.S. Bureau of the Census, 1997). Those figures do not imply that there are more women than men migrating to the U.S. However, Dominican immigrants in the United States tend to be female; that is, sixty percent of all immigrants are women (Hernandez & Rivera-Batiz, 1997). The most recent statistics for Puerto Ricans in the United States numbers 3,117,000 (U.S. Bureau of the Census, 1999) but sex distribution was not included.

Another aspect of the U.S. Cuban population in the U.S. is related to the migration policy. Rodriguez, (1997) states that since 1959, the United States migratory policy and legislation has encouraged, given privileges and politicized the exit of people from Cuba and their insertion in North American society. By the end of the sixties, the U.S. had allowed more than 14,000 children to enter the country without their parents ostensibly "to save them from communism"; and in 1966 a law was approved that normalized the legal condition of more than half a million Cubans as political refugees (Rodriguez, 1997). However, since 1994, Cubans are not allowed as refugees and they can only get Visas from the Interest Section of the United States in La Havana (Rodríguez, 1997).

Family continues to be the most important value for Latin American women. Latino family literature is framed by discussions of *familism*, the behavioral manifestations reflect strong emotional and value commitments to family life (Vega, 1995). A different point of view of the Latino family emerges from gender-role research that compares professed values about gender roles with the actual contexts of social behavior and functional relationships. In these studies gender role expectations are fluid, responsive to changing family structure and economic demands (Vega, 1995). However, these studies do not conduct an in-depth analysis of the differences between the professed values and the actual behavior of these women. Other research has demonstrated the importance of home for women's identities and as the place where resistance is created against injustices and oppression; and how Dominican women bring the values and roles associated with home to the place of migration (Pessar, 1985; 1986).

Caribbean women generally emigrate to the U.S. for economic reasons. Ortiz (1996) argues that Puerto Rican women's priority is to survive, with little space to explore their dreams and capacities. It can be added that housework is another limitation for their development. Many of the Caribbean women started in the garment industry. Sassen-Koob (1981) notes the following reasons for the concentration of Hispanic women in this sector: first, the job does not require knowledge of English;

second, many migrants have sewing skills needed for the garment industry; and third, the fact that salaries are lower than other industries reduces the competition with Anglo women who require higher salaries.

METHODOLOGY

A qualitative research design is used to describe and understand the life experiences of Spanish speaking Caribbean women living in urban areas of New York and New Jersey. This design is appropriate to conduct in-depth interviews with a small sample. The "snowball" sampling procedure was used to allow identification of women that met the study criteria. Sample criteria for inclusion were: residing in United States for a minimum of ten years, born and raised in Latin American and having at least one child. The majority of women identified were from Puerto Rico and the Dominican Republic, which is consistent with migration information for these states.

A life-history instrument guide consisting of sixty-three open-ended questions was developed in several sessions with the interviewers and revised by an anthropologist in the Department of Puerto Rican and Hispanic Caribbean Studies, and the author. Questions were selected to allow participants to express themselves in their own words. The guide included nineteen questions related to the migration process such as: reasons for leaving their countries, information they had about the United States, their expectations, arrival, experiences in the host country, and plans for returning or staying in the U.S. Eight questions were about salaried employment, including their job history, meaning of work, and sources of income. Participants were also asked about family and housework (18 questions), including their typical day, similarities and differences in the way they were raised and the way they are raising their children. Five questions were dedicated to participation in community organizations; and thirteen to the subjectivity of women. This last part includes their views about sexuality, fidelity in marriage, achievements of women in the U.S. and in their countries of origin, and their satisfaction with being a woman. At the end of the questionnaire, an opportunity was given for the respondents to express any advice they might want to share with other Latinas.

Students, primarily Latinas from Rutgers University, were trained to collect life histories from the study participants, in the Spring of 1997. The interviews were audio-taped and transcribed to create a data base. The narrations of twenty-three women, eleven from Puerto Rico, eight from the

Dominican Republic, and four from Cuba, were analyzed. Demographic characteristics of the women selected for the analysis are as follow: The women ranged in age from 28 to 79 years, with the majority in the 40 to 50 years of age category. They resided in the U.S. anywhere from 10 to 33 years with more than half reporting having had between 17 to 27 years residency in cities of New York and New Jersey. Educational attainment varied from elementary schooling to post-graduate degrees. Fourteen of the respondents indicated having attained some years of college including five of them with completed master's degrees. Only two women were on welfare, the others had steady jobs. The majority of the participants (19) were married while two were separated and two divorced. The median number of children was two, and only one woman reported having four children. Despite these similarities, none of the three groups of women were homogeneous and the results of the study should be generalized.

FINDINGS AND DISCUSSION

Migration Experiences

The city of New York has been the primary settlement area for the Dominican and Puerto Rican groups, while Cubans have preferred Miami. Hernandez and Rivera-Batiz (1997) stated that the Dominican population is the second-largest Hispanic group in New York City, after Puerto Ricans, and that close to sixty-percent of the Dominicans in the United States reside in this city. The principal settlement area is Washington Heights in Manhattan, and in northern Queens (Gilbertson, 1995). Besides Miami, there is a Cuban community in the state of New Jersey, and some life histories were collected there.

Dominican women expressed that migration laws were not as rigorous as at the present time. One of them commented:

> When my oldest sister, my mother and myself obtained Visas, we took an airplane and the first stop was Puerto Rico. We went to migration and at that time we got the green card immediately. Later the card arrived by mail and now people get a temporary card and two years later you get the permanent one, if all your documents are O.K.

Cuban women have been helped by strong organizations in Miami such as Casa de la Libertad (House of Freedom). One of them, a "marielitos" reported:

I arrived in the U.S. on a coast guard boat that rescued me and two other men from a raft that we had been on for about a week. I can't understand why I didn't drown that night when it stormed. As soon as I arrived at the coast guard headquarters I was pushed in and out of rooms and looked at by doctors as if I was an animal. I had not just gone through hell and back to be put in a camp that resembled a concentration camp.

My husband, who was already in the United States, and groups such as Casa de la Libertad helped me get out and get my papers. As soon as I could I took a plane to Newark and began my new life with my husband in Jersey City.

It is interesting to learn about help offers, especially from organizations in the Miami Cuban community. These organizations help newly arrived people to find their families, jobs, housing and legal papers. One of the study participants indicated that she belongs to a New Jersey organization called "Bridging the Gap" that helps Cubans to learn English and offers them legal orientation to complete the papers for residence and citizenship.

On the other hand, Puerto Ricans do not confront migration problems because United States citizenship was imposed in 1917, allowing them to travel freely to any state. However, citizenship has not ameliorated experiences of discrimination and racism in the United States. Even more, in these communities there is a high percentage of families living below the poverty levels; 185,631(29.6%) of Puerto Rican families and 16,559 (37.4%) of Dominican families (U.S. Department of Commerce, 1990). For Cubans, the percentage was as low as 8.6 percent (8,145) before 1980 but between 1980 and 1990 the amount increased to 12,426 (23.2%). Possible explanations are the composition of the population that emigrated in the eighties (marielitos) and the different treatment of these migrants.

The decision to migrate to the United States is usually made by men, mainly in their roles of fathers or husbands as well as the decision to return to their home countries. Women remembered that their fathers or husbands emigrated for economic reasons. Salgado de Snyder (1996) found in a study of international migration that it was common for Mexican women and young children to migrate forced by the head of the family (father and husband). All of the women interviewed had relatives living in the United States when they left their countries. The father or husband usually traveled first helped by those relatives and slowly the rest of the nuclear family. Only one of the Puerto Rican interviewees emigrated to study for a career because that had always been her goal. Her parents allowed her to go to the United States because they knew somebody (i.e., a relative or family friend), who could watch over her.

The lack of knowledge, high expectations or mythical thinking about the place of migration was frequent. Migrants tend to think that life will be easier for them. A woman who emigrated to the United States from the rural zone of the Dominican Republic in 1980 said:

> I believed that everything was going to be better, that here I was going to be wealthy and have everything. I saw people coming from here and at least they wore good clothes and I thought that things were going to be better. My husband traveled first and then he sent for me. When I arrived it was a great happiness. But after a week in New York, I wanted to go back . . .

Another Dominican who emigrated to work when she was eighteen thought that the "United States was beautiful and you can only see white people"; while one who emigrated when she was fifteen believed that "in the United States there were opportunities for everybody." A Cuban that emigrated in the 1980s commented:

> I thought that everyone was going to be nice and that I was going to be told that I was safe. I believed in the U.S. I was going to be free . . . .

Even Puerto Ricans with a longer history of emigration to the United States, do not have all the information. This was more evident in women who emigrated before the seventies. A Puerto Rican who emigrated in 1962 comments:

> I expected the roads to be gold. I thought that we were coming to the wealthiest and richest place in the world. I thought I was going to live in a castle. I pictured a perfect world with kind and perfect people.

Another aspect mentioned by the interviewees was the environment of the cities which they migrated too, especially New York City. These women came from different towns and cities of Puerto Rico, the Dominican Republic, and Cuba, where the weather and life styles were completely different. This is true, even in the capitals of these countries: San Juan, Santo Domingo, and La Havana. It was common to hear the women complain about darkness and closed doors in the buildings of the poor neighborhoods they live in. Such surroundings are a sharp contrast to the light and openness of some of even the poorest houses in many Caribbean towns.

One of the areas of great difficulty expressed by the women is the mastering of the English language. Even Puerto Ricans who study this English through the primary and secondary years of schooling, experience difficulties, particularly in understanding colloquial English. Learning the language does not always mean speaking without an accent. Several of the interviewees reported having negative experiences, such as the Puerto Ricans who expressed:

> Well, as you can see, I have a heavy accent. That has limited me the most. I had to fight to be the supervisor because they were going to give it to someone else who spoke English clearer and better.

Other women expressed that they did not learn to speak English because they live in areas where Spanish is spoken all the time, at the grocery stores, and for all kinds of services and recreation. It is when they have to visit government offices or resolve a legal or housing problem that they used their children as interpreters.

Some of immigrants return to their countries with the idea of staying, but they confront the same economic problems that initially forced them to go to the United States. A Dominican who emigrated with her two sisters when she was sixteen stated:

> I went again in 1990 with the intention of staying. I really did not want to ever come back here. But I never realized how bad were the social and economic conditions of the people there. Over here everybody has a refrigerator, TV, a car. All I wanted was to separate from my boyfriend. But he was desperate and he demonstrated that I was important to him. Then I returned.

Other Dominicans and Puerto Ricans dream of returning to their countries of origin after their children become adults and they themselves are eligible for retirement benefits. This idea is very clear in the following narration from a Dominican woman:

> When I get old, I will like to return to my country, stay there and die there. In this case my daughters will adapt and I will bring some money to start a business, any kind of business.

One Cuban woman dreams of returning to her native country when she says:

> I do think of returning to Cuba. I love my country a great deal. The U.S. has given me a lot but it is not the land of my birth and it is not where I want to die.

A Puerto Rican also expressed:

> I think that when my husband stops working I believe that the best place to be is Puerto Rico. You know, return to where you come from . . .

Although we observed the women's desire to return to their native countries associated with retirement, in the case of Dominicans, the average age of people who have returned is 36.8 years old (Guarnizo, 1995). Some life histories reflect that not all the women want to return, particularly the ones who had the opportunity of bringing the family to the United States and those who have obtained more independence. Related to this issue, Grasmuck and Pessar (1991) found that Dominican women enjoy more independence in New York and were less motivated than their husbands to return to the Dominican Republic. This new experience of independence often results in marital or partner separations, observed when husbands (or partners) return to the Dominican Republic and their wives decide to stay in New York.

Bueno (1995) also found that Dominican women who returned to their native country, considered the loss of rights and freedom previously unknown and obtained with migration. This includes, for example, a paid job and the independence to control their earned income, and the freedom for her daily activities. In both studies, the decision to migrate or to return to their native countries is reportedly made by the men. A Puerto Rican respondent, who was forced to return expressed:

> When my oldest daughter married, my husband wanted to return to Puerto Rico. That was the greatest sacrifice I ever made, completely against my wishes. I did not want to leave my son who was

> in college. Ah, also I have friends, but I had to follow him, and
> once there I was sad. . . .

She was so unhappy, that when she became a widow, she returned to
New Jersey. In contrast, one respondent wants to relocate to Puerto
Rico after they retire but her husband does not agree.

Family and Gender Roles

Motherhood continues to be seen as a fundamental activity for
women and the most important factor in defining the female gender in
Hispanic Caribbean societies. In Puerto Rico, women continue to celebrate motherhood and family life, and therefore may subconsciously re-
fuse to acknowledge their own subordination (Perez-Herrans, 1996).
Dominican women in the United States also value maternity. Besides
the family, other socializing institutions such as the education system,
church, and the mass media praise women as mothers while criticizing
or censoring those not conforming with the traditional maternal role.
None of these institutions however, value motherhood for the power it
gives women who are responsible for bringing new life to society.

The data shows that there is a tendency to consider family as those
that live under the same roof, usually the nuclear family. However, this
does not mean that extended family members are excluded. Respondents mentioned the constant communication with their extended families, mainly by phone and visits to them. This pattern of communication
is present even among Cubans with ideologies different from those who
did not emigrate, as shown in the following narration:

> We are a very close family. Even now with the ideology, some mem-
> bers agree with Castro and we don't, but when we talk on the phone
> Castro is not even mentioned. So I think that we will grow old together.

Several women reported that they teach domestic chores to both
daughters and sons, because they have paid jobs or they want their children to become independent. One Dominican woman understands that
the situation in the United States is different:

> Here you must teach them to be more independent because the sys-
> tem is more complicated. Children depend completely on their
> parents. Here they learn to be more independent in order to be-
> come able to deal with a fast daily lifestyle.

Others indicate equality between their husbands and themselves in the division of housework. One Puerto Rican admitted that she did not like house chores. Nevertheless, housework is the responsibility of mothers and wives with some contribution from children and very little from husbands. Pessar (1995) refers to the control Dominican women want to maintain when they do not share housework equally, even the ones who work outside the house. However, Pessar (1995) reports that when women contribute half or more of the family income, family members participate more in housework. Data demonstrated the efficiency in the distribution of time, particularly among the women who also work outside the home.

Marriage has a great value for the respondents, despite the actual frequency of divorce. Even today's women in the Dominican Republic prefer that their children marry well and do not have to get a divorce. Pessar (1995) indicates that for Dominican families in the United States, marriage is a symbol of stability and middle class status, in contrast to female-headed families that are usually poor and low class. However, statistics show that forty-nine percent of the Dominican population in New York City live in female-headed, single-parent households without the presence of a husband, in contrast to forty-one percent of the total Hispanic population (Hernandez & Rivera-Batiz, 1997). Similar statistics are reported among Puerto Ricans in New York: forty-three percent live in households headed by a woman (US Department of Commerce, 1990).

Resistance to the hostile environment is present among Caribbean women. They have a crucial role in the preservation of the traditions and family ties. We can observe their leading role in maintaining cultural traditions and a united family at a distance. Guarnizo (1995) argues that the impressive level of spatial atomization in the United States and the Dominican Republic does not mean that families are broken or in the process of dissolution. Rather, they are experiencing the emergence of a transnational family that is representative of the adaptation process of contemporary migrants. Likewise, when a Caribbean woman marries a North American man it does not mean that she will give up her culture. This is reflected in the following narrative of a Cuban woman:

> I teach my sons my nationality, my roots, my language, my culture always, despite being married to a North American.

Some changes in the socialization patterns were observed among the women interviewed. They learned that marrying well was a priority in their lives while teaching their daughters differently. Respondents told their daughters to obtain a profession first and then think about marriage. It is interesting to note the importance given to education, especially college degrees. Another observed attitudinal change involved sexuality and the value placed on virginity. Related to the issue of sexuality, a Dominican mother stated:

> I prefer to talk with my daughter when the time is appropriate and explain what she should do. I will tell her: I would not like you to do it because it is not right. But if you decide to do it, you must protect yourself against a pregnancy or an illness.

Likewise, a Puerto Rican mother expressed:

> I think one has to be mature, in this time of AIDS and everything else. If you protect yourself, it is your body and your life if you know what you are doing and you are prepared, then OK . . . I was like that but not my mother!

A Cuban mother commented:

> I don't judge them because the times have changed. I would just say to them to be sure that's what you want. The way I see sex is something so beautiful, you give yourself completely, there is nothing hidden. I don't see any problem with it as long as even if they are not married they decide to stay together.

These expressions clearly demonstrate changes in the way these women were raised and what they teach their children. Some of them learned that the first man who they bring home must be their future husband.

Another topic presented mainly by Dominican women was the "machismo" of Dominican men, observed more among those who live in the Dominican Republic than the ones living in the United States. Among the Puerto Ricans and Cubans, there exists a greater number of less traditional marriages, such as a Puerto Rican who studied for a masters degree in Puerto Rico while her husband took care of the home and children in New York. Another one considers her husband and herself as a team in the distribution of housework and economic responsibilities, and a Cuban who indicates that she is free and her husband does not interfere with her freedom. Nevertheless, the husbands of the two Puerto Ricans were born and raised in New York. Their parents were born in Puerto Rico but had also lived in New York City for many years. The Cuban respondent is married to a North American. We do not have a scale to measure levels of "machismo" or to test whether one country is more "machista" (masculine oriented) than another one. It is only fair to observe the presence of "machismo" in some homes while other relationships are more egalitarian. Nor can we assume that less traditional couples will stay that way if they relocate to Puerto Rico. Although there is legislation that promotes equality among Cuban families in Cuba, we do not know if family relations inside the home have changed.

Paid Work in the United States

The majority of Dominican women came to the United States as adolescents. They did not have work experience outside the home but knew how to do housework and some of them knew how to sew. Some of them stayed in service occupations but others were able to study and get business or professional jobs. Puerto Ricans also arrived in the United States at a young age with only a high school education and their work experience had been in the manufacturing sector. Cubans also arrived very young, and although they were members of higher socioeconomic classes, they also worked in manufacturing. Later they moved on to clerical and professional positions.

As expected, the definition of work given by respondents was the activity a person does for money. For example, a Dominican woman said that work is what she did in manufacturing. However, another Dominican expressed: "both are work, at home is a non-paid job and outside the home is more work." A Puerto Rican went on to say that she considers work as everything that a person must do that is not recreation. A Cuban commented, "work is any activity where you use your skills and dedicate time to achieve a goal." For Cuban women a job is vital not only for survival, but also for the upward mobility of the family (Prieto, 1992). No matter what jobs women hold, it gives them more autonomy, particularly among Latinas (Safa, 1995). Regardless of the amount of money, a salary is a symbol of recognition for a job done. On the contrary, women do not receive anything for housework, not even a thank you.

The majority of the women interviewed were married and employed. Similar to the findings of Gurak and Kritz (1996), in New York, employment is a hallmark of more stable marital unions for Dominican, Colombian and Puerto Rican women. Dominican women residing in New York with children and no spouse present are less likely to be employed than are either women who have spouses or no children while the opposite pattern holds in the Dominican Republic, where women living in households with the spouse present are least likely to be employed (Gurak & Kritz, 1996). However, many Latin American countries do not provide social welfare assistance for families of mothers and children. Their cultural patterns emphasize that married women should be homemakers and husbands the breadwinners.

Many Puerto Rican women initiated their work history in the garment industry. The influx of new immigrant female workers, predominantly from Cuba, Haiti, Dominican Republic, and Southeast Asia, were forced by a variety of circumstances to accept wages far below those set by federal law or union contracts. This resulted in job competition for Puerto Rican women as well as deteriorating work conditions, and declining wages (Ortiz, 1996). Likewise, the aggregation of "firms" of any size which are owned and managed by members of an identifiable cultural and national minority called the enclave, do not benefit Hispanic women the same way as it does Hispanic men in New York City. Moreover, many ethnic jobs provide women with very low wages, minimal benefits, and few opportunities for advancement (Gilbertson, 1995).

Puerto Rican and Dominican women show a work history and use welfare only when they don't have other alternatives. The two respondents who received economic assistance and medical services, prefer to have a job. One suffered a back injury in her previous job and the other could only find a low paying job. Candelario and Lopez (1995) argue that Dominican women are forced to apply for welfare when jobs available to them do not provide economic support for their children. In a similar study, Torruellas, Benmayor, and Juarbe (1996) demonstrate that Puerto Rican women considered motherhood and family as their primary responsibility, and received welfare support as a survival strategy in the United States. In the case of the Cubans interviewed, they were all employed. The studies reviewed for this article did not mention any use of welfare. However, the Cuban women who had refugee status received economic assistance and other kinds of benefits. It is possible that organizations assisting them upon arrival in the mainland have been effective in helping them find good jobs and other services.

CONCLUSION AND IMPLICATIONS

The main reason for emigration of Dominicans and Puerto Ricans is primarily an economic one, and to a certain extent similar for Cubans, although they also indicated political reasons for their immigration. The process of migration to the United States is similar for Dominicans and Puerto Ricans for three reasons: first, they receive distorted information prior to the trip; second, the tendency to settle in New York City; and third, the socio-economic conditions they confront in the new environment. For Cubans, it is somewhat different because they enjoyed privileges via a favorable U.S. migratory policy. However, Puerto Ricans, contrary to the other Latinos, have U.S. citizenship, which allows them to travel back-and-forth between the island and the mainland without restrictions.

It is possible to infer from existing statistics, that reports of high birth rates among young Dominican and Puerto Rican population, represent a future significant demographic increase of these groups in the United States. Landale and Ogena, (1995) point out that Latinos are expected to become the nations' largest ethnic minority within the next several decades. Nevertheless, there are some emigration changes that might reduce this increase. For instance, the new immigration laws may limit the entrance of Dominicans to the United States and Cubans have lost privileges from the migration authorities. On the other hand, among Puerto Ricans, the change is related more to the type of migrants. Recently, Puerto Rican migrants are composed of more skilled and technical workers, which some scholars referred too as a loss of human capital for the island (Santiago & Rivera-Batiz, 1997).

Family, especially motherhood, continues to be a fundamental value for the three groups of women. The changes discussed previously come from the contact with other cultures and the adaptations they make to survive in the new environment. Two important changes are the incorporation of women in the labor force and their more liberal views in the socialization of their daughters. Although the incorporation to the labor force has brought Caribbean women greater autonomy, it has also created some problems. These women need to deal with family and paid work while often confronting discrimination and a lack of opportunities for socioeconomic improvement.

Dominican women who shared their life histories consider that life conditions for women are better in the United States than those existing in their country. They expressed that women in the Dominican Republic occupy a lower status in relationship to their men. Pessar (1995) refers to paid work and living in the United States as important factors for success in changing traditional relationships. Landale and Ogena (1995) argue further that, Puerto Rican women living in the U.S. have markedly higher rates of family (i.e., marital or partner relationship) disruptions than those with no experiences in the mainland. They also note that the relatively high rates of family instability among first and second-generation U.S. residents and returned migrants is strongly related to recent and lifetime experiences.

This discussion leads us to point out that beyond future migratory movements, we must recognize the existence of a Dominican, Cuban and Puerto Rican community in the United States with significant problems, but a community which also contributes a great deal to the United States. Professions in the field of human services must listen to the voices of Hispanic Caribbean women in order to become aware of their needs, aspirations and their sense of identity. Services should be flexible, comprehensive and sensitive to their culture. The cultural understanding will help in the identification of protective mechanisms used in risk situations. For instance, the cultural pride mentioned by respondents, is a protective mechanism in dealing with some daily problems. Furthermore, the identification of natural support systems such as family, friends, neighbors, folk healers that can be partners in the provision of services and in coping successfully.

More attention should be given to the socialization process of Caribbean women. The value of maternity and familism must be taken into consideration in any intervention. Relationships with the family that stayed in their country of origin must be understood, not only for the affective ties but also for the economic contributions sent to them. Contacts among these families mean a lot of traveling, particularly among Dominicans and Puerto Ricans; and other forms of communication by telephone and mail.

More research is necessary in understanding the role of Latinas, not only in the migratory process, but also in community life and society. Other topics that deserve further study include: how children of migrants who stay with their grandparents are raised; the resistance or vulnerability of single-mother, head of households; networks developed in Latino communities; the role of religion in dealing with adversity; the importance of informal support systems; the interaction of gender, race, and class in Hispanic communities; cultural practices, and the impact of changing gender roles. The next phase of this qualitative research will focus on a group of Dominican women residing in Puerto Rico using similar variables as the ones used for the study presented in this article.

REFERENCES

Bueno, L. (1995). Experiencias de migración de retorno de mujeres dominicanas: Historias de vida de cinco mujeres. *Género y Sociedad*, 2, 1-52.

Candelario, G. & Lopez, N. (1995). The latest edition of the welfare queen story: An analysis of the role of Dominican immigrants in the New York City political and economical culture. *Phoebe*, 7, 7-21.

Georges, E. (1992). Gender, class, and migration in the Dominican Republic: Women's experiences in a transnational community. In N. G. Schiller, L. Basch, & C. Blanc Szanton (Eds.), *Towards a transnational perspective on migration.* New York: The New York Academy of Sciences.

Gilbertson, G. A. (1995). Women' Labor and enclave employment: The Case of Dominican and Colombian women in New York City. *International Migration Review*, XXIX, 657-670.

Grasmuck, S. & Pessar, P. (1991). *Between two islands: Dominican international migration.* Berkeley University of California Press.

Guamizo, L. E. (1995). Regresando a casa: clase, género y transformacion del hogar entre migrantes dominicanos/as retornados/as. *Género y Sociedad*, 2, 53-127.

Gurak, D. T. & Kritz, M. M. (1996). Social context, household composition and employment among migrant and nonmigrant Dominican women. International Migration Review, XXX, 399-422.

Hernández, R. & Rivera-Batiz, F. (1997). Dominican New Yorkers: A socioeconomic Profile, 1997. New York: The CUNY Dominicans Studies Institute.

Kritz, M. M. (1983). International migration patterns in the Caribbean Basin: An overview. In M. M. Kritz, C. B. Keely, & S. M. Tomasi, *Global trends in migration: Theory and research on international population movements.* New York: Center for Migration Studies.

Landale, N. S. & Ogena, N. B. (1995). Migration and union dissolution among Puerto Rican women. *International Migration Review*, XXIX, 671-690.

Linares, G. (1989). Dominicans in New York. *Centro Bulletin*, II, 77-84.

Martínez-San Miguel, Y. (1998). De ilegales a indocumentados: Representaciones culturales de Ia migarcion dominicana en Puerto Rico. *Revista de Ciencias Sociales*, 4, 147-171 (enero).

Ortiz, A. (Ed.). (1996). *Puerto Rican women and work: Bridges in transnational labor.* Philadelphia: Temple University Press.

Ortiz, V. (1995). Migration and marriage among Puerto Rican women. *International Migration Review*, 30, 460-484.

Pedraza, S. (1998). Cuba's revolution and exile: Manifold migrations. *Cumbre Caribeña Caribbean Summit '98.* Rio Piedras, P.R.: Universidad de Puerto Rico, Facultad de Educacion, 8-9, Octubre.

Pérez-Herranz, C. A. (1996). One two full-time jobs: Women garment workers balance factory and domestic demands in Puerto Rico. In A. Ortiz (Ed.), *Puerto Rican women and work: Bridges in transnational labor.* Philadelphia: Temple University Press.

Pessar, P. (1995). En el hogar y en el trabajo: Integracion de 1a mujer inmigrante al discurso feminista. *Género y Sociedad*, 2, 128-161.

Pessar, P. (1986). The role of gender in Dominican settlement in the United States. In J. Nash and H. Safa (Eds.), *Women and change in Latin America.* Massachussetts: Bergin & Garvey.

Prieto, Y. (1992). Cuban women in New Jersey: Gender relations and change. In D. R. Gabaccia (Ed.), Seeking common ground: Multidisciplinary studies of immigrant women in the United States. Westport, CT: Praeger.

Rodríguez, C. E. (1997). El flujo migratorio Cubano, 1985-1996: Balance y perspectivas. *Revista de Ciencias Sociales*, Nueva Epoca, 3, 37-81.

Safa, H. I (1995). *The myth of the male breadwinner: Women and industrialization in the Caribbean.* Colorado: Westview.

Salgado de Snyder, V. N. (1996). Problemas psicosociales de la migración internacional. *Salud Mental*, 19, 53-59.

Santiago, C. E. & Rivera-Batiz, F. (1997). La migración de los puertorriquenos durante la década de 1980. *Revista de Ciencias Sociales*, Nueva Epoca, 1, 178-206.

Sassen-Koob, S. (1981). Exporting capital and importing labor: The role of women. In D. M. Mortimer & R. S. Bryce-Laporte (Eds.), *Female immigrants to the United States: Caribbean, Latin American, and African experiences.* Washington, D.C.: Research Institute on Immigration and Ethnic Studies.

Torruellas, R. M., Benmayor, R., & Juarbe, A. (1996). Negotiating gender, work and welfare: Familia as productive labor among Puerto Rican women in New York City. In A. Ortiz, *Puerto Rican women and work.* Philadelphia: Temple University.

U.S. Bureau of the Census. (1999). *Statistical Abstracts of the United States*; Washington, DC: U.S. Government Printing Office.

U.S. Bureau of the Census (1997). *Selected Characteristics of Foreign Born Population by Citizenship and Selected Countries of Birth*; Washington, DC: U. S. Government Printing Office.

Vega, W. A. (1995). The study of Latino families: A point of departure. In R. E. Zambrana (Ed.), *Understanding Latino families.* Thousand Oaks, CA: Sage.

Another Kind of Rainbow Politics

Maria Vidal de Haymes
Keith M. Kilty
Stephen N. Haymes

SUMMARY. Race has been a particularly troublesome concept in the United States. It is especially problematic as it is applied to Latinos. While several perspectives are presented to examine race, race relations, and racial dynamics regarding Latinos in the U.S., this essay primarily relies on Omi and Winant's racial formation theory as a means for understanding the position of Latinos in the racial hierarchy of the United States. The authors argue that the experience of Latinos in the U.S. has taken place within a "racial" context, and as a result, have been involved in a racialization process throughout their history in this country. More specifically, the authors identify several contradictory racial projects that have shaped our current views of Latinos as a "racial group": Latinos as a panethnic group, a rainbow race and a race towards whiteness. These Latino racial projects are discussed within a racial formation framework. Furthermore, the role that

---

Maria Vidal de Haymes, PhD, MSW, is Associate Professor in the School of Social Work, Loyola University in Chicago.

Keith M. Kilty, PhD, is Professor in the College of Social Work, Ohio State University in Columbus.

Stephen N. Haymes, PhD, is Associate Professor of Education, DePaul University in Chicago.

[Haworth co-indexing entry note]: "Another Kind of Rainbow Politics." Vidal de Haymes, Maria, Keith M. Kilty, and Stephen N. Haymes. Co-published simultaneously in *Journal of Human Behavior in the Social Environment* (The Haworth Social Work Practice Press, an imprint of The Haworth Press, Inc.) Vol. 5, No. 3/4, 2002, pp. 175-188; and: *Latino/Hispanic Liaisons and Visions for Human Behavior in the Social Environment* (ed: José B. Torres, and Felix G. Rivera) The Haworth Social Work Practice Press, an imprint of The Haworth Press, Inc., 2002, pp. 175-188. Single or multiple copies of this article are available for a fee from The Haworth Document Delivery Service [1-800-HAWORTH, 9:00 a.m. - 5:00 p.m. (EST). E-mail address: getinfo@haworthpressinc.com].

175

the state plays in shaping the contours of race relations regarding Latinos is examined. *[Article copies available for a fee from The Haworth Document Delivery Service: 1-800-HAWORTH. E-mail address: <getinfo@haworthpressinc.com> Website: <http://www.HaworthPress.com> © 2002 by The Haworth Press, Inc. All rights reserved.]*

KEYWORDS. Race, identity, Latinos

INTRODUCTION

I can't check a circle that labels me black, white, Asian, or American Indian, because I'm not any of those things. . . . My sister and I have the same parents, but she's much darker than me. If it came down to choosing black or white, I'd have to choose white and she couldn't. That wouldn't make any sense. (Ada Nurie Pagan in Sandor, 1998)

The quote above captures the confusion that many Latinos face as they try to respond to the current definitions of race and ethnicity used by the Census Bureau. The Census Bureau defines race and ethnicity as two different demographic characteristics and has separate questions for each on its survey forms. This distinction dates back to the 1978 adoption of the Statistical Directive 15 by the Office of Management and Budget (OMB). The Directive created four official racial categories to be utilized by all federal agencies: American Indian or Alaskan Native, Asian or Pacific Islander, black, and white (Sandor, 1998).

The 1990 census questionnaire had two separate items, one asking respondent to report their race using the four official categories and a second item asking them to indicate their "ethnicity." Nearly ten million (9.8%) respondents could/would not classify themselves as American Indian or Alaskan Native, Asian or Pacific Islander, black, or white, so they checked the "other" category. Of those who checked the "other race" category, ninety-eight percent reported Hispanic origin on the ethnicity questionnaire. This number accounted for over forty percent of the twenty-two million Hispanics counted in the 1990 census, indicating a substantial resistance to the official racial categorization scheme (Sandor, 1998).

The Census 2000 has a similar two-question scheme. The first, asks if the respondent is Spanish/Hispanic/Latino and if the respondent answers yes, s/he is prompted to identify his/her ethnicity. The second question asks the respondent to identify his/her race from a list that offers the following choices: white, black/African American, American Indian/Alaskan Native, Asian Indian, Chinese, Filipino, Japanese, Korean, Vietnamese, Native Hawaiian, Guamanian or Chamorro, Samoan, or other Pacific Islander. The respondent is instructed that s/he may select one or more of these categories in answering the second question. This second question provides a confounding combination of racial, national, and ethnic terms under the category of "race." Rather than address the confusion/resistance elicited by the 1990 Census categorizations, the Census 2000 racial categorization scheme appears to further deepen the quandary about racial and ethnic configurations.

While some authors have questioned the current conceptualization of race in the United States, some question the utility of "race" as an analytical category as applied to the Latino question. In this paper, we will examine the concept of race as applied to analysis of the current situation of Latinos by contemporary scholars.

CONCEPTUALIZING RACE AND RACIAL GROUPS

Race is a complex and confusing notion. It has had different meanings from one society to another and from one historical era to another. It has been a particularly troublesome concept in the United States, continuing to raise controversy and adversity as a new century dawns. At the beginning of the twentieth century, W. E. B. DuBois identified the "problem of the colorline" as the defining problem of the century (Wilkins, 1996), while at the end William Julius Wilson (1980) made his reputation by declaring its "declining significance." A recent national bestseller, in fact, was titled *The End of Racism* (D'Souza, 1995), arguing that race no longer mattered and must be eliminated as an ingredient in public policy.

Yet race matters. It remains a powerful and divisive force in our society (Hacker, 1992). It may not be meaningful as a biological concept, but it certainly has social substance. As Schaefer (2000, p. 15) notes,

> In modern complex industrial societies, we find little adaptive utility in the presence or absence of prominent chins, epicanthic folds of the eyelids, or the comparative amount of melanin in the skin. What is important is not that people are genetically different but that they approach one another with dissimilar perspectives. It is in

the social setting that race is decisive. Race is significant because people have given it significance.

At the heart of the concept of race is inequality. Individuals occupy different positions in the social hierarchy, often on the basis of group characteristics. How individuals fit into the hierarchy directly affects their opportunities to compete for the valued resources in a society. In the contemporary U.S., an observer can readily perceive that racial status is expressed through patterns of behavior, which demonstrate that "different races rank unequally along several dimensions and that there are specific mechanisms for maintaining separateness and inequality among them" (Smedley, 1993, p. 21).

THE NATURE OF RACE

Since different groups have been recognized as "racial groups" in different places and at different times, it is important to examine how race becomes defined and accepted, both among the general public and the scientific community. Noel Ignatiev (1995, p. 1) illustrates this point in his book *How the Irish Became White*, in asking "how the Catholic Irish, an oppressed race in Ireland, became part of an oppressing race in America" and thus became white in a new land. This has led to further confusion about what exactly race is. Because of the fact that some immigrant groups to the U. S. were once identified as racial groups but are typically now identified as ethnic groups, some writers have now taken to using "ethnicity" interchangeably or in place of "race."

Smedley (1993, p. 15) maintains that race is a modern concept, originating in colonial expansion by Europeans: "Expansion, conquest, exploitation, and enslavement have characterized much of human history over the past five thousand years or so, but none of these events before the modern era resulted in the development of ideologies or social systems based on race." While racial and ethnic distinctions have existed for most, if not all, of human history, Smedley rejects the common assumption that racial classifications as they are expressed in Western societies are a universal human phenomenon. That idea also implies that racial categories are fluid and can be applied by powerful groups to virtually any group that they may wish to appropriate as a labor supply or eliminate as a barrier to the acquisition of territory. Before exploration throughout the Americas, Africa, and Asia, European colonialists practiced on their neighbors, including the Irish.

In the Americas, though, race took on certain defining characteristics, particularly after the development of plantation farming and slavery. While there were differences among the European colonial powers, Smedley (1993) argues that the most rigid and exclusionary of racial ideologies were developed by the English in North America. Skin color became the prime characteristic for defining different groups, particularly for distinguishing between African and European. This led to the "one drop rule" as the basis for the social construction of race in colonial America and the United States. That is, in this country, to be black means that one has any ascertainable trace whatsoever of "black blood" in one's family history (Schaefer, 2000). This is not merely a popular belief; it has had legal acceptance at least since the 1886 case of *Plessy v. Ferguson*:

> This case challenged the Jim Crow statute that required racially segregated seating on trains in interstate commerce in the state of Louisiana. The U.S. Supreme Court quickly dispensed with Plessy's contention that because he was only one-eighth Negro and could pass as white he was entitled to ride in the seats reserved for whites. Without ruling directly on the definition of a Negro, the Supreme Court briefly took what is called "judicial notice" of what it assumed to be common knowledge: that a Negro or black person is any person with any black ancestry. (Davis, 1991, p. 8)

As recently as 1983, the U.S. Supreme Court upheld the racial classification laws of the state of Louisiana (Omi & Winant, 1994).

Similar distinctions were made between white European colonialists and the indigenous population of Native American Indians. However, race consciousness was less critical here, since the Native American population was nearly destroyed by the end of the nineteenth century and had been steadily declining for centuries (Thornton, 1987).

PERSPECTIVES ON RACE

Omi and Winant (1994) identified four perspectives that social scientists have developed to explain race. The first is described as "ethnicity theory," the core of which is group identity. From this perspective, there are two competing pressures on ethnic groups: one of assimilation or merger with the dominant group and the other one of maintaining group identity. The second focuses on "class," and the core concept is inequality. Race, then, is seen as a critical element with regard to advantage and disadvantage in the social hierarchy, where discrimination is an outcome of the economic structure rather than a core element in the social structure. The third revolves around the concept of "nation," particularly the impact of colonial expansion of Europeans throughout the non-European world. Race was a means for colonialists to maintain their domination, and the resolution of racial difference and conflict is part of larger dynamics of national oppression and liberation. The fourth perspective is described as "racial formation."

According to Omi and Winant, the first three approaches to understanding race, race relations, and racial dynamics, do not stand alone. They overlap and help us to understand some aspects of racial matters. But they do not explain race. Instead, we need to take a sociohistorical approach that shows how racial categories are created and transformed. The racial formation approach argues that understanding race can be achieved only by treating it as a matter of both social structure and cultural representation where the two are linked together.

Omi and Winant's theory of racial formation presents race as a social construction. By this they mean that race is neither a fixed, concrete, objective reality, nor is it a pure illusion, fiction or ideological construct. They argue that it has elements of both in that race is "a concept which signifies and symbolizes social conflicts and interests by referring to different types of human bodies" (Omi & Winant, 1994, p. 55). From this vantage point, racial categories are created, lived, and transformed through a sociohistorical process of "racial projects" that ideologically link structure and cultural representation:

> *A racial project is simultaneously an interpretation, representation, or explanation of racial dynamics, and an effort to reorganize and redistribute resources along particular racial lines.* Racial projects connect what race *means* in a particular discursive practice and the ways in which both social structure and everyday experiences are racially organized, based upon that meaning. . . These projects are, of course, vastly different in scope and effect. They include large-scale public action, state activities, and interpretations of racial conditions in artistic, journalistic, or academic fora, as well as the seemingly infinite number of racial judgements and

practices we carry out at the level of individual experience. (Omi & Winant, 1994, p. 6, 60-61)

Within the racial formation perspective, Omi and Winant examine the role that the state plays in shaping the contours of race relations. From this viewpoint, government is seen as playing a substantial hand in setting the terms of race and inter/intra-racial relationships through the passage of legislation. Some explicit examples include the enactment of restrictive immigration policies, the setting of racial categories for the census, and voting district boundary determinations. Other government actions such as zoning, public school financing, and police deployment policies have less explicit consequences for the shaping of race relations.

THE CREATION OF LATINOS:
A PAN-ETHNIC RACIAL PROJECT

Winant (1994) asserts that the social category of "Latino" resulted from the racialization of the various Latin American ethnic groups in the U.S. context. Latin American groups with distinct identities, national origins, histories, cultures, and antagonisms were amalgamated into one group through a process of pan-ethnicity.

According to Lopez and Espiritu (1990, p. 198), pan-ethnicity replaces both "assimilation and ethnic particularism as the direction of change for racial/ethnic minorities." Pan-ethnic formations, argues Winant (1994), emanate from the dynamic relationship between the group being racialized and the state. The intellectual and political elite of the group strategically utilizes the numbers and resources that a pan-ethnic bloc can wield to make political demands, while the state benefits from recognizing and responding to a large bloc, rather than an unmanageable multitude of ethnic interest groups.

According to Munoz (1987, p. 36), the term Hispanic emerged in the corridors of the federal government in the 1970s after the decline of the Chicano Power Movement. For federal bureaucrats, it provided a convenient category to group all immigrants from Latin America and their descendants in the context of social welfare programs. For the five elected congressmen of Latin American origins (1 Puerto Rican and 4 Mexican-American), it provided a vehicle to promote coalition politics amongst their respective Spanish-speaking constituents, as well as aiding them in forming a caucus which elevated their power in the U.S. Congress.

Nevertheless, Lopez and Espiritu (1990) argue that pan-ethnic forma-tions are more than simple "alliances of convenience," they are associ-ated with the convergence of shared cultural and structural factors. For example, some of the cultural factors may include language and religion and structural factors can include class and geographic concentration. However, Lopez and Espiritu (1990, p. 219-220) conclude that, "those . . . groups that, from an outsider's point of view, are most racially homoge-neous are also the groups with the greatest pan-ethnic development." Thus race is seen as a central factor in the construction of pan-ethnicity.

While common structural and cultural factors are necessary for pan-ethnic formation, so is the minimization of or distraction from dif-ference. From the perspective of the dominant culture, these differences between national groups are often unknown and/or ignored. Munoz (1987) addresses the implications of this with regard to Latinos in the following quote.

> The major problem with the term (Latino/Hispanic] is that it ignores the complexities of a multitude of different cultural groups, each with its own special history, class realities, and experiences in the United States. It can be said that all may share the common denomi-nator of the Spanish language, but it cannot be said that all share the same position of racial and class inequality–and relatedly the same prospects for upward class mobility. (Munoz, 1987, p. 36)

LATINO RACIAL PROJECTS: RAINBOW RACE OR RACING TO WHITENESS

La Raza, the *cosmic race*, *mestizo, Creole* and the *rainbow race* are all terms that have been applied internally by Latinos to describe the ra-cial-hybridity that has characterized the people of Latin America. As an internal-racial project, the rainbow race has meant something different to Latinos than it has to white Americans. As an external racial project it has meant a non-white racialization process for Latinos in the U.S. Grosfoguel and Georas (1996, p. 195) address the latter in their discus-sion of the racialization of Caribbean Latinos immigrants in New York:

> Unable to place Puerto Ricans in a fixed racial category, either as white or black, due because of the mixed racial composition of the community, white Americans increasingly perceived them as a racialized Other. Puerto Ricans became a new racial subject, dif-ferent from whites and blacks, sharing with the latter a subordinate

position to whites. . . . In many instances the racism experienced by Afro-Puerto Ricans is no more profound than that experienced by lighter-skinned Puerto Ricans. However, no matter how "blonde or blue-eyed" a person may be, and no matter how successfully he can "pass" as white, the moment that person self-identifies as Puerto Rican, he enters the labyrinth of racial Otherness. Puerto Ricans of all colors have become a racialized group in the imagination of White Americans, whose racist stereotypes cause them to see Puerto Ricans as lazy, violent, stupid, and dirty. Although Puerto Ricans form a phenotypically variable group, they have become a new "race" in the United States.

In Latin America, the rainbow race construct has been part of a different racial project. According to Roman (1996, p. 9), it has historically been the official ideology and popular discourse that racism does not exist in Latin America, at least not in the virulent form associated with the United States. The great "racial" mixture of Indian, African, and Spaniard are said to have created a distinct "creole" or "mestizo" society in which the "cultural" takes precedence over the "racial." This society, unlike that of the United States, is characterized as a homogeneous whole, a nation of "rainbow people" free of racial preoccupations and racism. Any admission of racism is explained as a "vestige of slavery" or a more contemporary U.S. "import."

Roman (1996, p. 11) argues that what is most problematic about the prevailing Latino "rainbow people" construct is that it doesn't "allow for protest by those excluded because in theory there is no exclusion." Those claiming racial exclusion are positioned as "overly sensitive" or victims of an "alien racial ideology" or an "inferiority complex."

Roman (1996) offers a second, albeit related, racial ideology popular in Latin America: *mejoramiento de la raza* (improvement of the race). This ideology is based on a belief of white superiority and black inferiority. Based on Spanish colonial white supremacist ideas and fears of racial imbalance (blacks outnumbering whites) and black slave uprisings, interracial unions were encouraged. Promoters of this thought that the wide spread *mestizaje* resulting from such unions would eventually culminate in the elimination of *blacks*. Thus mestizaje was seen as a progression in a *race towards whiteness*, or in Roman's words: "From this perspective, mestizaje is only laudable–or even acceptable–as a transitional phase and not, as the *rainbow people* construct would seem to suggest, as an end in itself (1996, p. 10). Fusco (1995, p. 23-24), summarizes the convergence of these two ideologies in the following:

In the South, at least two centuries of ideological celebration of hybridity (the many discourses of *mestizaje*) often brings Latin American intellectuals to reject binary understandings of race. Latino cultural critics tend to insist on the historical difference of a more variegated racial classification system, claiming that class counts more than race, that Latinos have always had a higher rate of interracial unions and a progressive, nationalist, anticolonialist tradition, which is at least in theory, integrationist. Although it is true that the independence struggles and nationalist discourses of the Spanish Caribbean stipulated racial equality whereas the American Revolution did not, it is also true that no multiracial Latin American society has eliminated racial inequity. What is often left out of these equations are the similarities between northern and southern segregationist legislation, social practices, and economic hierarchies. What is also occluded is the political manipulation of hybridity, by Latin American official cultures in the nineteenth century, which encouraged miscegenation (without legitimate interracial marriage) as a strategy for diminishing the threat of black political power. Finally, in the twentieth century, this rhetoric has been used by both to mask the racialized economic disparities and to fuel the popular perception that blackness is something Latinos get rid of with socialization, miscegenation with whites, and hair straightener.

The Rainbow Race and U.S. Politics

In the context of the U.S., the in-betweeness of the rainbow race has been engaged in two contradictory ways as advanced by different political tendencies within the Latino leadership. The ambiguity regarding the question of race inherent in the rainbow race construct, when inserted in a binary understanding of race which characterizes the U.S., has created a situation in which Latinos can make claims at either end of the rainbow spectrum: white or black. In other words, two distinct racial projects have been advanced by Latino political elites, one racial project attempts to align Latinos more closely with whites, while the other attempts to do so with nonwhite groups.

In his analysis of Chicano politics, Munoz (1987) argues that middle class Mexican American political organizations, such as the League of United Latin American Citizens (LULAC), the Mexican American Political Association (MAPA) and the Political Alliance of Spanish Speaking Organizations (PASSO) have all pursued a politics of assimilation and accommodation, choosing to identify with whites in exchange for acceptance. More specifically, Munoz (1987, p. 39) asserts that while some groups have not rejected their Mexican culture, they have fostered a white identity outside of the Chicano community as a political strategy. In other words, pan-ethnic, rainbow race, cultural identity and solidarity is advanced internally while a white assimilationist strategy is advanced outwardly.

In contrast, Munoz argues that the Chicano Power Movement of the 1960's and 1970's attempted to "shape a politics of Chicano unification on the basis of nonwhite identity and working class interests." This movement had its beginnings in the farm workers struggle lead by Cezar Chavez and the Chicano student movement, which produced several organizations across the nation, such as MECHA, El Movimiento Estudiantil Chicano de Aztlan. Later, non-student youth groups such as the Brown-Berets and other community organizations formed to support the same political trend. This reformulation of Latino identity, in this case specifically Mexican American, directly challenged middle class Mexican-American, political organizations. While the aforementioned organizations such as LULAC and MAPPA sought incorporation into the dominant institutions, the central objectives of the Chicano Power Movement were a "quest for a non-white identity and the struggle for political and economic power through the development of independent Chicano institutions and community control over existing institutions" (Munoz 1987, p. 42).

More recent maneuvers around the *fixing* of census categories continue the exploitation of the racial ambivalence of Latinos for varied political projects. Goldberg identifies that major purpose of the census "has always been to manage effective resource distribution and voting access" and "these economic and political mandates in the United States have always been deeply racialized" (1995, p. 245). He also asserts that due to the racial hybridity of Latinos, their racial self-identification in the census is vulnerable to the changing interest of those who have the power to define the categories. As Latinos will soon become the largest *minority* group in the U.S., Goldberg argues, the political stakes are heightened in regard to which end of the *rainbow* spectrum Latinos will identify with in the census:

> One of the subtly silent ways remaining available to dilute blacks' voting rights, perhaps one of the only permissible alternatives now, is to set them against "other" statistically dominant "minori-

ties," minorities whose racial configurations are precisely ambiguous. Blacks are marked hegemonically as politically and socially liberal (and in the 1980s liberal came to be cast as literally un-American); Hispanics (and perhaps also Asian Americans) are often cast as socially (and perhaps economically) conservative . . . seventy-eight percent of black voters support the Democratic Party compared to 54 percent of the "Hispanic" voters, and only thirty-four percent of Whites. In the managed tensions between liberals and conservatives that characterize U.S. politics, the drive to bring Hispanics under the "right" wing is on. A social statistics that purports to report the truth may be party to the next big lie, the new racialized dynamics. This new dynamic of racialized fabrication may be fueled, paradoxically by the very instrument designed to democratize the social body count, namely, racial self-identification. (Goldberg 1995, p. 246)

A parallel tension between white vs. non-white identification has occurred among the Latino intellectual leadership. Here the discussion has vacillated between ethnic vs. racial frameworks for understanding the situation of Latinos in the U.S. Some theorists examining the Latino condition have advanced the ethnicity paradigm, which is based on the process of incorporation for white ethnic immigrants. Others have rejected ethnicity-based theories for a racial analysis of social relations, building on the theories advanced to explain the condition of non-whites in the United States (Darder and Torres, 1998).

Darder and Torres (1998) place these theoretical shifts in the context of larger social movements. They trace the resistance of Latino scholars to the use of "ethnicity" as a framework to analyze social relations to a rejection of assimilation theories. These theories, advanced to describe the process of European immigrant incorporation, were discarded in the 1960s by Latino scholars for a theory internal colonialism, cultural imperialism, and racism, aligning Latinos with African Americans in the social analysis and social movements of the times.

However, the theoretical landscape appears to be shifting again, as contemporary Latino scholars seem to be moving from a racial to an ethnic or cultural framework. For example, Darder and Torres (1998) call for a critical reconceptualization of the concept of ethnicity to understand the Latino experience. Yet others, such as Klor de Alva (1998), argue that culture and language, not race, are the relevant analytical categories for examining the encounters and incorporation of Latinos in the United States.

CONCLUSION

A racial formation approach appears to be a useful means for understanding the position of Latinos in the racial hierarchy of the U. S. Some analyses have conceptualized Latinos as an "ethnic group," but the American experience of Latinos has taken place within a "racial" context, and they have been involved in a racialization process throughout their history in this country. More specifically, several contradictory racial projects have shaped our current views of Latinos as a "racial group."

AUTHOR NOTE

Maria Vidal De Haymes, PhD, MSW, teaches courses in the areas of social welfare policy, community organizing, and multiculturalism. She has published research concerning Latino immigrants in the U.S, child welfare practice and policy, and social work education. Dr. Vidal de Haymes has served as a consultant to numerous local and state agencies and has served on the board of several Latin community-based organizations and state agency boards. She is a member of the Society for the Study of Social Problems, and the Latino Social Workers Association.

Keith M. Kitty, PhD, has published or presented more than 50 papers and is a member of the editorial board for the *Journal of Studies on Alcohol* and Assistant Editor for the *Journal of Drug Issues*. Dr. Kilty is a member of the Society for the Study of Social Problems and is currently Chair of its Division on Poverty, Class and Inequality. He is also a member of the National Steering Committee of the Social Welfare Action Alliance (formerly the Bertha Capen Reynolds Society) and Vice President of the Ohio State University Chapter of the American Association of University Professors.

Stephen N. Haymes, PhD, received a PhD in Education and Cultural Studies from Miami University at Oxford, Ohio. Professor Haymes is a Ford Post-doctoral Fellow and Scholar-in-Residence in the Education Department, Afro-American Studies Department and the Center for the Study of Race and Ethnicity in America at Brown University at Providence, Rhode Island. He is the author of the book *Race, Culture and the City: Pedagogy for Black Urban Struggle* which received a national award from the Gustavus Myers Center at Boston College for "The Outstanding Book on the Subject of Human Rights in North America." He has also written numerous essays on the politics and pedagogy of race, culture and education in the United States

REFERENCES

Darder, A. & Torres R. D. (1998). Latinos and society: Culture, politics, and class. In A. Darder & R. D. Torres (Eds.), *The Latino Studies reader: Culture, economy and society* (pp. 3-26). Malden, MA: Blackwell.

Davis, J. F. (1991). *Who is black?* University Park, PA: Pennsylvania State University Press. D'Sousa, D. (1995). *The end of racism.* New York: Free Press.

Fusco, C. (1995). *English is broken here: Notes on cultural fusion in the Americas.* New York: The New Press.

Goldberg, D. T. (1995). Made in the USA. In N. Zack (Ed.), *American mixed race: The culture of microdiversity* (pp. 237-256). Lanham, MA: Rowman & Littlefield.

Graham, R. (Ed.). (1997). *The idea of race in Latin America, 1870-1940.* Austin, TX: University of Texas Press.

Grosfoguel, R & Georas, C. (1996). The racialization of Latino Caribbean migrants in the New York metropolitan area. *Centro, 8,* 191-201.

Ignatiev, N. (1995). *How the Irish became white.* New York: Routledge.

James, W. (1996). Afro-Puerto Rican radicalism in the United States: Reflections on the political trajectories of Arturo Schomburg and Jesus Colon. *Centro, 8*(1/2), 92-127.

Klor de Alva, J., Shorris, E., & West, C. (1998).Our next question: The uneasiness between Blacks and Latinos. In A. Darder & R. D. Torres (Eds.), *The Latino Studies reader: Culture, economy, and society* (pp. 180-189). Malden, MA: Blackwell.

Lopez, D. & Esperitu, Y. (1990). Panethnicity in the United States: A theoretical framework. *Ethnic and Racial Studies, 13.*

Martinez, E. (1998). Seeing more than black and white: Latinos, racism, and the cultural divides. In M. Anderson & P. H. Collins (Eds.), *Race class and gender: An anthology* (3rd ed.) (pp. 112-119). New York: Wadsworth.

Munoz, Jr., C. (1987). Chicano politics: The current conjecture. In M. Davis, M. Marable, F. Pfeil, & M. Sprinker (Eds.), *The year left* 2: *An American socialist yearbook* (pp. 35-52). Stony Brook, NY. New Left Books.

Omi, M., & Winant, H. (1994). *Racial formation in the United States.* New York: Routledge.

Rodríguez-Morazzani, R. P. (1996). Beyond the rainbow: Mapping the discourse on Puerto Ricans and "race." *Centro, 8*(1/2), 128-149.

Román, M. J. (1996). Un hombre (negro) del pueblo: Jose Celso Barbosa and the Puerto Rican "race" toward whiteness. *Centro, 8*(1/2), 8-29.

Sandor, G. (1998). The "other" Americans. In M. Anderson & P.H. Collins (Eds.), *Race, class and gender: An anthology* (3rd ed.) (pp. 106-112). New York: Wadsworth.

Schaefer, R. T. (2000). *Racial and ethnic groups.* (8th ed.)Englewood Cliffs, NJ: Prentice Hall.

Smedley, A. (1993). *Race in North America.* Boulder, CO: Westview.

Thornton, R. (1987). *American Indian holocaust and survival: A population history since 1492.* Norman, OK: University of Oklahoma Press.

Wilkins, D. B. (1996). Introduction: The context of race. In K. A. Appiah & A. Gutman, *Color conscious. The political morality of race. Princeton, NJ: Princeton University Press, pp. 3-29.*

Wilson, W. J. (1980). *The declining significance of race. (2nd. ed.). Chicago: University of Chicago Press.*

Winant, H. (1994). *Racial conditions: Politics, theory, comparisons.* Minneapolis, MN: University of Minnesota Press.

Creating a Latino/Hispanic Alliance: Eliminating Barriers to Coalition Building

José B. Torres

SUMMARY. The author presents an overview of the significance that key cultural elements such as race, color, and language have on affecting coalition building between and among Latinos/Hispanics in the U.S. A discourse on a proposed paradigm for coalition building is also presented. *[Article copies available for a fee from The Haworth Document Delivery Service: 1-800-HAWORTH. E-mail address: <getinfo@haworthpressinc.com> Website: <http://www.HaworthPress.com> © 2002 by The Haworth Press, Inc. All rights reserved.]*

KEYWORDS. Latino/Hispanic, alliance, barriers, coalitions

INTRODUCTION

Almost four decades after the civil-rights movement directed Americans toward improving relations between blacks and whites, we ad-

José B. Torres, PhD, MSW, is Associate Professor of Social Welfare at the University of Wisconsin-Milwaukee, and is also Associate Scientist with the Center of Addictions and Behavioral Health Research at the UW-Milwaukee. He teaches courses that focus on direct social work practice, social work with multicultural populations, and social work supervision and consultation. His research interests and publications include multicultural mental health education and training, supervision of clinical training and practice, cultural aspects of gender roles, and domestic abuse. He is a certified marriage and family therapist, and an approved supervisor of the American Association for Marriage and Family Therapy.

[Haworth co-indexing entry note]: "Creating a Latino/Hispanic Alliance: Eliminating Barriers to Coalition Building." Torres, José B. Co-published simultaneously in *Journal of Human Behavior in the Social Environment* (The Haworth Social Work Practice Press, an imprint of The Haworth Press, Inc.) Vol. 5, No. 3/4, 2002, pp. 189-213; and: *Latino/Hispanic Liaisons and Visions for Human Behavior in the Social Environment* (ed: José B. Torres, and Felix G. Rivera) The Haworth Social Work Practice Press, an imprint of The Haworth Press, Inc., 2002, pp. 189-213. Single or multiple copies of this article are available for a fee from The Haworth Document Delivery Service [1-800-HAWORTH, 9:00 a.m. - 5:00 p.m. (EST). E-mail address: getinfo@ haworthpressinc.com].

vance into the 21st century amidst a variety of painful and embarrassing conflicts over race, ethnicity, and class. At the same time, we are entering the new millennium as our nation is once again being transformed by significant demographic changes. Across the United States, we are becoming a multiracial, multiethnic, and multicultural society. As diverse racial, ethnic, and cultural minority groups rapidly become a larger share of the U.S. population, national economic and political competition has intensified as different ethnic groups struggle for their equal share of scarce resources and an equal footing in the round table of access to opportunity. Latinos/Hispanics have not been immune to this phenomenon.

Efforts to challenge myths, erroneous stereotypes, and assumptions have introduced important cultural perspectives of Latino/Hispanic families and communities. Although traditional notions of Latinos/Hispanics, as "deviant, deficient, and disorganized" have been successfully challenged, important advances, notable problems, and limitations remain silent in the study of the more inclusive Latino/Hispanic context in the United States (Baca-Zinn & Wells, 2000).

In Wisconsin, we are just beginning to see and face the simple fact that relations between whites and Latinos/Hispanics are being mediated by interactions with other ethnic groups, including African Americans/Blacks. Though blacks remain the largest minority group in Wisconsin, local, state, and national census information indicate that whites in Milwaukee will soon be outnumbered by the aggregate of blacks, Latinos/Hispanics, Asians and other newly arrived immigrants. This projection reflects two national trends: *First,* racial and ethnic groups in the U.S. will outnumber whites for the first time, during the early part of the new millennium; *Second,* Latinos/Hispanics will become the nations' largest ethnic minority in the country, overtaking non-Latino/Hispanic blacks within the next decade. According to the U.S. Bureau of the Census (1999), the Latino/Hispanic population has grown by almost 32 percent since 1990, subsequent to a phenomenal 53 percent increase between 1980 and 1990. Latinos/Hispanics represent 11.7 percent (31.7 million) of the total U.S. population, growing at a rate of 53 percent faster than the total U.S. population. Should the Census Bureau projections prove to be accurate, the Latino/Hispanic population will account for 52 million persons (16.3%) of the total population by the year 2020, and will subsequently account for 97 million persons, nearly one-quarter of the population, by the year 2050 (U.S. Bureau of the Census, 1996).

In light of their projected growth and potential impact in the economic, political, and social life of American society, it is imperative that

Latinos/Hispanics begin the process of assessing the possibility of developing a common vision focused on their mutual well-being. An agenda for a shared goal to obtain the necessary resources and opportunities for emotional, physical, and economic survival would promote a sense of kinship, and reduce the friction and hostile relationships held by many Latinos/Hispanics towards each other prior and subsequent to coming to the United States (Ayala, 1999).

Working with groups from different ethnic groups isn't easy. Regardless of similarities of cultural norms, language, and religion, there is much we don't know or understand about each other. Not to be denied is the presence and need for greater understanding of how Latino/Hispanic subgroups experience discrimination, prejudice, and racism, within our own communities, a strong force that has promoted division amongst the different subgroups. To relieve discomfort, we often support stereotypes that may extend misinformation, based on ignorance of Latino/Hispanic life experiences and struggles for survival in the U.S. How can we work together, with all the differences-some subtle, some glaring-in the way we approach reaching a degree of unity to confront mutual problems? There is a need for Latinos/Hispanics to acknowledge and understand intra-group, as well as inter-group differences. Issues for understanding include, for example, cultural backgrounds, patterns of immigration, demographics, and language.

The following discussion focuses on some basic cultural background characteristics that can help Latinos/Hispanics maximize the possibilities for a constructive dialogue for the purpose of resolving the isolation and desperation to protect against the fear that their individual group voices (i.e., issues), will not be addressed in a unified voice. Although relevant to the Milwaukee community—where a common, shared experience remains elusive among its Latino/Hispanic population (predominantly Mexican American and Puerto Rican), this discussion examines the larger context of how we misunderstand each other as groups competing with each other. It is imperative that Latinos/Hispanics be educated about the similarities and differences between the different subgroups, but that each group also comprehend, with empathic understanding, the urgency to promote eradicating barriers which impinge on any efforts toward collective collaboration and coalition-building (Betances, 1993). However, caution must be exercised to avoid assuming or generalizing that a shared ethnic or cultural heritage among Latinos/Hispanics produces homogeneity of thought, feeling, or behavior, or even group loyalty (Cafferty & Engstrom, 2000). In fact, it is their distinct heritages, among other social and cultural dimensions, which influences their heterogeneous ethnic identity, and defies any validity to an existing "typical Latino/Hispanic" or "typical Latino/Hispanic family."

A LATINO/HISPANIC RAINBOW:
AN EMERGING AND EVOLVING POPULATION
IN THE UNITED STATES

Despite some moderate progress in socioeconomic and educational developments since the early 1960s, concerns remain high among Latinos/Hispanics, about enduring problems that have long plagued their communities. Some of these problems include poverty, high levels of unemployment, low levels of educations, poor housing, violence, crime, gangs, and poor health care. Understanding these conditions in Latino/Hispanic communities is often lost due to scholars inappropriately using incompatible data and erroneously characterizing Latino/Hispanic subgroups as a homogeneous entity.

Much of the literature on poverty among ethnic minorities is based on examining the experiences of poor African Americans living in large northwestern and midwestern communities. This has led to occasional angry and confusing discourses about American race and ethnic relations reflecting a history of blindly assuming that the only major axis of racial division in the United States is black-white. Such a dualistic and dichotomous racial perspective fails to account for the increased conflicts between whites and other non-white minority groups, such as Latinos/Hispanics, over political power, economic development, cultural autonomy, and ethnic identity (Gibbs, 1999; Torres, 2000). The outcome has been a lack of serious attention given to the relationship between the nation's two largest ethnic minority populations, African Americans and the Latino/Hispanic population in the context of the dominant white European American society. Although studies on Latinos/Hispanics, primarily focused Mexican Americans in the southwest have been addressed, there remains a paucity of data pertaining to the health and socially related conditions of Latinos/Hispanics in general, and particularly their increasing numbers in the Midwest (i.e., Chicago, Detroit, Indianapolis, and Milwaukee). Unfortunately, data relative to Latinos/Hispanics in other Midwestern communities are limited and difficult to obtain because of their lower aggregate numbers (Aponte, 1993; Torres, 1991).

Table 1 illustrates a general overview from the 1999 census data on the Latino/Hispanic, population in the United States (U.S. Bureau of the Census, 1999) that summarizes and contrasts the ambient socio-demographic characteristics of Latino/Hispanic sub-groups and non-Latino/Hispanic whites (Anglo Americans). In 1999, the Census Bureau estimated that in contrast to non-Latino/Hispanic whites, the Latino/Hispanic population increased from 9 percent (i.e., 22.4 million) in 1990 to an estimated 11.7 percent (i.e., 31.7 million) in March 1999, making them the second largest ethnic minority in the United States. This growth reflects immigration trends and natural increase.

Among the 31.7 million U.S. Latinos/Hispanics, nearly two thirds (65.2 percent), were of Mexican American heritage. Puerto Ricans accounted for 9.6 percent, while Cubans, Central and South Americans, and those described as "Other Hispanics," each accounted for 4.3 percent, 14.2 percent, and 6.6 percent respectively (U.S. Bureau of the Census, 1999). Socioeconomic indices for levels of well being on Table 1 indicate that Latinos/Hispanics did not fare well during the 1990s. Comparisons between Latinos/Hispanics and non-Latino/Hispanic whites, reflect that Latinos/Hispanics are younger; less educated; have lower mean and median household income; higher rates of unemployment, and higher rates of lower paying labor and service jobs, many of which fail to provide adequate or any health care benefits. They also have lower rates of professional jobs, large families, more families with a female head of household, and more families who live below the poverty level. Further comparisons between Latino/Hispanic subgroups indicate that Cubans are the oldest and generally the best off in terms of income, education, employment status and other indicators. By contrast, the Puerto Rican and Mexican American populations trade places as the least well off, depending on the sociodemographic indicator examined. Regardless of indicators examined however, most Latino/Hispanic scholars regard Puerto Ricans as the least well off of the Latino/Hispanic subgroups. For example, when measured by the percentage of families who lived below poverty level, Puerto Rican families showed the highest percentage (i.e., 26.7%), living below poverty level in 1998 (see Table 1).

The socioeconomic conditions among Latinos/Hispanics, noted in Table 1, suggest that opportunities for successful life changes are diminished for some subgroups more than others (i.e., Mexican Americans and Puerto Ricans versus Cuban Americans), conditions that impair their chances of enjoying socioeconomic security and well-being. Although Latinos/Hispanics share a number of socioeconomic and historical char-

TABLE 1. Selected Characteristics of Latinos/Hispanics and White/European Americans (March 1999)

	Total U.S Population	Non-Latino/ Hispanic White	Total Latino/ Hispanic	Mexican American	Puerto Rican	Cuban American	Central/ South American	Other Latino
Total Population (1999)	271.7 mil	193.0 mil	31.7 mil	20.6 mil	3.0 mil	1.3 mil	4.5 mil	2.1 mil
Percent of Total Population	100%	71.1%	11.7%	65.2%	9.6%	4.3%	14.3%	6.6%
Median Age	34.9	37.5	26.1	24.2	27.5	41.3	29.9	28.3
Median Household Income (1998)	$38,885	$42,439	$28,330	$27,361	$26,365	$32,375	$31,636	$30,463
Median Total Family Household Income (1998)	$46,737	$51,607	$29,608	$27,883	$28,953	$39,530	$32,676	$35,264
H.S. grad or more (25 years and over)	83.4	87.7	56.1	49.7	63.9	70.3	64.0	71.1
Bachelors Degee or More	17.0	27.7	10.9	7.1	11.1	24.8	18.0	15.0
Unemployment (16 years and over) (1999)	4.6	3.6	10.9	7.1	11.1	24.8	18.0	15.0
Female Householder, No	17.9	13.0	23.7	21.3	37.2	17.0	23.7	30.6
Spouse Present								
Family Below Poverty Level(1998)	12.7	6.1	22.7	24.4	26.7	11.0	18.5	18.2

Source: U.S. Bureau of the Census, Department of Commerce (1999). The Hispanic Population in the United States: March 1999. Current Population Reports, pp. 20-527.

acteristics, they are nevertheless, a diverse population. The cultural, economic, and political similarities and differences, and their wide geographical dispersal across the United States, suggests the need to avoid the tendency of Latinos/Hispanics being the object of generalizations. The realities of Latinos/Hispanics whether they are migrant workers (documented or undocumented), descendants of residents settled prior to territorial incorporation into the U.S., long-settled immigrants, recent arrivals, or the children and grandchildren of immigrants, or political refugees-present interesting and varied patterns of Latino/Hispanic enclaves, including varying patterns of cultural adaptations such as assimilation, acculturation, isolation and marginalization (Kromkowski, 1996).

In Wisconsin, the 1990 Census indicated that Latinos/Hispanics, the state's second largest ethnic minority group, represented 1.9 percent of the state's total population. According to 1998 U.S. Census population estimates for Wisconsin, the Latino/Hispanic population experienced a 30.4 percent growth between 1990 and 1998, from 93,197 (1.9%) in

1990 to 133,970 (2.6 %) in 1998 (Zaniewski & Rosen, 1998). Among the Latino/Hispanic population, Mexican Americans and Puerto Ricans claim the largest proportion of the states' Latino/Hispanic population, 65 and 20 percent respectively. Other selected demographic and socio-economic characteristics of the state's Latino/Hispanic population indicated that their data was consistent with the national data.

Latinos/Hispanics in the U.S. are unprecedented in terms of their diversity, defying easy designation. They reflect an increasing varied, heterogeneous population that compliments current national changes, dynamics and challenges to the scholarship of Latinos/Hispanics. A diverse population that represents twenty-one Spanish-speaking countries and two with the native language of the Portuguese, Latino/Hispanic sub-groups have distinct histories and varied patterns of surviving in the U.S. that distinguish them from each other while also connected by unifying cultural characteristics. They identify culturally through degrees of commonality with the native Spanish language, assumed to be shared equally among all Latinos/Hispanics (Cafferty & Engstrom, 2000), distinctive cultural features such as the importance of the collective family system, an emphasis on spiritual and interpersonal relationships, respect for authority, changing gender dynamics, and an emphasis on the here-and-now rather than on the future-time orientation valued by the dominant European American culture. They are also differentiated by physical or (racial) criteria (i.e., skin color). These physical differences often, but not always, overlap with cultural distinctions like language or religion and reinforce the separation of Latinos/Hispanics from non-Latinos/Hispanics.

The following discussion focuses on the Latino/Hispanic population and its major subgroups: Mexican Americans, Puerto Ricans, Cuban Americans, and Central and South Americans. Also discussed is the group, Dominicans, who are sometimes counted with Central Americans or with South Americans.

Mexican Americans comprise about two-thirds of the Latino population, primarily in the Southwest, especially Texas, California, New Mexico, and Arizona. Large numbers of Mexican Americans also reside in communities throughout the Midwest, particularly Illinois and Michigan, with the city of Chicago having the second largest concentration after Los Angeles. It's socio-historical identity is traced back to the outcome of the Mexican-American War of 1848 and subsequent actions by the U.S. which resulted in the loss of extensive land areas that were part of Mexican territory. Although some Mexican Americans are realizing the American Dream in rising educational levels, occupational opportunities, and incomes, the majority of Mexican Americans have not kept pace with white European American gains, in part due to the large influx of unskilled, poorly educated newcomers.

Significant increases in the Mexican American population have impacted the growing racial and ethnic diversity in the U.S. Most Mexican Americans, like their Mexican counterparts, reflect a *Mestizo* identity, a blend of Caucasian, from their European ancestry (predominantly Spanish), and Native American Indian, including Aztec and Mayan tribes (Novas, 1994). Approximately two-thirds are native born and the remainder is foreign horn (Rumbout, 1995). Almost half of Mexican Americans residing in urban communities live in central cities (i.e., *barrios*), where life is filled with distinct socioeconomic disadvantages. Mexican Americans are the youngest of all Latino/Hispanic subgroups (24.2 years), have the lowest family household income ($27,883), and lowest levels of education. Despite some socioeconomic improvements Mexican Americans remain overrepresented in low-wage occupations, especially service, manual labor, and low-end manufacturing (U.S. Bureau of the Census, 1999).

Puerto Ricans in the U.S. have various common features with Mexican Americans, but they also reflect numerous differences, including racial characteristics. Shared characteristics include variations in use of the Spanish language, economic or labor-migrant status, low levels of skills, and formal education. Whereas most Mexican Americans are Mestizos, today's Puerto Rican culture reflects a blend of Spanish, African (Afro-Caribbean), European, and native Taino Indian ancestry. In contrast to Mexican Americans, Puerto Ricans are U.S. citizens by birth, are not considered immigrants, and have the right to migrate back-and-forth between Puerto Rico and the mainland without regulation (i.e., no need of passports), a result of their "commonwealth" status with the U.S. The majority reside in or near large metropolitan cities of the Northeast with the New York City-New Jersey area continuing to be the leading enclaves, followed by Massachusetts, Pennsylvania, Connecticut, Florida, California, and Midwest communities in Chicago, Indianapolis, and Milwaukee.

In spite of U.S. attempts to influence adoption of the English language as the official language of the island (De Montilla, 1975), Puerto Rican's long held belief that one cannot separate a Puerto Rican identity from the Spanish language, has unquestionably influenced the island's social and political policy. They affirm that Spanish will always be the language of Puerto Rico. The issue of Puerto Rico's political status in relationship to the U.S. remains the "issue of issues" (Betances, 1993).

The island's political identity has been a long-standing conflicting, stressful, and painful theme with personal, family, community, and political divisions struggling over the best political prescription for continuity of the Puerto Rican way of life.

While the political status issue remains at center stage among many Puerto Ricans, there continues to be increasing concern about the poor socioeconomic conditions among Latino/Hispanic subgroups in the U.S., Puerto Ricans in particular. In fact, compared to all other Latino/Hispanic groups, Puerto Ricans experience the highest degree of social dysfunction and exceed that of African Americans on some socioeconomic indicators. Among the Latino/Hispanic subgroups, Puerto Ricans are the most economically disadvantaged as evidenced by their reported lowest median income, highest unemployment and poverty rates, highest rate of children under 18 years of age living in poverty, and highest rate of female-headed households (U.S. Bureau of the Census, 2000). The latter characteristic, argues Chavez (1991), encourages welfare dependency and also subverts the socioeconomic mobility characteristics of other immigrant groups.

Cuban American immigration and the circumstances surrounding their entry into the U.S. during the early 1960s, subsequent to the revolution that resulted in Fidel Castro's ascent to power in 1959, are strongly related to their relatively superior levels of living in subsequent years. The Cuban population also reflects a rich blend of mestizos and mulattos of Afro Caribbean, Spanish, and other European and American Indian heritage (Falicov, 2000). The initial migration of Cubans in 1960, were primarily white European looking well-to-do political refugees (i.e., business persons, lawyers, teachers, nurses, and skilled workers), who set up their own businesses, settled for the most part in south Florida, primarily in the Miami area, in New Jersey, New York, and more recently, California, Texas, and Illinois (Bernal, 1988). The favorable background characteristics of this initial migratory wave along with the positive social and financial reception accorded their arrival by' the U.S. Government, provided Cubans with a far more advantageous base for advancement and upward mobility, than that afforded other Latino/Hispanic immigrant groups (Aponte, 1993: Pedraza-Bailey, 1985: Perez-Stable & Uriate. 1993).

According to 1999 Bureau of the Census figures, Cubans are older than other Latinos/Hispanics (i.e., median age is 41.3). Their socioeconomic success in comparison to other Latino/Hispanic groups is reflected in their higher levels of education, lower unemployment rate, higher median family income, lower poverty rate, and greater middle-class composition. Among the more recent Cuban migrants however, a significant number have not been protected from the effects of different forms of discrimination including racism and poverty. While a segment of this population is benefiting from upward socioeconomic mobility, another segment remains or moves downward into the ranks of the lower socioeconomic class, less educated, individuals with drug/alcohol and psychiatric problems. and others with legal

The newest immigrants to the U.S. since the mid-1970s are primarily from *Central and South America*, especially from El Salvador, Guatemala, and Nicaragua. In response to the traumatic effects of political repression, civil wars and human rights abuses, more than a million Salvadorans and about 200,000 Guatemalan refugees have entered the U.S. alone, many of them being children or young adults. As a consequence of their migration under difficult war-related circumstances and stresses of immigration. many of these individuals face a set of serious challenges and exhibit special problems such as posttraumatic stress disorders, academic difficulties, and other adjustment problems. Other factors affecting their adjustment process in the U.S. include a high percentage of undocumented individuals, marginal employment, and high poverty rates. Complicating their socioeconomic conditions is the refusal by the U.S. government to recognize them as political refugees (Lopez, Popkin, & Telles, 1996). Consequently, this is a group with urgent needs requiring attention from social and mental health services. Approximately one-third of Central and South Americans settled in California with others settling in New York, Florida, New Jersey, Texas, Virginia, Illinois, and Maryland, particularly metropolitan areas with visible Latino/Hispanic communities.

A diverse population which defies generalizations, Central and South Americans, as a group, present higher levels of education and less susceptibility to poverty than all other Latino/Hispanic groups except Cubans, but also falling behind Anglos in both categories. They reflect numerous dissimilarities such as the economic development in their native countries, their rural or urban backgrounds, social class, racial composition, and differences in Spanish dialects are found among several groups.

In addition to Central and South American immigrant populations, a significant number of immigrants from the *Dominican Republic*, one of the Caribbean Islands, are also making its presence in the Latino/Hispanic mosaic, with a little more than half a million Dominicans immigrating to the U.S. since the mid-1960s. The majority of this population is heavily concentrated in the New York City area (primarily Washing-

ton Heights in Manhattan and South Bronx), with smaller numbers settling in Florida. Many of them are reported to locate in areas with other
visible Latinos/Hispanics, particularly Puerto Ricans. This population
also enters the Latino/Hispanic community with many socioeconomic
challenges from a resistant community (Grasmuck & Pessar, 1996).
Numerous Dominicans arrive in New York from the Dominican Republic via Puerto Rico. Known for their industriousness, many of the
Dominicans enter the mainland illegally, are ineligible for any kind of
social-welfare programs, go into the undesirable, illegal, or disorganized end of the labor market, working in sweatshops, driving gypsy
cabs, dealing drugs, and operating nightclubs and other perilous small
businesses. Meanwhile, some Dominicans are successfully adapting to
their new environment and accepting responsibility for contributing to
their communities (Lemann, 1991).

The Latino/Hispanic experience encompasses a colorful mosaic of a
diverse collection of natural origin groups with unique socio-historical
backgrounds and widely discrepant welcoming experiences by the dominant society. As younger Latinos/Hispanics struggle to define, redefine,
and claim their heritage, learning and/or maintaining proficiency in
Spanish, must be part of the journey to creating a bilingual/bicultural La-
tino/Hispanic identity, an enriched Latino/Hispanic being.

Freire's Conscientization: Latinos Learning About Themselves and Each Other

In 1970, Paulo Freire, in his classic book, *Pedagogy of the Oppressed*, defines the concept of *conscientisacao* (conscientization), and
gives recognition to the fact that oppression has caused unjustified
self-blame and identity-denial among marginalized groups. A tenet of
Freire's (1970) pedagogy of the oppressed is that all people can have
knowledge of and understand the systems that oppressed them. This includes "learning to perceive social, political, and economic contradictions, and to take action against the oppressive elements of reality"
(p.19). Through such awareness, or *conscientization*, people become
more fully human, transform their experience, and then transform the
world. Conscientization, stresses the self-identity of poor and minority
people, and sets up a new process of recognition of marginality and the
emergence of self-identity and pride of heritage. Within this process,
one must not only have knowledge, but use it as a basis for action. As
we enter the new millennium, how will Latinos respond to the continu-

ing oppressive factors in our society such as racism, inadequate education, unemployment, poor housing and heath care? How will they respond to the endangered success of conscientization (i.e., learning to perceive social, political, and economic contradictions and to take action against the oppressive elements of reality), with an anti-pluralistic backlash exaggerated by the changing demographics of the United States?

An examination of the Latino/Hispanic experience in the U.S. reveals a history of futile attempts to integrate the different subgroups to promote a national "umbrella organization" (Fox, 1996). Endeavors to convene Hispanic/Latino dialogues ultimately become discussions almost exclusively focused on issues pertaining to Mexican Americans while minimizing themes which are also of importance and inclusive to the Latino/Hispanic population. Two important themes which tend to be ignored are, *first*, elements of their heterogeneity, such as nationalities, histories, language, negative socioeconomic factors, health issues; *second*, characteristics of their strengths and perseverance for surviving in often hostile environments. Although Latino/Hispanic struggles have resulted in some gains which have benefited many Latinos/Hispanics, continued interaction amongst each other and other ethnic minority groups in the U.S. (i.e., African Americans), leaves much to be desired and much more to be accomplished. Can Latinos/Hispanics organize and create a complementary socio-political agenda, focused on a vision for social justice, while recognizing and appreciating their similarities and differences? Instead of responding to the changing demographics, defensively and with fear, a new paradigm and dialogue of race and ethnic relations and economic, social, and political barriers with which they struggle may be in order among Latinos/Hispanics.

A call for unity among Latinos/Hispanics, a call that is long overdue, should unequivocally resonate well with Latinos/Hispanics, eliminating a history of division and competition for socio-political power and resources. For much of the history of Latinos/Hispanics in the United States, Mexican Americans, have revered the position at the center of the Latino/Hispanic group racial vortex, exerting their influence alone, on issues affecting other Latino/Hispanic subgroups (Jimenez, 1991). In view of the expanding multicultural and multiethnic nature of the country, this behavior among Latinos/Hispanics is inappropriate, influencing further division among the different groups, resulting in increasing the adverse socioeconomic and political conditions experienced within their communities in decades to come. Similarities in their group structure and socio-political conditions should reinforce the need for Latinos/Hispanics to consider the need to regroup.

Will Latinos/Hispanics in the U.S. allow themselves to move beyond their differences, fears, lack of trust, and instead make workable coalitions of interest so as to promote a common agenda for social justice? A more challenging question is: Can Latinos/Hispanics afford not to celebrate their similarities, embrace their differences, and create a working liaison in order to avoid finding themselves divided and in different corners of the political ring? Responding to either questions would require that critical attention be given to certain premises and conditions which must be understood by Latinos/Hispanics. These include sharing an adequate understanding of the elements, which encapsulate their ethnic identity, issues of race and color, political issues in their respective cultural context, and their ability to reach an agreement on the significance of language within each group. They must also reach a consensus on a set of guiding principles that would clearly define what constitutes a joint-coalition project or theme. A joint conference or structure to facilitate communication among the groups in order to develop priorities, resolve conflicts, and to promote goodwill among members of all Latino/Hispanic groups should also be established (Betances, 1993).

On Being Latino/Hispanic in the United States

The development of an understanding of ethnicity and how Latinos/Hispanics have evolved as an ethnic interest group in the United States is essential to discussing the meaning of race, color, and language in the context of coalition building. Ethnicity, contrary to some popular beliefs is not synonymous with race or culture. For the purposes of this discussion, ethnicity refers to a group of people seen by others and themselves as having distinct cultural features and history and a clearly defined socio-cultural history (Smedley, 1993). Similar to other U.S. ethnic minority groups, Latinos/Hispanic are considered ethnic groups who have been forced to operate as interest groups for the purpose of removing barriers to social progress in often-hostile environments (Betances, 1993). Within the hostile cultural environments, they share the common experience of rejection through the processes of domination, discrimination, racism, and unequal treatment by institutions, traditions, history, and individuals of the white dominant culture.

In contrast to the issue of race (i.e., skin color-blackness), as the major thread that connects most African American people's experiences in the U.S., *language* is the most salient factor identifying and binding most Latinos/Hispanics. However, it's imperative that Latinos/Hispanics understand the significance which African Americans and Caribbean's place on the theme of "blackness," since the issue of skin color is also an important component of the Latino/Hispanic identity, particularly among Puerto Ricans, Cubans, and Dominicans (Betances, 1993; Rodriguez, 1994). Any dialogue between and among Latinos/Hispanics that fails to address these themes will result in an incomplete and frustrating discourse (Betances, 1993).

Until recently, in the white European American culture, the concept of race has been perceived as binary, a dualistic and dichotomous model of traditional black-white polarization: one is either black or white. Not only has the dominant society defined categorization of racial membership, laws of the land, but also explicitly defined who is black and who is white. Under the rule of *hypodescence*, "one drop of black blood rule," persons with even a small fraction of African ancestry, were considered black (Higginbotham, 1978). This North American dictum which states the one drop of African blood makes the person a contaminating factor, remains a powerful belief among many white European Americans, and to some degree, among some African Americans and Latinos (Nash, 1982; Betances, 1993). As a group, Latinos/Hispanics, similar to African Americans, share a distinctive history of subordination, segregation, and discrimination. Like other groups who experience rejection by a dominant society, they seek to reject rejection, end oppression, and create a united front by embracing a theme, a particular issue of mutual appeal, intended to confront different levels of power and domination and eliminate oppressive barriers (Betances, 1993).

Within the Latino/Hispanic population, race has traditionally been viewed not as a dichotomy between black and white, but as a continuum. Among natives of the Caribbean region and their descendants, the color continuum runs from White to Black with other diverse terms used to describe various shades of color and physical appearances between white European looking individuals, Africans, and Latinos/Hispanics (Rodriguez, 1990). Thus, color and racial differences among Latino/Hispanic groups constitute central factors bearing significant implications in most aspects of their experiences. In fact, Comas-Díaz, (1994) indicates that color differences is one of the most disturbing issues within U.S. Latino/Hispanic communities, where the individual and institutional racism prevalent in the United States increases the level of racial ambiguity, often encouraging a racial division among many Latinos/Hispanics.

BLENDS OF SKIN COLOR
AND A LATINO/HISPANIC IDENTITY

Latinos/Hispanics exhibit a wide range of racial traits, skin colors, and physical appearances that are perceived through myopic cultural lenses and conceptual categories sharply at odds with the strict racial dichotomy characteristic of the U.S. culture. The color and racial differences evident among Latinos/Hispanics constitute central factors bearing significant implications for understanding their ethnic identity. Unlike non-Latino/Hispanic Blacks, Latinos/Hispanics do not possess a single, unifying identity; rather, they recognize racial differences running along a continuum from White to Black or White to Indian, and unlike U.S. Whites, they do not view racially mixed identities in strictly negative terms (Massey, 1993). This by no means suggests that color prejudice or racism does not exist among Latinos/Hispanics. Compared to white European American racism, racism among Latinos/Hispanics reflects a different construct: a dynamic, fluid, and contextual concept that is often intertwined and associated with social class, and does not follow as well a defined color line (Comas-Díaz, 1994). Whereas White racism creates a coherent racial identity and a unifying ideology among African Americans, it fragments the Latinos/Hispanics along racial lines. A willingness to understand the complex issue of color in the Latino/Hispanic communities must be a priority for members of this population.

In contrast to African Americans, Latinos/Hispanics present no dominant racial or ethnic identity across its subgroups, and even within groups racial identity can be problematic. Montalvo (1991), notes that some Latinos/Hispanics reflect European or Caucasian physical characteristics while others do not. Regardless of their phenotype characteristics, there are socio-historical reasons for the meanings of racial and cultural blending that Latinos/Hispanics have given to those experiences. Long-standing issues that capture Latinos/Hispanics in the racial classification debate has placed them in a totally different position. Like other Americans, Latinos/Hispanics can be of any race. What distinguishes them or makes them unique from all other Americans is culture, not race. However, in this society, White racism continues to insidiously act to divide ethnic and cultural populations on the basis of skin color and appearance. Subsequently, many Latinos/Hispanics with darker skin and more obvious African and/or Indian ancestry are relegated to lower incomes, live in more segregated communities with poor housing, and experience more prejudice and discrimination.

The impact of racial, ethnic, and cultural mixing has presented a dilemma for many Latinos/Hispanics in the U.S., particularly those that include African phenotypic characteristics. Historical circumstances and incidents leading to interracial/intercultural sexual relationships was given different values based on preferred mixed heritage. Traditional intermixing of heritages often affected upward mobility provided that these unions produced offsprings with more European/Caucasian characteristics. Betances (1993) and Roman (1996), describe the concept of *"mejorando la raza"* ("bettering the race"), as a traditionally honored value in Latino/Hispanic society. This phenomenon, similar to the undertaking of "whitening or bleaching" among African Americans is to some degree rooted in the idea that one should *adelantar la raza* (improve the race) by always attempting to marry individuals who are lighter in hue than one is (Rodriguez, 1994). Among African Americans and Latinos/Hispanics, relationships between individuals with different racial designations are mediated by historical, political, social, and economic factors. Ultimately destructive psychologically and socially, adaptation of white standards of skin color and distortions of such preferences leads many African Americans and Latinos/Hispanics to believe that light skin represents beauty, intelligence, charm, and grace, which is reflective of the "double consciousness" discussed by DuBois (1986).

For Latinos/Hispanics, the issue of race is a divisive factor. As a racially heterogeneous population made up of a variety of ancestries (European, Spanish, African, Asian, Indian, and various mixtures thereof, Latinos also differ in individual group encounters with the Anglo culture. The history of discrimination against Puerto Ricans in the U.S. differs from that of Mexican Americans, although both groups are lumped together with Cubans, Dominicans, Central Americans, and others under the classification of Hispanic or Latino. They are further divided from one another in being alienated from their own cultural system of racial classification. Reflecting the racial taxonomy of the dominant culture, Latinos/Hispanics tend to make invidious distinctions among themselves on the basis of skin color and appearance, creating conflicts that can be particularly acute in the case of Caribbean Latinos (Denton & Massey, 1993).

The traditional and current meaning of color tends to be more fluid among Latinos/Hispanics, than among other ethnic minority groups, including African Americans. In acknowledging their racial and cultural backgrounds, many Caribbeans, for example, view their mixed racial background of Indian, Spaniard, and African heritage as a rainbow.

Within certain Latino Caribbean countries, the North American dictum of the "one drop of black blood rule" takes on a different meaning: one drop of white blood minimizes the stigma of being black. The historical recognition of the Latino Caribbean racial composition was, in part, influenced by the Catholic religion's position of discouraging intermarriage while also condemning sexual cohabitation as living in sin. The solution to this dilemma was the church's facilitating the legalization of interracial unions. The offspring's of such unions were often religiously and legally recognized by the society.

Among some Latinos/Hispanics there is a perception that racism is not a part of the culture. This perception is challenged as Latinos/Hispanics' experiences with racism in the United States is complicated by the observed existence of within-group segregation and hierarchy of racism that exists among Cubans, Mexicans and Puerto Ricans (Betances, 1972; 1993; Falicov, 2000). Betances (1972; 1993) argues that "yes," Latinos/Hispanics are racists, "to the degree the culture experiences internalized racism manifested in behaviors that accommodate the conquest of indigenous Indians and the enslavement of Africans" (Betances, 1993; Brady, 1992). A history of enduring discrimination within the American context of the workplace, in housing, education, and in political representation, has resulted in Cubans, Mexican Americans, and Puerto Ricans to project their experiences of racism and exercise similar patterns of stereotypes and behaviors toward each other (Falicov, 2000).

Essential to any discussion of skin color as a significant factor in the psycho-social dynamics and experiences of Latinos/Hispanics is the highly sensitive and often circumvented issue whereby the hue of one's skin is placed in a positive or negative category dependent on lighter versus darker degrees of "Blackness." Among many African Americans and Latinos/Hispanics, to a certain degree, a high value is placed on light skin because white society is more accepting of others whose skin color more closely approximates European standards. Harvey (1995) argues that among African Americans who adapt white standards of skin color, there is a belief that light skin represents beauty, intelligence, charm, and grace, which is reflective of the double consciousness that DuBois (1986) referred to in his work *Souls of Black Folk*. Similar attitudes about skin color are evident among Latinos/Hispanics. One of its manifestations observed in our racially polarized society is observed in situations where light-skinned Latinos/Hispanics may face less racism than their darker skinned *hermanos* (siblings). The social pressure for Latinos/Hispanics to feel proud of their heritage and to embrace their individual and subgroup Latinos/Hispanics identity and language as the theme which empowers them as an inclusive entity, is a socio-political reality that must not escape promoters of coalitions among Latino/Hispanic communities. The failure of Latinos to appreciate the complexity and significance of this issue may further frustrate efforts at coalition building (Betances, 1993). Betances (1993) further argues that the racism reflected among some Latinos/Hispanics is supported by white European Americans' assumption that being Spanish and white is always better than any of the categories of color that emerges from the mixing, which is often caused by oppression. He asserts that Latino/Hispanic racism is also influenced by the degree that pseudo theories have been promoted, which suggest that differences have to do with class and not with the historically racist justification invented to prevent equal access to wealth, power, and prestige for those "lower" classes, more often that not made up of individuals from ethnic minority groups.

Racismo or Latino-style racism is reflected in all spheres of the society from education, politics, religion, arts, and business to social, personal, family, sexual, and interpersonal relationships. Although not institutionalized as North American racism, patterns of internalized racism among some Caribbean Latinos transcend to their experiences in the U.S. and are nurtured by the racism of the dominant society. Although considered to be different by some Latinos/Hispanics, racismo is as painful, dysfunctional, destructive, and divisive among them as is its North American counterpart, and in need of repair.

The uneasiness among Latino/Hispanic groups demands that leaders of the different populations agree to discuss the growing dissatisfaction with the persistent racial and political conflicts (i.e., issues of skin color, immigration) among Latinos, attempt to deal with identity issues and overall positive and negative views on Latino's failures and successes (Stavans, 1995). They must challenge their respective group membership to "purge themselves of racist assumptions and traditions" (Betances, 1993, p. 220). They must also reevaluate the significance and usefulness of racial categories, develop a new and common ground for collaboratively joining to eradicate oppression, and realize the longing for social justice. Understanding race as a social construct, a concept referring to some biological basis for including and excluding human beings into particular groups, some prescribed and determined categories, is greatly needed. The challenge for confronting this phenomenon is long overdue.

Betances (1993) suggests that Latinos/Hispanics must circumvent any expectations of confirming their being free of racism by claiming a Black identity and align themselves with Black issues/causes. They must stop their denial of not being racist and abstain from being used as pawns of the dominant racist ideology, without automatically attempting to adopt a black identity. Whether Puerto Rican, Cuban, Dominican, or others with African ancestry, Latinos/Hispanics must embrace their Spanish, African and/or Indian heritage, using this component of their racial and cultural identity as a complementary element, not an abandonment, of an enriched individual and ethnic group identity. Not an easy endeavor, the success of such an integrated identity requires a personal commitment to one's group identity. Any expectation or demand for Latinos/Hispanics to assimilate with African Americans culturally, and into their movement would be culturally irresponsible and unrealistic. Their diverse socio-historical and contemporary experiences are grounded in different sets of socio-cultural realities including their individual and collective Latino/Hispanic identity, and as people of the Americas (Moore, 1988). A responsible action is to put aside culturally tinted lenses and create a coalition of individual groups in a collective identity committed to work and move toward a common agenda (Betances, 1993).

Traditionally, many Latinos/Hispanics' feelings of pride and self-esteem are rooted in family and community and culturally related to *familismo* (familism), *respeto* (respect), and *dignidad* (dignity). Regardless of their status in the racial-color continuum, Latinos/Hispanics must be given the respect rightfully theirs, and the dignity to be recognized as invaluable partners in the struggle to eradicate the abhorrent nucleus and tentacles of racial stigma in the dominant society-at-large, and Latino/Hispanic community as well. Their collectivist orientation demands they not be excluded or isolated from the conflicting social encounters of the Latino/Hispanic communities and labeled anything but Latino/Hispanic.

LANGUAGE:
THE COMMON INGREDIENT
THAT BINDS LATINO/HISPANICS

Despite ongoing national public debates about retention of the Spanish language among Latinos/Hispanics, language is the most salient factor identifying and binding most Latino/Hispanic subgroups. It specifically plays a significant role mediating the relationship with American society, and is a central theme to their efforts in determining an inter-ethnic Latino/Hispanic common ground. However, the meaning that language holds for Latinos/Hispanics and non-Latino/Hispanic whites is perceived and evaluated quite differently by the larger society and Latino/Hispanic subgroups. Issues of poverty, education (including debates over English-only or bilingual education), immigration, and cultural preferences, represent only a few indicators of the significance that changing Latino/Hispanic demographics is already creating throughout the nation. Bilingual education, for example, has been a major controversial issue in public education and in non-Latino/Hispanic work settings.

Conflicts over English-only or bilingual education programs have moved beyond the boundaries of bilingual education as a tool for "understandable learning," (Betances, 1993). For some, it symbolizes more than differences in educational or linguistic philosophies, but fundamental differences in perspective on cultural diversity and access to equal educational opportunities through our tax-supported public education and other institutional systems (Gibbs, 1999). It's an issue often dividing Latino and non-Latino populations, as well as exposing major ideological differences within the Latino population. Failure to appreciate the significance of the "two-languages-are-better-than-one" issue to the Latino population is impractical and impedes the process of coalition building as well (Betances, 1993). In fact, the costs and benefits of speaking Spanish versus "English only," have moved in diverged directions as the U.S. economy has globalized and become more integrated with markets in Latin America (Mazzey, 1993). While recognizing that there are and will always be differences between them, dialogues for reconciling differences must be a priority. Diversity among Latino/Hispanic subgroups, language, particularly bilingualism, demands the utmost accuracy and attention no less than addressing how being black for African Americans must be understood in the context of its socio-historical identity.

In the U.S., Latinos are confronted with the distinct goal of being bilingual. A lack of facility in English has inevitable socioeconomic consequences for any immigrant or native ethnic minority group. Among Latinos, it lowers earnings and reduces occupational status primarily by hampering access to opportunities for higher-level and higher paying jobs. However, for Latinos, the inability to speak English poses a barrier more for occupational advancement than for employment. For most Latinos, adapting English skills does not translate into a rejection of Spanish per se: in fact, most Latinos are bilingual (Tienda & Nieder, 1984). A decision to learn English is simply a means of getting ahead in the U.S., and implies nothing about the relative merit of one's native tongue and culture. Although there is no particular shared vision that serves as a major unifying force among Latinos across the United States, they share a common language and certain cultural values from their Spanish heritage, such as familismo, respeto, personalismo, dignidad, and *confianza* (trust).

The unique racial and cultural history of Latinos/Hispanics defies any prospect to exercise the theme of race as the social adhesive to bond Latinos/Hispanics to each other. While sharing some similarities reflecting their Spanish heritage, they differ significantly in terms of national histories, sub-cultural experiences, geographic experiences, ideologies, or a common experience of oppression outside the U.S. In a society becoming more and more a culturally multifaceted mosaic, supporters and mobilizers of the theme that two languages are better than one, and that the Spanish language is an asset, not a liability, for all Latinos/Hispanics must be cheered (Betances, 1993). The dominant theme embraced by most Latinos is the compelling significance of their personal and cultural identity, the Spanish language.

CREATING A NEW PARADIGM FOR COALITION BUILDING AMONG LATINOS/HISPANICS

What are the implications for enlightened community leaders to transcend their personal comfort levels and extend beyond the incipient tension between and among Latinos? Mobilizing needs to capitalize on the efforts of past struggles will require coalitions among diverse ethnic minority groups. Traditional frameworks focused on questions and concerns of power and ethnicity are no longer limited to black-and-white themes. Changing demographics requires a different framework that extends beyond this dichotomous model of race relations. Challenging this dichotomy requires acknowledging its heuristic limitations and barriers to variable realities in the social landscape of the nation.

A major barrier that has hindered building workable ethnic coalitions has been the ethnocentrism that various Latino/Hispanic groups express about their own ethnic identity, parochial interests, turf battles, as well as the ideological differences within each group that impede consensus over goals (Aguirre & Saenz, 1991; Gibbs, 1999). This obstacle must be directly challenged and reconciled in the best interest of the Latino/Hispanic community. Resolved to appeal accommodating compromises, "enlightened leaders" from participating communities must intensify existing dialogues accentuating the benefits of developing a functional coalition and disadvantages in division. Latinos/Hispanics must attend to their limited understanding of each other's cultural determinants of identity and unity. The challenge is to begin as collaborators, learning from each other, affirming and respecting each other's unique ethnic and cultural differences, and struggle to remove barriers which impact negatively on individual groups. Issues of race, color, class, and language must be confronted within and across the different groups.

Eradicating the malignancies of discrimination, oppression and different forms of racism requires Latinos/Hispanics "walk the talk" in partnership. They must acknowledge feelings of outrage and grief at the gross indignities, injustices, and destruction of humanity experienced by Latinos/Hispanics and others. Developing a realistic appreciation of what it means to experience being Latino/Hispanic in the various Latino/Hispanic enclaves across the U.S. is greatly needed. A healthy survival of the Latino/Hispanic community requires that the leadership of the communities they are part of, commit themselves to find a common ground, a shared self interest, and a common humanity with one another. Within the Latino/Hispanic community at large, a concerted multidimensional effort to facilitate cultural contacts among members of the various groups must be seriously considered. Aguirre and Saenz (1991) suggest, for example, joint national arts festivals, mutual economic ventures exploring the Latino/Hispanic market in the U.S., and educational/student exchanges. The latter suggested activity could include, for example, adapting aspects of the American Foreign Student (AFS) Intercultural Program, currently available to high school students in the U.S. and foreign countries. A modified intercultural program such as this, focused on Latino/Hispanic high school and college students, would promote inter-ethnic educational activities in which students from Puerto Rican families in New York, for example, would spend time living with working class Cuban American families in Hialeah, Florida, or with Mexican American families in Los Angeles, and vice versa (Aguirre & Saenz, 1991). Latinos/Hispanics should also consider coalitions with African Americans and progressive-liberal white European American groups, in order to leverage Latino/Hispanic growing political and economic power to achieve specific goals. Coalition building, not competition with other oppressed groups, is necessary for success (Morales & Reyes, 1997).

Whether the proposed mechanisms for eliminating barriers to coalition building between among Latinos/Hispanics are realistic or not depends on whether the groups can clearly understand the complex issues of race, color, culture, and language (Betances, 1993). Ultimately, coalition building will be hampered unless there s a dramatic transformation in ideology. Ideological changes intended to create lasting linkages versus short-lived ones must be included in any dialogue for coalition building. Essential to this effort is the willingness and commitment to establish a united presence. and to seek and address a common ground on issues that negatively impacts Latino/Hispanic communities. Among the issues to be considered are education, employment, housing, health care, and overall poverty and common suffering, regardless of color or culture. Highlighting a common agenda without minimizing the significance of race, color, language, and culture should be the complementary self-interest that may result in long-lasting coalitions among Latinos/Hispanics.

In the final analysis, Latinos/Hispanics will survive as they have for decades. The previously noted concerns and discussion will hopefully challenge further dialogue from which understanding the need for a common humanity with one another will influence respect and appreciation of diverse and flourishing collectives embracing the benefits of coalitions.

NOTE

The literature on Latinos/Hispanics has no consensus regarding the preferred term to use when referring to such collective groups as Puerto Rican, Mexican American, Cuban, Central and South Americans who live in the United States. It is essential therefore, with all due respect for the different definitions of "Hispanic" and "Latino," to acknowledge that for the purpose of this discussion, the terms Latino and Hispanic are used interchangeably, referring to U.S. residents of Mexican/Mexican American, Puerto Rican, Cuban, Central and South American, and "Other Hispanic" heritage living in the mainland.

REFERENCES

Aguirre, B. E. & Saenz, R. (1991). A futuristic assessment of Latino ethnic identity. *Latino Studies Journal*, 2, 19-32.

Aponte, R. (1993). Hispanic families in poverty: Diversity, context, and interpretation. *Families in Society: Journal of Contemporary Human Services*, 36, 527-537.

Ayala, D. N. (1999). The cultural beat: An inter-ethnic Hispanic alliance for the year 2000! *Psychline*, 3, 32.

Baca Zinn, M. & Wells, B. (2000). Diversity within Latino families: New lessons for family social science. In D. H. Demo, K. R. Allen, & M.A. Fine (Eds.), *Handbook of family diversity* (pp. 252-273). New York: Oxford University Press.

Bernal, G. & Gutierrez, M. (1988). Cubans. In L. Comas-Díaz, & E. H. Griffith (Eds.), Clinical guidelines in cross-cultural mental health (pp. 233-261). New York: Wiley.

Betances, S. (1972). The prejudice of having no prejudice. *Rican*, 1, 41-54.

Betances, S. (1993). African-Americans and Hispanics/Latinos: Eliminating barriers to coalition building. In S. Battle (Ed.) *The State of Black Hartford*, (pp. 206-226). Hartford, CT: The Urban League of Greater Hartford, Inc.

Brady, V. (1992). Black Hispanics: the ties that bind. In P. S. Rothenberg (Ed.), *Race, class, and gender* (pp. 218-226). New York: St. Martin's Press.

Cafferty, P., SJ., & Engstrom, D. W. (2000). *Hispanics in the United States*. New Brunswick, NJ: Transaction.

Chavez, L. (1991). Out of the barrio: *Toward a new politics of Hispanic assimilation.* New York: Basic Books.

Comas-Díaz, L. (1994). LatiNegra: Mental health issues of African Latinas. *Journal of Feminist Family Therapy*, 5, 35-74.

de Montilla, A. N. (1975). *Americanization in Puerto Rico and the public school system.* Rio Piedras, PR: University of Puerto Rico Press.

Denton, N. A. & Massey, D. S. (1989). Racial identity among Caribbean Hispanics: The effects of double minority status on residential segregation. *American Sociological Review*, 54, 790-808.

DuBois, W. E. B. (1986). *The souls of black folk*. New York: Random House.

Fox, G. (1996). *Hispanic nation, culture, politics, and constructing of identity.* Secaucus. Carol Publishing Group.

Freire,, P. (1970/1996). *Pedagogy of the oppressed [Translated into English by Myra Bergman Ramos]*. New York: Continuum.

Gibbs, J. T. (1999). The California Crucible: Toward a new paradigm of race and ethnic relations. *Journal of Multicultural Social Work*, 7, 1-18.

Grasmuck, S. & Pessar, P. (1996). Dominicans in the United States: First- and Second-generation settlements, 1960-1990. In S. Pedraza & R. G. Rumbaut (Eds.), *Origins and destinies: immigration, race, and ethnicity in America* (pp. 280-292). Belmont, CA: Wadsworth.

Harvey, A. R. (1995). The issue of skin color in psychotherapy with African Americans. *Journal of Contemporary Human Services*, 76, pp. 3-10.

Higginbotham, A. L. Jr. (1978). *In the matter of color, race, and the American legal process: The colonial period*. New York: Oxford University Press.

Jiménez, F. (1991). Dangerous Liaisons. *Hispanic Magazine*, April, pp. 13-18.

Lemann, N. (1991). The other underclass. *The Atlantic Monthly*. December, 96-110.

Lopez, D. E., Popkin, E., & Telles, E. (1996). Central Americans: At the bottom struggling to get ahead. In R. Waldinger & M. Bozorgmehr (Eds.), *Ethnic Los Angeles* (pp. 279-204). New York: Russell Sage Foundation.

Massey, D. S. (1993). Latinos, poverty, and the underclass: A new agenda for research. *Hispanic Journal of Behavioral Sciences*, 15, 449-475.

Montalvo, F. F. (1991). Phenotyping, acculturation, and biracial assimilation of Mexican Americans. In M. Sotomayor (Ed.), *Empowering Hispanic families: A critical issue for the 90s* (pp. 97-119), Milwaukee, WI: Family Service of America.

Moore, C. (1988). *The Blacks, and Africa*. Los Angeles, CA: University of California's Center for Afro-American Studies.

Morales, J. & Reyes, M. (1998). Cultural and political realities for community social work practice with Puerto Ricans in the United States. In F. Rivera & J. L. Erlich (Eds.), *Community organizing in a diverse society* (3re. Ed.), (pp. 75-96). Boston, MA: Allyn & Bacon.

Nash, G. B. (1982). *Red, black, and white: The people of early America* (2nd ed.). Englewood Cliffs, NJ: Prentice Hall.

Pedraza-Bailey, S. (1985). *Political and economic migrants in America: Cubans and Mexicans*. Austin, TX: University of Texas Press.

Perez-Stable, M., Uriate, M. (1993). Cubans and the changing economy of Miami. In R. Morales & F. Bonilla (Eds.), *Latinos in a changing U.S. economy: Contemporary perspectives on growing in equality* (pp. 133-159). Newbury Park, CA: Sage.

Rodriguez, C. E. (1990). Racial classification among Puerto Rican men and women in New York. *Hispanic Journal of Behavioral Sciences*, 12, 366-380.

Rodriguez, C. E. (1994). Challenging racial hegemony: Puerto Ricans in the United States. In S. Gregory & R. Sanjek (Eds.), *Race* (131-145). New Brunswick, NJ: Rutgers University Press.

Roman, M. J. (1996). Un hombre (negro) del pueblo: Jose Celso Barbosa and the Puerto Rican "race" toward whiteness. *Centro, 8*(1/2), 128-149.

Rumbout, R. G. (1995). *Immigrants from Latin America and the Caribbean: A socioeconomic profile* (Statistical Brief No. 6). East Lansing: Julian Samora Research Institute, Michigan State University.

Smedley, A. (1993). *Race in North America: Origin and evolution of a worldview*. Boulder, CO: Westview Press.

Stevans, I. (1995). *The Hispanic condition: Reflections on culture and identity in America*. New York: Harper Collins.

Tienda, M., & Niedert. L. J. (1984). Language, education, and the socioeconomic achievement of Hispanic origin men. *Social Science Quarterly*, 65, 519-536.

Torres, R. E. (1991). Health status assessment of Latinos in the Midwest. *Latino Studies Journal*, 2, 53-70.

Torres, J. B. (2000). African/Black Americans and Hispanics/Latinos: Eliminating Barriers to Coalition Building. In S. F. Battle (Ed.). *State of Black Milwaukee* (pp. 139-167). Milwaukee, WI: Milwaukee Urban League.

U.S. Bureau of the Census. (1996). *Statistical Abstract of the United States*, 116 ed. (Washington, D.C.: Government Printing Office, 1996). Table 19 [middle projection].

U.S. Bureau of the Census. (1999). *The Hispanic Population in the United States: March 1999*. Current Population Reports. P20-511. Washington, DC: U.S. Government Printing Office.

Zaniewski, K. J. & Rosen, C. J. (1998). *The atlas of ethnic diversity in Wisconsin*. Madison, WI: University of Wisconsin Press.

Epilogue

Reflecting personal and professional perspectives throughout the previous ten chapters, nineteen authors have presented what they view as problems encountered by many Latinos and/or Hispanic communities. These academicians and practitioners have been victims and helpers, immigrants and native born, fair skinned and dark skinned. Our community of scholars is representative of the roles played by social workers. Some have had experiences as activists, clinicians, educators, group workers, legal workers, researchers and community workers, to mention a few areas of expertise.

They bring a cultural richness and political awareness to this anthology, honed by a panoply of concerns about their communities' continued oppression, mental health problems, and economic struggles. They have also focused on our communities' strengths through cultural vitality. Their chapters have been written from the perspective of scholars and practitioners who have lived close to the realities they write about. Their postures have not been that of outsiders but as insiders who have struggled with the problems of their communities and, for some, their families.

It is difficult to be a detached academician when one is writing about family. Our authors have communicated this passion powerfully. Their unique amalgamation of theories and personal experiences has helped shape a praxis perspective to our book, *Latino/Hispanic Liaisons and Visions for Human Behavior in the Social Environment*.

[Haworth co-indexing entry note]: "Epilogue." Rivera, Felix G. Co-published simultaneously in *Journal of Human Behavior in the Social Environment* (The Haworth Social Work Practice Press, an imprint of The Haworth Press, Inc.) Vol. 5, No. 3/4, 2002, pp. 215-216; and: *Latino/Hispanic Liaisons and Visions for Human Behavior in the Social Environment* (ed: José B. Torres, and Felix G. Rivera) The Haworth Social Work Practice Press, an imprint of The Haworth Press, Inc., 2002, pp. 215-216. Single or multiple copies of this article are available for a fee from The Haworth Document Delivery Service [1-800-HAWORTH, 9:00 a.m. - 5:00 p.m. (EST). E-mail address: getinfo@ haworthpressinc.com].

215

Although the Latino/Hispanic community shares a language in common, historical events, nationalism, and economics have forged life experiences unique to our authors. Their experiences, while varied, have helped conceptualize a unified vision of the severity and magnitudes of the problems faced by our barrios, and ways our communities have triumphed over oppression, disenfranchisement and powerlessness. Their approaches are culturally sensitive, of course, but they are much more than that. The passion and love for their communities comes across in their writing. They have not just shared paradigms; they have also shared personal experiences that resonate throughout our extended *familias* (families).

It is always challenging for scholars that are part of communities of color with inordinately high at-risk groups and individuals to be lumped into the litany of particularisms of experiences rather than their universalisms. The reality is that the quality of life of an Afro Cuban, Afro Puerto Rican or Afro Dominican is significantly more challenging than that of fair skinned Latinos. How should they be categorized? Should the fair skinned Latino social worker or professor be filled with guilt? Or, should we all be aware of oppressions' multiple layers and how that oppression cuts across class, racial and cultural lines? The dilemmas presented by these realities are both particularistic–for she or he who suffers is suffering uniquely–and universalistic, for the ugliness of oppression is color, class, and gender specific. Thus, our authors have been and continue to be proud of who they are and where they have come from, while also addressing their individual trials in getting to where they are today as respected community leaders, educators and scholars. We must continue addressing and sharing our overlapping strengths and be cognizant of our overlapping social problems.

It really does not matter what we call ourselves as long as we act, teach, research and write from a common bond of cultural identification and progressive action. We must be professional but we must not let professionalism get in the way of our cultural identification and our passion for social justice and social change.

There is much scholarship yet to be written by our academicians and practitioners, but we believe this book is a vigorous contribution in that direction. The very perspectives taken by our authors demonstrate this vigor. The fact that some chose to emphasize cultural differences while others chose to identify cultural uniqueness point towards a very healthy duality that has been part of the tradition of *nuestra gente* (our people) for centuries. The diversity we represent is what makes us strong and resolute.

Felix G. Rivera, PhD

Index

Numbers followed by "f" indicate figures; "t" following a page number indicates tabular material.